# THE GERMAN ARMY HANDBOOK OF 1918

# The German
# Army Handbook
# of 1918

Introduction by James Beach

Frontline Books, London

*The German Army Handbook of 1918*

This edition published in 2008 by Frontline Books, an imprint of Pen and Sword Books Ltd,
47 Church Street, Barnsley, S. Yorkshire, S70 2AS

www.frontline-books.com

ISBN: 978-1-84415-711-2

*The German Army Handbook of 1918* was originally issued by The General Staff
as *Handbook of the German Army in War, April, 1918*. It was republished in 1977
by Arms and Armour Press as *German Army Handbook, April 1918*.

A CIP data record for this title is available from the British Library.

For more information on our books, please visit

www.frontline-books.com, email info@frontline-books.com
or write to us at the above address.

Prelims typeset by MATS www.typesetter.biz
Printed and bound in Great Britain by Biddles Ltd, King's Lynn

# INTRODUCTION

. . . **Shoulder cords (officers').**–'Field shoulder cords' will be worn by officers on the jacket (*Bluse*) and greatcoat; for officers below the rank of General they will have a uniform width of 1¾ inches without any stiffening; they consist of a cloth strap of various colours, corresponding to those of the shoulder straps of the rank and file (in the infantry and *Jäger* the colours correspond to those of the *edging* of the shoulder straps of the rank and file). This strap forms a foundation for the cords and badges, which are 'dull' and of a size corresponding to the present size for captains.

In April 1918 the British Expeditionary Force (BEF) in France was reeling from the blows delivered by the German army in their Lys offensive. The outlook seemed gloomy, the Germans were threatening to break through to the Channel ports, and Field Marshal Sir Douglas Haig, the Commander-in-Chief, felt it necessary to issue his famous 'backs to the wall' order imploring his army to an even greater defensive effort. By coincidence in the same month the General Staff in London reissued this intelligence handbook on the German army. The modern observer might ask why, at this moment of titanic struggle, such things as 'shoulder cords (officers')' of the German army might be worthy of official record? The simple answer is that a British intelligence officer in the path of the German offensive, seeking to identify the units to which prisoners belonged, would need to understand the German army's uniform distinctions; particularly if the prisoners would not volunteer such information orally or sought to deceive him. When taken out of context the extract quoted above seems rather absurd, but it is upon such apparently trivial things that an intelligence system often depends. Taking a step back, it is important to realise that this handbook, in spite of its sometimes unusual detailing, is one expression of an almost intangible phenomenon: British intelligence's perception of their enemy. We now have the benefit of hindsight, derived from comparing accounts from both sides of the conflict. The modern reader can find out a great deal about the reality of the situation on both sides of the Western Front and the danger is that this leads to unrealistic critiques of contemporary decisions. For the actual participants their perception of the enemy was incomplete, sometimes misleading, and constantly changing. Snippets of information would be accrued from multiple sources and it was the unenviable task of the intelligence staffs to collate and analyse them in order to generate an intelligence picture which would then inform operational decision-making.

This handbook was one of the tools available to the intelligence staff in their work. It was not the only one and it was perhaps not the most important, however it can perhaps be seen as one of the cornerstones of the intelligence library of documents available to them. It distilled all the underlying intelligence data concerning the German army. In modern parlance it was a compendium of 'basic intelligence' over which more up-to-date 'current intelligence' could be overlaid. For example, an intelligence officer might receive reports suggesting a re-organisation of certain German units. The handbook would provide the datum against which he could judge the significance of this change. The handbook also provided a number of useful *aide memoires*. At the simplest level, Appendix B would assist in the interpretation of captured German maps. Perhaps more importantly, Chapter 1 provided the intelligence officer with an exhaustive explanation of German manpower policy since 1914. Therefore when the intelligence officer came to interrogate prisoners or examine their pay-books, he would have a point of reference for such significant factors as the call-up dates of new classes of conscripts, the re-deployment of older men, or the duration of training for new soldiers. At the BEF level this would allow strategic judgements as to the German manpower situation, but for lower-level intelligence officers it would contribute to their assessment of the character of the German units opposite them in the frontline. The handbook could also assist in the induction of new intelligence personnel. Its layout made it an ideal textbook for the Intelligence School in Harrow where officers of the Intelligence Corps were trained. Alternatively the staff officer assigned to intelligence from other duties could use it as a primer.

For the modern reader the handbook has many potential uses. Its most obvious utility is as a source on the German army in the First World War. Thanks to the unwelcome attention of RAF Bomber Command in 1945, the archival sources on the German Imperial army are not all that they could be. Although other sources do exist in English, such as the recently-translated version of Herman Cron's 1937 work *Imperial German Army, 1914–18: Organisation, Structure, Orders of Battle* (2002), the sheer detail contained in this handbook makes it useful to a variety of historians studying the Kaiser's army. As well as being written in English, it also has the advantage of being compiled contemporaneously rather than retrospectively. As David Nash pointed out in his introduction to the 1977 reprint of the handbook, it does contain some factual errors regarding the

German army but on balance this is outweighed by the quality and quantity of the material presented. The range of material presented is vast: from lists of recruiting districts to the average age of divisional and corps commander; from a detailed explanation of how the army expanded after August 1914 to technical performance data for various weapons; and from the colours that carrier pigeons were dyed for easy recognition to the average speed of transport trains. Regarding the last point, the handbook suggests that in the early part of the war 'trains started for a destination, getting through as best they could, passing from station to station as the line became clear'. This stands in contrast to the usual stereotypes of Teutonic efficiency in running railways.

## Organisational Context

The other benefit of this handbook is what it tells us about British intelligence. Intelligence documents reveal the interests of their creators. Their emphasis and their omissions say something about the intelligence system that created them. The establishment of the modern British intelligence community is usually dated to 1909 when the establishment of a 'Secret Service Bureau' under Captain Vernon Kell and Commander Mansfield Cumming led to the development of the Security Service and the Secret Intelligence Service, known colloquially as MI5 and MI6. However the military intelligence component of the intelligence community has a much longer pedigree. Both the Royal Navy and the British army evolved intelligence staffs in the second half of the Nineteenth Century and by 1914 these were well rooted in the military hierarchies. In August 1914 the intelligence staff of the War Office deployed to France and Belgium with the General Headquarters (GHQ) of the BEF. The intelligence effort was led by Colonel (later Major-General Sir) George Macdonogh. At the end of 1915, when Haig took over command of the BEF, Macdonogh moved back to London to galvanise the growing but still rather moribund intelligence staff at the War Office. Macdonogh was replaced at GHQ by Brigadier-General John Charteris; a controversial figure who, it has been alleged, misled his commander as to the true state of the German army in 1916 and 1917. Charteris was removed from his post in January 1918 and his place was taken by Brigadier-General Edgar Cox, a former protege of Macdonogh's. These changes of senior personnel reflect two things. First, during the attritional battles of 1916 and 1917 there were often tensions between the War Office and GHQ intelligence staffs. At the heart of this was the perception of the German army, particularly whether or not it was declining in the face of the Allied offensives. Second, was the fact that until 1917 the analytical centre of gravity probably lay at GHQ rather than at the War Office.

In 1914 the regular intelligence officers' posts in London had been taken over to a great extent by retired officers, known as 'dug-outs'. After his return to the War Office Macdonogh gradually improved the size and quality of his analytical staff. He seems to have deliberately targeted the recruitment of academic experts. For example the international historian (later Sir) Charles Webster was languishing as a minor functionary in the Army Service Corps' supply chain when he was summoned to utilise his talents on the War Office intelligence staff. At the time of the Handbook's publication, the War Office sub-section responsible for analysing the German army was MI3(c). This group of five officers resided in Room 331 of the War Office (now known as the Old War Office Building) along with their colleagues of MI3(b) who analysed Austria-Hungary. MI3(c) included Captain Thomas Joyce, an anthropologist from the British Museum, who had worked in this section since 1916. They were led by Major Gilbert Shepherd, an intelligence staff officer who had been assigned previously to GHQ in France. In the context of the earlier GHQ / War Office rivalry, the 'ownership' of various intelligence publications was of some importance. By 1918 the division of labour was that the War Office assumed responsibility for documents related to the German army as a whole, while GHQ published material related only to the Western Front. But although this handbook was a War Office document, much of its information would have been derived from GHQ's intelligence products. This was not the only publication published by MI3(c). They also compiled and updated the various orders-of-battle that were vital reference books for frontline intelligence officers. These books were known colloquially by the colour of their covers. Thus the publication *German Forces in the Field*, which went through six editions between March 1915 and April 1918, was known as the 'Brown Book'.

### The Handbook

Whereas the format for the *German Forces in the Field* had been developed by Edgar Cox during his time as a junior intelligence analyst at GHQ in 1915, the contours of the handbook were determined by its pre-war version. The introduction to the 1912 edition explained that it was intended 'for the use of officers who desire to obtain a comprehensive view of the German army during peace-time, or who may wish to follow its operations during manoeuvres or other training'. Before 1914 the War Office issued and revised a number of these handbooks covering almost all the armies of Europe. The handbook can therefore be seen as quite a 'traditional' intelligence publication.

A comparison between the pre-war and 1918 versions of the handbook is interesting. Although the earlier edition has nearly 350 pages, compared to the almost 200 in 1918, the latter is printed in a much smaller font and so the volume of information is considerably greater. Both adopt a similar structure. They begin with a discussion of the manpower available to the German army and the processes by which men were recruited and trained. Both then move on to the German command and staff arrangements before examining the various arms of service and concluding with communications, logistics and various appendices. The most striking difference is the omission of any analysis of tactics in the 1918 edition, whereas the pre-war version included a short section on the 'tactics of the three arms'. This gap is understandable. In comparison to other intelligence products, the handbook was designed to have quite a long shelf-life. Therefore any pronouncements on German tactics could be overtaken by developments on the ground and could become dangerously misleading. Second, the analysis of German operational behaviour fell within the remit of GHQ rather than the War Office. To this end GHQ Intelligence would often publish analyses of German tactics; sometimes as standalone documents, or as part of their daily intelligence summaries.

In many ways this handbook stands as a testimony to the development of the intelligence system over the previous four years. By 1918 the British army had evolved a variety of intelligence collection techniques. On the frontline the Germans would be observed round the clock by specially-trained observers looking for indications of forthcoming operations. Periodically the infantry would launch raids into the opposing trenches with the express purpose of capturing prisoners for interrogation. The German trenches and rear areas would be systematically photographed by British aircraft, with the pictures examined and annotated by specialist draughtsmen looking for the infrastructural changes that presaged enemy attacks. German wireless messages would be intercepted, with the codes being attacked by teams of female soldier clerks. British offensives would yield numerous prisoners but, perhaps more importantly, large hauls of documents which would have to be translated before analysis. This analysis might involve the examination of sacks full of letters, using Field Post Office designations to ascertain the location of units, or it might be the collation of hundreds of soldiers' pay books to create a profile of new recruits. At the same time technical experts would comb the battlefield for discarded weapons and pieces of equipment to be subjected to technical examination. Finally, deep behind German lines on the railway networks of occupied Belgium and France, local agents would risk their lives to spy upon and report German movements, through a network of couriers, back to British officers based in neutral countries. This collection system was also complemented by a sophisticated analytical structure.

By 1918 British formations, often down to battalion-level, had officers responsible for the functioning of intelligence. Every division had an Intelligence Corps officer and from Corps level upwards teams of these officers would be overseen by dedicated intelligence staff officers.

Looking at the handbook's sections, one is struck by its often encyclopaedic detail. It also seems clear from frequent quotations that captured German documents probably formed the bedrock of the handbook's information. For example the extract quoted at the beginning of this introduction reads as though it has been précised from German regulations. Although prisoners would have provided useful early indications and subsequent corroboration of developments, such official German documents were greatly prized as incontrovertible intelligence sources. Many were translated and presented verbatim in GHQ intelligence products. In some ways the British were fortunate that the bias towards the offensive between 1915 and 1917 meant that German documents were likely to fall into their hands. This is not to say that this justified the strategy, just that this effect has not really been given sufficient prominence.

Unfortunately the destruction of many GHQ records in 1919 and the *Luftwaffe's* impact on the War Office records in 1940 means that the working files of the intelligence staffs have not survived. Therefore, unlike some government publications, it is it difficult to ascertain exactly how intelligence publications, such as the handbook, were compiled. However the survival of the American Expeditionary Force's intelligence files almost in their entirety provides some indication. The Americans studied the work of GHQ Intelligence very closely and would seem to have imitated their practices. For example, subject files would be collated with paragraphs from daily intelligence summaries cut out and pasted into the file or book. Over time this material would accumulate and, if required, could be used as the basis of an assessment regarding that subject. It therefore seems a reasonable assumption that the analysts of MI3(c) would have maintained files on the various subjects contained within the handbook and then, when tasked with producing a new edition, would have simply incorporated any fresh material.

In summary; what at the time was perhaps viewed as a rather dull military publication is now, for the modern reader, a fascinating compendium of information that hopefully will be put to use in a multiplicity of historical purposes. It provides a window, albeit a slightly imperfect one, into an organisation that has been described as the 'motor' of the First World War. It also provides an echo of the British intelligence system that sought to understand that organisation.

### Guide to Further Reading

The interwar period saw the publication of numerous accounts of spies and their doings. Many of these are very entertaining but their value as history is rather limited. They are often simply compilations of numerous unverifiable anecdotes or more narrow autobiographical accounts that usually boil down to 'how I changed the course of the war with my secret service exploits'. Frankly, some of these are rather fraudulent and the reader must proceed with care. Modern historians have drawn upon these accounts but have usually sought to verify them with other sources. Therefore the reader is advised to begin with later works of synthesis before venturing into the earlier sources. The following guidance provides some suggestions for those interested in British intelligence during the era of the First World War. In 2009 these books are due to be reinforced by the appearance of the official histories of the Security Service and the Secret Intelligence Service written by Christopher Andrew and Keith Jeffery respectively. Hopefully these publications will contain some revelations for the period of the First World War.

The reader would be advised to begin with general surveys of intelligence history. The obvious start-point is Christopher Andrew's *Secret Service - The Making of the British Intelligence Community* (1985). Despite its advancing age, it remains a good introduction to Twentieth Century British intelligence and his treatment of the First World War is extensive. Using an array of memoirs and private papers, the book is accessible and often entertaining. An alternative but much wider survey is contained in Jeffrey Richelson's *A Century of Spies: Intelligence in the Twentieth Century* (1995). Richelson looks beyond just Britain and although his treatment of the First World War is very limited, his is also a relatively easy read. Readers who prefer a more biographical approach to their history might prefer David Stafford's *Churchill and Secret Service* (1997) as an introduction. This examines Churchill's influence upon and interaction with British intelligence including the period of the First World War. However Stafford's coverage is understandably narrower than Andrew's work.

The period leading up to the First World War is served by some useful books. Thomas Fergusson's *British Military Intelligence, 1870–1914* (1984) is a dense work of organisational history which is not for the faint-hearted. Matthew Seligmann's *Spies in Uniform: British Military & Naval Intelligence on the Eve of the First World War* (2006) is a much more accessible and fascinating academic study of how Britain's military and naval attachés collected and reported intelligence on Germany up to 1914. A wider European context is provided by the first half of the volume edited by Ernest May entitled *Knowing One's Enemies:*

*Intelligence Assessment before the Two World Wars* (1984). However Paul Kennedy's chapter on Britain contains only very limited references to intelligence activities.

The only serious book-length survey focused on First World War British intelligence is Michael Occleshaw's *Armour Against Fate: British Military Intelligence in the First World War* (1989). Derived from the author's doctorate on the subject, it is able to go into more depth than Andrew's *Secret Service* on a number of important subjects. It is an interesting read and contains colourful stories, interesting pictures, and some very useful original documents and organisational charts. His annotated bibliography is also rather helpful to the novice. However, as his title suggests, Occleshaw's focus is upon the military intelligence system. Although this overlaps with many other areas of intelligence activity, his account is not wholly comprehensive and so ought to be augmented by further reading. The contribution of the Intelligence Corps to military intelligence in this period is summarised well in the early chapters of Anthony Clayton's *Forearmed: A History of the Intelligence Corps* (1993). Three of the chapters in *Strategy and Intelligence: British Policy during the First World War* (1996) edited by Michael Dockrill and David French make a good contribution to our understanding of intelligence, albeit in narrow areas. John Ferris explores the air defence of Britain with particular reference to signals intelligence, David French examines operational intelligence on the Western Front in 1917 and 1918, and Michael Dockrill looks at the Foreign Office's intelligence analysts. The intelligence dimensions of British campaigns in the Mediterranean theatre have been admirably served by two books. Yigal Sheffy's *British Military Intelligence in the Palestine Campaign, 1914–1918* (1998) is an exhaustive examination of how intelligence influenced the conduct of operations. More recently, Peter Chasseaud and Peter Doyle's *Grasping Gallipoli: Terrain, Maps and Failure at the Dardanelles* (2005) debunks the old assumptions that the invasion force had no knowledge of terrain they were to fight over.

Unsurprisingly the world of spies and secret agents has probably received greater attention than other aspects of intelligence. Augmenting Christopher Andrew's earlier survey, there is now Alan Judd's *The Quest for C: Mansfield Cumming and the founding of the Secret Service* (1999). Judd was given access to still-classified documents, including the diary of Captain Mansfield Cumming, the first head of the Secret Intelligence Service. He is therefore able to provide a good explanation of how that organisation conducted itself in the era of the First World War. More recently Janet Morgan's *Secrets of Rue St Roch: Intelligence Operations behind Enemy Lines in the First World War* (2004) has illuminated the actions of one sub-section of the army's secret service operations. Partly a work of 'family history', this delightful book often reads like the plot for an espionage thriller. More academic in its focus, but equally interesting, is Tammy Proctor's *Female Intelligence: Women and Espionage in the First World War* (2003). At the heart of her book is an examination of the women who spied for the Allies during the First World War, although she also examines female involvement in non-espionage activities in intelligence organisations. She does an admirable job of providing a broader and more sober context to the oft-recycled tales of Mata Hari that are beloved of intelligence writers.

Those interested in Britain's counter-espionage and counter-subversion efforts during the First World War have a number of works to choose from. Richard Thurlow's *The Secret State: British Internal Security in the Twentieth Century* (1994) is a useful survey that gives the First World War due prominence. The Public Record Office (now known as the National Archives) published MI5's 1946 internal history *The Security Service, 1908–1945* (1999) with an introduction by Christopher Andrew. Until the appearance of Andrew's aforementioned new official history, this book's seventeen pages on the period of the First World War will have to suffice. More revealing is Andrew Cook's *M: MI5's First Spymaster* (2004). This book describes the career of William Melville one of the 'founding fathers' of the Security Service. Although most of the book deals with events before 1914, there is some interesting coverage of the wartime period. A useful context is also provided by Bernard Porter's *The Origins of the Vigilant State: The London Metropolitan Special Branch before the First World War* (1987). The 'other side of the hill' to the British work is explained admirably in Thomas Boghardt's *Spies of the Kaiser: German Covert Operations in Great Britain during the First World War Era* (2004). Using the surviving German naval intelligence records, he documents the reality that MI5 and others were seeking to uncover. Those interested in the British imperial dimension to counter-intelligence and counter-subversion would profit from reading Richard Popplewell's *Intelligence and Imperial Defence: British Intelligence and the Defence of the Indian Empire, 1904–1924* (1995) or Frank Cain's *The Origins of Political Surveillance in Australia* (1983).

The standard introductory survey of signals intelligence remains David Kahn's *The Codebreakers* (1967, updated 1996). Lengthy but very accessible, it has three chapters on the First World War. Patrick Beesly's *Room 40: British Naval Intelligence 1914–18* (1982) is dated but a useful starting point for naval signals intelligence. In addition to his chapter on air defence mentioned above, John

Ferris also edited a collection of documents for the Army Records Society called *The British Army and Signal Intelligence during the First World War* (1992). Although the documents themselves might seem a little bewildering to the new reader, his introduction is a pithy and very helpful summary of the broader subject. British photographic intelligence is less well-served. Peter Mead's *The Eye in the Air: History of Air Observation and Reconnaissance for the Army* (1983) and Roy Conyers Nesbit's *Eyes of the RAF: A History of Photo-Reconnaissance* (1996) both examine the First World War, but this is as part of a wider survey of the discipline.

In comparison to the Second World War, the number of works on British intelligence during the First World War remains rather limited. Given that the period has inspired a growing historical literature over the past two decades, it can only be hoped that more intelligence historians will be drawn to the First World War as the centenaries of that conflict approach.

James Beach, 2008

# TABLE OF CONTENTS.

## CHAPTER I.—RECRUITING AND RECRUIT TRAINING.

3

# CHAPTER IV.—COMMAND AND STAFFS.

CHAPTER X.—AIR SERVICE—*continued.*

## B.—Anti-aircraft Organization.

## CHAPTER XI.—SIGNAL SERVICE.

## CHAPTER XII.—SURVEY.

## CHAPTER XIII.—TRANSPORTATION.

### A.—Railway Service.

### B.—The Mechanical Transport Service.

## CHAPTER XIV.—INTENDANCE AND SUPPLY.

## CHAPTER XV.—MEDICAL AND VETERINARY SERVICES.

## CHAPTER XVI.—LANDSTURM UNITS.

## CHAPTER XVII.—UNIFORM.

8

## APPENDICES.

## LIST OF PLATES.

# HANDBOOK OF THE GERMAN ARMY IN WAR.
## APRIL, 1918.

### CHAPTER I.

### RECRUITING AND RECRUIT TRAINING.

**1. Liability to serve.**—In peace, every male German was liable to military service *wehrpflichtig*) from his 17th to his 45th birthday.

Although not liable in peace to service in the standing army until his 20th year, every German, on reaching the age of 17, automatically became liable to serve in the *Landsturm*, *.e.*, the category intended primarily for home defence. Every man belonged to the *Landsturm 1st Ban* between the ages of 17 and 20.

**2. Recruiting in peace.**—In peace, liability to service in the standing army commenced when a man had reached the age of 20, and consisted of 2 years' "*aktiv*" colour-service (3 years in the cavalry and horse artillery), followed by successive periods in the *Reserve* (4 or 5 years), *Landwehr* (11 years), and *Landsturm 2nd Ban* (7 years). All men passed to the Landsturm 2nd Ban on the 1st of April in the year on which they reached the age of 39.

After completing his period of colour-service, a man was, in peace, liable to be called out for two annual trainings while in the Reserve, and after passing to the Landwehr 2nd Ban was free from further service.

**3. Annual enrolment.**—The annual recruit contingent, or "class" (*Jahresklasse*), comprises all men who attain their 20th birthday during the year in question. Thus, the men of the 1900 "*Jahrgang*" form the 1920 Class (*Jahresklasse*).

In peace the preliminary enrolment or mustering (*Musterung*) of the annual recruit contingent took place in the spring of each year. At this muster the following different categories came up for medical examination :—

    (*a.*) All men who would attain their 20th birthday in that particular year.

    (*b.*) "*Restanten*"* from the two previous years.

    (*c.*) A few older men who for special reasons had been allowed to postpone their service.

---

* *i.e.*, men who for any reason are not taken for any form of service, but are put back for one or more years.

(*d.*) Younger men who had been allowed to come up before their normal time; *i.e.*, chiefly men who wished to adopt the army as their profession.

The final classification and disposal of the above categories in the three years preceding the war were as under :—

| Number of men called up for examination by the *Ersatzkommission*. | | Posted to the Landsturm. | To the Ersatz Reserve. | Annual contingent of recruits for colour service. | Number finally disposed of, inclusive of Naval contingent and final rejections. | Annual balance (*Restanten*). |
|---|---|---|---|---|---|---|
| **1911,** 20 years old .. | 563,024 | 16,680 | 6,141 | 106,249 | | |
| 21 ,, .. | 367,688 | 13,925 | 4,817 | 53,185 | 565,520 (including volunteers). | 705,864 |
| 22 ,, .. | 289,098 | 102,821 | 77,486 | 62,510 | | |
| Older and younger | 51,574 | 8,881 | 3,699 | 1,981 | | |
| Total .. | 1,271,384 | 142,307 | 92,143 | 223,925 | | |
| **1912,** 20 years old .. | 557,608 | 15,022 | 5,969 | 112,624 | | |
| 21 ,, .. | 385,163 | 12,366 | 4,621 | 57,757 | 572,168 (including volunteers). | 717,700 |
| 22 ,, .. | 294,825 | 101,475 | 73,243 | 67,261 | | |
| Older and younger | 52,272 | 9,059 | 3,873 | 2,075 | | |
| Total .. | 1,289,868 | 137,922 | 87,706 | 239,717 | | |
| **1913,** 20 years old .. | 587,888 | 12,825 | 5,521 | 125,001 | | |
| 21 ,, .. | 380,331 | 10,371 | 4,439 | 80,767 | 622,360 (including volunteers). | 705,659 |
| 22 ,, .. | 305,619 | 87,189 | 73,064 | 97,371 | | |
| Older and younger | 54,181 | 7,915 | 3,887 | 2,536 | | |
| Total . | 1,328,019 | 118,300 | 86,911 | 305,675 | | |

*Notes.*—(1.) The increase in the annual contingent for 1913 was due to the passing of the *Friedenspräsenzstärkegesetz* (Peace-strength law) of 1912, which provided for an increase in the strength of the standing army. This increase was to have been fully effected by October, 1915, had not war broken out.
(2.) The bulk of the men posted to the Ersatz Reserve and to Landsturm I are those who have come up for the third and last time, *i.e.*, who are 22 years old.
(3.) Rejected men are said to be *ausgemustert* (mustered out). They are not liable to any form of military service. The percentage of absolute rejections on account of total physical incapacity for service (classified as *Dauernd-untaugliche*) amounts to about five to six per cent. of the total number of men examined at the annual muster. This is not shown above.

Men on the *Restanten-Liste*, after having been put back at three successive musters, were finally released from their obligation to serve, and posted to the Untrained Landsturm. The actual calling of the annual class, *i.e.*, its assembly in the depôts, took place on the 1st October in each year.

For the years 1914--1919 a gross total of 650,000 may be assumed for each annual class, before the elimination of the unfits. Actually, during the war, the net figures for the various classes have only averaged between 400,000 and 500,000 men each year. The reduction in the net figures has been due partly to the number of men who anticipated their calling up by volunteering, partly to the physical deficiency of men called up before their time, and partly to the necessity of retaining men in skilled occupations.

4. **The Ersatz\* Reserve.**—In peace, the annual contingent necessary to maintain the Army and Navy was about 240,000 men in 1912, but had risen to 305,000 in 1913, for the Army alone, owing to the passing of the Peace Strength Law of 1912.

As the annual class was greatly in excess of this figure, even after the weeding out of the unfits, a certain number of men (87,000 in 1912) were turned over each year to the *Ersatz-Reserve* (Supplementary Reserve).

The Ersatz Reserve was made up of—

(*a.*) Men fit for active service, but excused for family or economic reasons, and

(*b.*) Men with minor physical defects.

These men nominally remained in the Ersatz Reserve for 12 years, during which time they were liable to be called up for three annual trainings. Only a small proportion of the Ersatz Reserve underwent training.

After passing 12 years in the Ersatz Reserve, the trained men were transferred to the Landwehr 2nd Ban, while the untrained men were transferred to the Landsturm 1st Ban.

On mobilization, the Ersatz Reserve amounted to a total of about one million men, aged between 20 and 32.

As regards the employment of the Ersatz Reserve in war, it should be borne in mind that men of this category have not necessarily been incorporated in *Ersatz* formations; for instance, a very high percentage of Ersatz Reservists filled the ranks of the first series of new formation Reserve divisions in 1914. Conversely the brigade Ersatz battalions in the original Ersatz divisions contained a majority of reservists and Landwehr men.

5. **One-year volunteers.**—In peace, young men of good education who undertook to clothe, feed and equip themselves during their period of service, and who attained a satisfactory standard of proficiency in their duties, were permitted to transfer to the Reserve as "aspirant officers" at the end of one year's service only. After undergoing two annual trainings with the Reserve, and passing a military examination, they were graded as Reserve Officers.

These men were known as "one-year volunteers" (*Einjährig-freiwillige*), and wore an edging of twisted cord of the State colours on their shoulder straps as a distinguishing mark.

6. **Categories.**—The following diagram shows the different classes forming the categories, trained and untrained, which were liable for service in July, 1914, and also the annual classes which have become liable for service since that time. Men of all the

---

\* Care should be taken to avoid confusing the various meanings of the word "*Ersatz.*" In its original sense it means "Supplement" or "Reinforcement." It was applied to the pre-war recruiting category "*Ersatz-Reserve*" in this sense, and was also used to denote the depôt units in Germany. The word *Ersatz* is also prefixed to a certain number of field units (regiments, brigades and divisions) which have been formed by the depôts during the war.

undermentioned classes and categories were serving in the German field army at the end of 1917 :—

| Year of birth. | Forming the class of | Men fit for service. | Men fit for service, but not required. | Men unfit for war service. |
|---|---|---|---|---|
| 1900 | 1920 | | | |
| 1899 | 1919 | | | |
| 1898 | 1918 | | | |
| 1897 | 1917 | Landsturm, 1st Ban. | | |
| 1896 | 1916 | | | |
| 1895 | 1915 | | | |
| 1894 | 1914 | | | |
| 1893 | 1913 | Active .. .. .. | | |
| 1892 | 1912 | | | |
| 1891 | 1911 | | | |
| 1890 | 1910 | | | |
| 1889 | 1909 | Reserve .. .. .. | Ersatz Reserve (only a small number trained) | Landsturm, 1st Ban. (untrained). |
| 1888 | 1908 | | | |
| 1887 | 1907 | | | |
| 1886 | 1906 | | | |
| 1885 | 1905 | | | |
| 1884 | 1904 | Landwehr, 1st Ban. .. | | |
| 1883 | 1903 | | | |
| 1882 | 1902 | | | |
| 1881 | 1901 | | | |
| 1880 | 1900 | | Trained men in Landwehr 2nd Ban. | |
| 1879 | 1899 | Landwehr, 2nd Ban. | | |
| 1878 | 1898 | | | |
| 1877 | 1897 | | Untrained men in Landsturm 1st Ban. | |
| 1876 | 1896 | | | |
| 1875 | 1895 | | | |
| 1874 | 1894 | | | |
| 1873 | 1893 | | | |
| 1872 | 1892 | Landsturm, 2nd Ban. | | Landsturm, 2nd Ban. |
| 1871 | 1891 | | | |
| 1870 | 1890 | | | |
| 1869 | 1889 | | | |

**7. Recruiting in war.**—In war, the period of liability to be called up for military service is, as in peace time, between the ages of 17 and 45, with the following differences:—

(a.) The annual classes can be called up and sent to the front before reaching the age of 20.

(b.) All transfers from one category to another (*i.e.*, from Active to Reserve, from Reserve to Landwehr, and from Landwehr to Landsturm) are suspended, except in a few cases of men who have been incapacitated by wounds or sickness, and are on that account definitely transferred to the Landsturm.

(c.) Men are not released from service on reaching the age of 45.

(d.) Men previously rejected as " permanently unfit " can be re-examined and called upon to serve. (Law of 9th September, 1915.)

In war, the enlistment of the recruits of a new class involves three distinct processes :—

(a.) Inscription on the Landsturm Lists (*Meldung zur Stammrolle*), which takes place from time to time in each recruiting district (*Aushebungsbezirk*) for all youths who have reached the age of 17.

(b.) Medical inspection (*Musterung*), when the men of the annual class in each district are assembled, medically examined and classified according to their fitness or otherwise for service.

(c.) Calling up (*Einziehung*) for active service, when the reservists are actually incorporated in the standing army and join a depôt.

At the medical inspection the recruits are classified as follows :—

(a.) K.V.—*Kriegsverwendungsfähige* (= fit for active service).

(b.) G.V.—*Garnisonsverwendungsfähige* (= fit for garrison duty in Germany, on the Lines of Communication, or in the field).

(c.) A.V.—*Arbeitsverwendungsfähige* (= fit for labour employment).

(d.) D.U.—*Dauernd-untaugliche* (= permanently unfit).

When a class is called up, the K.V. men are at once sent to the depôts of field units ; the G.V. and A.V. men are sent to Landsturm formations (*see* Chapter XVI.). The " *Dauernd-untaugliche*," although temporarily exempted, are always liable to be re-examined ; if then considered fit they are posted to a depôt.

After the medical inspection, and before being called up for service, a recruit engaged on an essential trade may be exempted on the application of his employer (" *reklamiert* "). These men have been combed out from time to time during the war.

**8. War volunteers.**—During the war a certain number of young men, between the ages of 17 and 20, have been allowed to volunteer for active service before the calling up of their class. These men are known as war volunteers (*Kriegsfreiwillige*).

In 1914, volunteers came forward in very large numbers and included a fair percentage of men, over 20 years of age, who had been posted to the untrained Landsturm, and were thus released from their obligation to serve in peace. In 1915 there was a marked falling off, and from that time onwards it may be estimated that about 5 per cent. of each class has anticipated its calling up by volunteering.

9. **Stages of recruiting during the war.**—The accompanying diagram shows the stages of recruiting since the beginning of the war.

The **Reserve** and **Landwehr** were practically all absorbed by the expansion of the Army which took place on or shortly after mobilization.

The Ersatz Reserve began to come into the depôts in considerable numbers in September, 1914, when it contributed towards the first series of " new formation Reserve divisions." The rest of this category was called up during 1915.

The **1914 Class** was called up about the time when it was normally due (end of September, 1914), together with the *Restanten* of the 1914 muster, and a certain number of war volunteers. The total number of men thus produced was probably over a million. The calling up of these men was spread over a period of 3 months, as the depôts were full of Ersatz reservists. They were sent to the front after 3 or 4 months' training, and, in addition to providing drafts for existing units, they helped in the creation of the second series of new formation Reserve divisions numbered 75–82 and 8th Bavarian.

The **Landsturm** was then extensively drawn on to make good the losses of the winter campaign, and the Landsturm classes, called up in successive batches, continued to supply drafts until the close of 1915, when the last of the 2nd Ban was exhausted.

Meanwhile, the **1915 Class** had been called up during the months of April, May and June, 1915, followed by the **1916 Class** between August and November of the same year. The 1915 Class was sent to the front after 4 months' training, the 1916 Class after an average of 4 to 5 months' training.

The heavy fighting of the summer and autumn of 1915 had proved such a heavy drain on Germany's man-power that drastic measures had to be adopted in the autumn of that year to tap fresh resources.

The men who had been previously rejected as " **permanently unfit** " for service were re-examined under more stringent conditions. As this source provided only indifferent material, the next resort was to " **comb out** " labour, first agricultural, and finally industrial. Even munition factories were called upon to provide their quota.

The **1917 Class** was called up between January and May, 1916, *i.e.*, over 18 months in advance of its normal time. This class was rapidly exhausted owing to the heavy losses at Verdun and on the Somme. Part of the 1917 Class was sent to the front after only 3 months' training.

The calling up of the **1918 Class** took place between September, 1916, and January, 1917, 2 years before it was due. The first recruits of this class were posted to field units in January, and the class was exhausted as a source of drafts by the end of July, 1917. It contributed to a large extent towards the formation of the new infantry regiments numbered from 442 onwards (231st to 242nd and 15th Bavarian Divisions).

Although elements of the **1919 Class** were called up in some parts of Germany during January and February, 1917, the class as a whole was not called up until May and June, 1917, 2½ years before it was due. The appearance of the 1919 class in units on the Western Front during 1917 was avoided by drafting the recruits of this class to the Russian Front, and by withdrawing seasoned troops from that front to replace the losses suffered on the Western Front during the autumn.

The **1920 Class** had not been called up for military service by the end of 1917, but was mustered in the spring of 1918.

10. **Territorial recruiting organization.**—The German recruiting system is based on the territorial organization of the Empire; the Army Corps is the unit for purposes of recruiting and administration.

# Stages of Recruiting during the War.

The length of the black lines shows the number of men raised from each class or category, the slope of the black lines denotes the duration of calling up in each case.

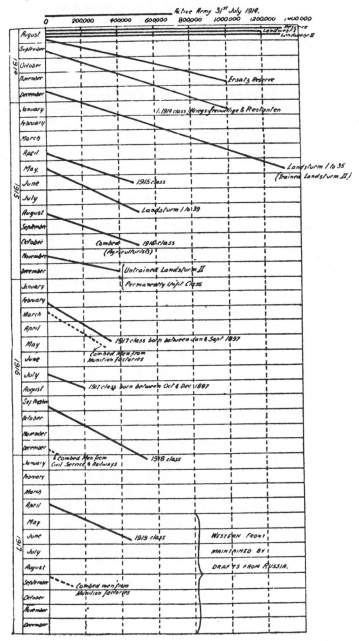

The German Empire is divided into 24 Army Corps Districts, in each of which a complete Army Corps is, in peace, stationed and recruited, except in the case of the XV., XVI. and part of the XXI. Army Corps, stationed in Alsace-Lorraine, which are partially recruited from other districts of the Empire. The Prussian Guard Corps was stationed in Berlin in peace, but was recruited from the whole of Prussia and from Alsace-Lorraine.

In peace, each of these Army Corps Districts was divided into 4 or 5 brigade districts, each subdivided into 2 or 3 Landwehr districts (*Landwehr-Bezirke*); each *Landwehr-Bezirk* had a small permanent staff for recruiting and mobilization.

In addition to these 4 or 5 brigade districts, there existed in the areas of certain large towns so-called *Landwehr-Inspektionen*, whose task it was to deal with the inevitable surplus of men in thickly populated areas.

## 11. The Army Corps Districts.—The 24 Army Corps Districts* are as follows.—

| Army Corps. | Area. | Principal towns. |
|---|---|---|
| I. | East Prussia ..  ..  .. | **Königsberg**, Insterburg, Memel, Tilsit. |
| II. | Pomerania ..  ..  .. | **Stettin**, Bromberg, Stralsund, Swinemünde. |
| III. | Brandenburg ..  ..  .. | **Berlin**, Brandenburg, Frankfurt a/O, Potsdam. |
| IV. | Prussian Saxony ..  ..  .. | **Magdeburg**, Halle a/S, Halberstadt, Torgau. |
| V. | Duchy of Posen ..  ..  .. | **Posen**, Liegnitz, Görlitz, Glogau. |
| VI. | Silesia ..  ..  ..  .. | **Breslau**, Schweidnitz, Glatz, Gleiwitz, Neisse. |
| VII. | Westphalia ..  ..  .. | **Münster**, Wesel, Düsseldorf, Crefeld. |
| VIII. | Rhineland ..  ..  .. | **Coblenz**, Cöln, Aachen, Trier, Bonn, Düren. |
| IX. | Schleswig-Holstein ..  .. | **Altona**, Hamburg, Bremen, Lübeck, Flensburg. |
| X. | Hanover ..  ..  .. | **Hannover**, Braunschweig, Oldenburg, Osnabrück. |
| XI. | Thuringia and Hesse-Nassau .. | **Cassel**, Erfurt, Gotha, Weimar, Jena, Marburg. |
| XII. | Eastern Saxony ..  ..  .. | **Dresden**, Bautzen, Pirna, Zittau, Meissen. |
| XIII. | Württemberg ..  ..  .. | **Stuttgart**, Ulm, Ludwigsburg, Tübingen. |
| XIV. | Baden ..  ..  ..  .. | **Karlsruhe**, Mannheim, Freiburg i/B., Heidelberg. |
| XV. | Alsace ..  ..  ..  .. | **Strassburg**, Colmar, Zabern, Neu-Breisach. |
| XVI. | Western Lorraine ..  .. | **Metz**, Diedenhofen, Saarlouis, St. Avold. |
| XVII. | West Prussia ..  ..  .. | **Danzig**, Graudenz, Thorn, Marienwerder. |
| XVIII. | Hesse ..  ..  ..  .. | **Frankfurt a/M.**, Mainz, Darmstadt, Worms. |
| XIX. | Western Saxony ..  .  .. | **Leipzig**, Chemnitz, Döbeln, Zwickau, Plauen. |
| XX. | South-east Prussia ..  .. | **Allenstein**, Braunsberg, Elbing, Lyck, Deutsch-Eylau. |
| XXI. | Eastern Lorraine..  ..  .. | **Saarbrücken**, Saarburg, Hagenau, Bitsch. |
| I. Bav. | Southern Bavaria ..  .. | **München**, Augsburg, Kempten, Passau. |
| II. Bav. | Lower Franconia and Palatinate | **Würzburg**, Bamberg, Zweibrücken, Landau. |
| III. Bav. | Northern Bavaria ..  ..  .. | **Nürnberg**, Ingolstadt, Bayreuth, Regensburg. |

The towns printed in heavy type are the headquarters of Army Corps Districts.

In war, the headquarters of Army Corps Districts are known as *stellvertretende Generalkommandos* (acting Army Corps Headquarters).

## 12. Contingents furnished by the different States of the Empire.—Although organization, equipment and training are practically homogeneous throughout the whole of

---

* See map at the end (Plate 1).

the German Army, the four Sovereign States have each their own army and separate Ministry of War. The Bavarian Army is the one which varies most from the Prussian model.

Officers of the Bavarian and Saxon Armies are on separate lists for promotion ; officers of the Prussian and Württemberg armies are interchangeable.

The contingents furnished by the different States are fixed by law in the following ratio :—

|  | Per cent. |
|---|---|
| Prussia and the smaller States.. .. .. .. .. .. | 78 |
| Bavaria .. .. .. .. .. .. .. .. .. | 11 |
| Saxony .. .. .. .. .. .. .. .. .. | 7 |
| Württemberg .. .. .. .. .. .. .. .. | 4 |
|  | 100 |

This proportion has not altered during the war, and corresponds almost exactly to the relative populations of the four Sovereign States.

In peace, the Bavarian Army consisted of three Army Corps, namely, the I., II. and III. Bavarian Corps. Bavarian units, from Army Corps downwards, are numbered separately* from the units of the Prussian Army. Saxon and Württemberg units conform to the Prussian numerical series. The Saxon Army consisted in peace of two Army Corps, the XII. and XIX., and the Württemberg Army of one, the XIII. Corps.

The remaining States of the Empire do not furnish separate contingents, but are merged in the Prussian Army.

Badensers and Alsace-Lorrainers are mixed in the formations raised in the XIV. Corps District. A certain number of Alsace-Lorrainers are to be found in the formations raised in the XIV., XV., XVI. and XXI. Corps Districts, but they are scattered for the most part in other units, mainly on the Russian Front, and a large proportion is to be found in Guard units as well as in new formations raised in the Guard Corps depôts (e.g., 43rd Reserve, 79th Reserve and 80th Reserve divisions). The XVI. and XXI. Corps (Lorraine) are principally recruited in Westphalia and Rhineland.

The Polish population of the Duchy of Posen is distributed over the Silesian and Vistula provinces (V. and VI. Corps Districts). There are also large colonies of Polish labourers in the mining and industrial regions of Westphalia and Rhineland, so that Poles are numerous in units recruited from the VII. and VIII. Corps Districts.

13. **The depôt system.**—In peace, each Army Corps District provided the machinery necessary for recruiting, equipping and training :—

> 2 infantry divisions,
> 2 cavalry brigades, and
> The necessary proportion of technical troops.

On mobilization, each infantry, cavalry and artillery regiment left behind at its peace station a depôt to provide it with reinforcements during the campaign. In the case of the different arms these depôts are known as follows:—

| | |
|---|---|
| *Ersatz-Bataillon* .. .. .. | For each infantry and foot artillery regiment, and for each *Jäger* and pioneer battalion. |
| *Ersatz-Eskadron* .. .. .. | For each cavalry regiment. |
| *Ersatz-Abteilung* .. .. .. | For each field artillery regiment. |

---

* There are a few exceptions amongst sector troops.

The majority of Active infantry regiments have two Ersatz battalions, but towards the end of 1917, the 2nd Ersatz battalion was disbanded in a number of cases.

In addition to supplying their affiliated field units with drafts, each of these depôts also serves as a nucleus for the formation of new units.

The new units formed during or since mobilization are similarly provided with depôts.

Normally each depôt only provides drafts for its affiliated field unit, but on emergency it sometimes happens that men trained in the depôt of one regiment are sent as reinforcements to another regiment, occasionally even to a regiment belonging to another Corps district. Cases have occurred of regiments changing their depôt from one Corps district to another, e.g., the regiments of the 50th Reserve Division and 52nd Reserve Division.

**14. Organization of regimental depôts.**—Each Active infantry regiment has normally two depôts (Ersatz battalions) situated at different places in its Corps district in Germany. Reserve and Landwehr infantry regiments have usually only one depôt battalion each.

A normal depôt battalion comprises—

> 3 or 4 Ersatz companies.
> 1 convalescent company (*Genesende-Kompagnie* or *Genesungs-Kompagnie*).
> 1 company of men fit for garrison duty (*Garnisonsverwendungsfähige*).
> 1 or 2 " recruit depôts" (*Rekruten-Depots*).

The strength and composition of depôt battalions vary from time to time according to recruiting requirements and the resources available, but the strength is usually from 1,000 to 1,200.

Untrained men on joining are posted to the " recruit depôt" which is, on an average, 400 strong and divided into 4 sections (*Züge* or *Abteilungen*). After a preliminary course of training the recruits are posted to the Ersatz companies, and are then ready to be sent as drafts to the field recruit depôts behind the front. The Ersatz companies are 100–200 strong.

In some cases recruits pass directly from the " recruit depôt" to the field recruit depôt, the Ersatz companies being filled with recovered wounded (*hergestellte*) and combed men who have already had some training.

The men of the " convalescent company" and " garrison duty company" are kept at light duty. Their progress is closely watched and they are subjected to frequent medical examinations. As soon as they are passed as fit they are transferred to the Ersatz companies.

The depôt battalions of Landwehr infantry regiments are organized in a similar manner, but they are made up of older men of a considerably lower physical standard.

**15. Field recruit depôts.**—Up to the beginning of 1915, recruits enrolled in the German Army went direct from their regimental depôt in Germany to join their units at the front. Since the month of February, 1915, recruits of all categories, after a training varying in length from 1 to 3 months, have been sent to field recruit depôts (*Feld-Rekruten-Depots*) behind the front. The field recruit depôt is a kind of training camp where the recruits' training is completed; from these depôts the recruits are sent to the front as required. Returned wounded also pass through the field recruit depôts in order to learn the latest methods of trench fighting. During the Somme battle, recruits were often passed hurriedly through the field recruit depôts after only 2 or 3 weeks' training.

The field recruit depôts are generally attached to a division, or sometimes to a Corps, to which they act as an advanced reserve of personnel. Being situated only a few miles from the front, these depôts can quickly send up the necessary reinforcements in the event of severe losses being sustained; they can also, during periods of quiet, receive from the front men whose military training has proved to be insufficient.

The field recruit depôts constitute units which can be employed, if the necessity arises, on work behind the front, and they have occasionally been used in front line in quiet sectors.

At the beginning of the Somme battle, a recruit battalion employed on the construction of rear defences actually became engaged in the battle, and companies from a field recruit depôt were also employed in the Cambrai battle in 1917, as an emergency measure.

As the field recruit depôts usually follow the formations to which they are attached, in the event of their moving from one sector to another, there is a system of exchange between the cadres of the regiments at the front and those of the field recruit depôts, so that officers and non-commissioned officers, temporarily unfit for service in the trenches, can be employed for instructional purposes at the depôt.

The fact that the field recruit depôts act as a reserve of personnel causes their effective strength to vary from time to time; on an average, however, they seem to consist of a battalion per division, composed of from four to six companies of 200 men each.

The recruits generally arrive at the field recruit depôt in a combined draft from the home depôts of all the regiments of the division. Sometimes, however, the field recruit depôt receives elements from a district other than that from which it normally draws recruits.

The reinforcements from the field recruit depôts are distributed as required among the regiments which have gaps to fill; cases have occurred of reinforcements being sent from the field recruit depôt of one division to regiments belonging to another division at the front, and even from a field recruit depôt on the Western Front to a unit in Russia.

16. **Training centres.**—As the depôts are for the most part in towns and thickly populated districts where training facilities are restricted, a number of training grounds (*Truppen-Übungs-Plätze*) existed in peace for carrying out combined training. These training grounds were situated at:—

| | |
|---|---|
| Döberitz (III). | Königsbrück (XII). |
| Jüterbog (III). | Zeithain (XII). |
| Zossen (III). | Münsingen (XIII). |
| Altengrabow (IV). | Heuberg (XIV). |
| Neuhammer (V). | Oberhofen (XIV). |
| Warthe (V). | Gruppe (XVII). |
| Lamsdorf (VI.) | Hammerstein (XVII). |
| Friedrichsfeld (VII). | Darmstadt (XVIII). |
| Senne (VII). | Orb (XVIII). |
| Elsenborn (VIII). | Arys (XX). |
| Lockstedt (IX). | Bitsch (XXI). |
| Munster (X). | Lechfeld (I. Bav.) |
| Ohrdruf (XI). | Hammelburg (II. Bav.) |
| | Grafenwöhr (III. Bav.) |

At most of these training grounds large permanent camps have been instituted during the war, *e.g.*, Senne-Lager, Munster-Lager and Warthe-Lager. The new divisions formed during the war have generally been assembled and trained in these camps.

Besides the training camps in Germany, two very large training centres have been formed in the occupied territories, namely at Beverloo (east of Antwerp) and at Warsaw. The training centres at Beverloo and Warsaw act as reservoirs for the supply of drafts to the Western and Eastern Fronts respectively. Each has a permanent training establishment known as an *Infanterie-Ersatz-Truppe*.

The *Infanterie-Ersatz-Truppe* at Beverloo consists of 11 battalions; that at Warsaw of 4 battalions.

Recruits are sent from these camps as required, either direct to units in the field or to the field recruit depôts.

During the summer and autumn of 1917, in consequence of the collapse of the Russian Army, the training centre at Warsaw, as well as the field recruit depôts on the Russian Front, were largely drawn on to provide reinforcements for units in the west.

In several of the German armies there is an instructional formation (*Uebungs-Division*) for training units out of the line. This is formed from the units in the army area. The instructional staff is found by detaching officers and non-commissioned officers temporarily from their units.

17. **Boys' Defence Corps.**—An official organization for giving boys, between 14 and 17 years of age, preliminary military training and instruction in the use of the rifle and machine gun is now in operation in Germany. This work is under the supervision of a youths' military training society called the *Jugendwehr*.

The boys are organized in companies and battalions throughout the German Empire.

The training received in the *Jugendwehr* does not entirely replace the recruit training undergone when the members are ultimately called up for military service, but it is meant to make them acquainted with military discipline and the elementary rifle exercises, thus reducing the time spent on routine drill during the period of recruit training in the army.

# CHAPTER II.

## OFFICERS AND NON-COMMISSIONED OFFICERS.

**1. Combatant officers.**—In peace, the German corps of officers formed a distinct class or caste in social life. The appointment and promotion of officers remained a royal prerogative, and the holding of a combatant commission carried with it many material privileges in addition to a distinct social status.

At the same time the standard of professional efficiency was maintained at a very high level. Promotion to higher command or appointment to the General Staff was carefully restricted to those who were efficient in every sense.

Although the system of a social caste possessed advantages in peace time, partly in ensuring the supply of officers, partly in maintaining the strict disciplinary standard of the German Army, it had to give way in war to more democratic relations. The rigid barriers which separated the German officer from his men have in fact disappeared. The wastage of war has caused a corresponding decrease in the standard of professional efficiency. Consequently, the confidence placed in their officers by the rank and file has diminished to a certain extent.

**2. Technical officers.**—In addition to the corps of officers belonging to the combatant arms, there are other classes of officers employed in connection with various technical services, namely:—

Medical officers (*Sanitätsoffiziere*).
Veterinary officers (*Veterinäroffiziere*).
Ordnance and artificer officers (*Zeug- und Feuerwerks- Offiziere*).
Fortress-construction officers (*Festungsbauoffiziere*).

These officers are graded on a scale corresponding to the ranks of combatant officers.

**3. Military officials.**—There is also an important branch of military officials (*Militärbeamten*) in charge of administrative services. They are divided into upper (*obere*) and lower (*untere*) classes. Those of the former class rank as officers.

The upper class includes—

Judge-Advocates (*Kriegsgerichtsräte*).
Intendants (*Intendanturräte*).
Paymasters (*Zahlmeister*).
Chaplains (*Militärgeistliche*)

**4. Grades of combatant officers.**‡—The grades of combatant officers in the German Army are as follows:—

(a.) **General officers** (*Generalität*).—      *Nominal command or equivalent rank*

| | |
|---|---|
| *Generalfeldmarschall* (Field-Marshal) .. | Commands a Group of Armies. |
| *Generaloberst* .. .. .. .. | Commands an Army. |
| *General der* { *Infanterie*\* *Kavallerie*\* *Artillerie*\* } .. .. | Commands a Corps. |
| *Generalleutnant* .. .. .. .. | Commands a division. |
| *Generalmajor* .. .. .. .. | Commands a brigade. |

(b.) **Regimental officers.**—

| | |
|---|---|
| †*Oberst* (Colonel) .. .. .. .. | Commands a regiment. |
| †*Oberstleutnant* (Lt.-Col.) .. .. .. | Second-in-command of a regiment. |
| †*Major* (Major) .. .. .. .. | Commands a battalion. |
| { *Hauptmann* .. .. .. .. .. | Captain of Infantry, Artillery and Engineers |
| { *Rittmeister* .. .. .. .. .. | Captain of Cavalry and Train. |
| *Oberleutnant* . .. .. .. .. | Lieutenant. |
| *Leutnant* .. .. .. .. .. | 2nd Lieutenant. |
| { *Feldwebelleutnant* (not commissioned) .. | Serjeant-major-lieutenant. |
| { *Offizierstellvertreter* (not commissioned) .. | Acting officer. |

**5. Promotion and seniority of officers.**—The promotion of officers is the prerogative of the Sovereigns of the four kingdoms of Prussia, Bavaria, Saxony and Württemberg. The first principle of promotion is that the officer promoted is thoroughly fitted in every respect for his new position. Even in peace this was determined by inspection and not by examination.

Except on the General Staff, promotion up to the rank of captain or major takes place within the regiment. Above the rank of major promotion takes place on a general list.

Promotion was slow in peace according to our standard, but is now slightly more rapid for the junior ranks. The following table shows the average age at which officers reach the various ranks in peace and war respectively, on the assumption that an officer is first commissioned as a 2nd lieutenant at the age of 20:—

| — | Peace. | War. |
|---|---|---|
| Lieutenant .. .. .. .. .. .. .. .. .. | 29 | 25½ |
| Captain .. .. .. .. .. .. .. .. .. .. | 36 | 29¼ |
| Major .. .. .. .. .. .. .. .. .. .. | 45½ | 42 |
| Lieut.-Colonel .. .. .. .. .. .. .. .. | 52 | 50 |
| Colonel .. .. .. .. .. .. .. .. .. | 54½ | 54¼ |
| Major-General (Brigade Commander) . .. .. .. .. .. | 58 | 57 |
| Lieut.-General (Divisional Commander) .. .. .. .. .. | 61 | 61 |
| General (Corps Commander) .. .. .. .. .. .. .. | 65½ | 65 |

\* Denotes the arm of the service to which he belongs. A pioneer officer who rises to General's rank called "*General der Infanterie.*"      † Field officers are known as "*Stabsoffiziere.*"

‡ For the badges of rank, *see* page 151.

At present the average age of divisional commanders is 58, and that of Corps commanders is 62.

Accelerated promotion is given to General Staff Officers in the ranks of lieutenant and captain; in peace, they reach the general list of majors about 6 years ahead of contemporary regimental officers. In war, the promotion of General Staff Officers is also accelerated. For instance, a number of General Staff Officers, who became captains in March, 1912, were promoted to the rank of major in December, 1916, thus gaining nearly 2 years' seniority over the regimental officers of the same service.

The names, ranks and appointments of officers are given in the annual Army List (*Rangliste*). The Bavarian and Saxon Armies have separate Army Lists.

A Seniority List (*Dienstaltersliste*) is also published, giving the date of promotion to present rank.

Promotions, appointments and transfers are published under the heading of *Personal-Veränderungen* in the Official Gazette (*Reichsanzeiger*).

An Officer's Commission (*Patent*) is issued by the Emperor through the Military Cabinet. When an officer is confirmed in his rank he is said to be "*patentiert.*" When he receives brevet-rank he is said to be "*charakterisiert.*"

## 6. Grades of medical and veterinary officers.

—The grades of medical and veterinary officers, who are assimilated in rank to combatant officers, but have no combatant titles, are as follows :—

| Medical grade. | | Corresponding rank. |
|---|---|---|
| *Generalstabsarzt* | | Lieutenant-General. |
| *Obergeneralarzt* (with an Army) | | Major-General. |
| *Generalarzt* (with a Corps) | | Colonel. |
| *Generaloberarzt* (with a Division) | | Lieut.-Colonel. |
| *Oberstabsarzt* (with a regiment) | | Major. |
| *Stabsarzt* } (with a battalion) | | { Captain. |
| *Oberarzt* } | | { Lieutenant. |
| *Assistenzarzt* | | 2nd Lieutenant. |
| *Veterinary grade.* | | |
| *Generalveterinär* | | Colonel. |
| *Korpstabsveterinär* | | } Major. |
| *Oberstabsveterinär* | | } |
| *Stabsveterinär* | | Captain. |
| *Oberveterinär* | | Lieutenant. |
| *Veterinär* | | 2nd Lieutenant. |

## 7. Grades of non-commissioned officers.

—The principal grades of non-commissioned officers are as follows :—

| | | |
|---|---|---|
| { *Feldwebel* | = | Company-serjeant-major (infantry, foot artillery or engineers). |
| { *Wachtmeister* | = | Battery or squadron-serjeant-major (cavalry, field artillery or train). |
| { *Vizefeldwebel* | = | Vice-serjeant-major (infantry, foot artillery or engineers). |
| { *Vizewachtmeister* | = | Vice-serjeant-major (cavalry, field artillery or train). |
| *Fähnrich* | = | Ensign. |

The above non-commissioned officers are entitled to wear a sash (*Portepee*), and are classed as *Portepeeträger*.

| | |
|---|---|
| *Sergeant* | = Lance-serjeant. |
| { *Unteroffizier* | = Corporal. |
| { *Oberjäger* | = Corporal in *Jäger* battalions. |
| *Obergefreiter* | = Bombardier (artillery). |
| *Gefreiter* | = Acting-bombardier or lance-corporal. |

There is no rank exactly corresponding to the British serjeant or lance-serjeant, but the status of an *Unteroffizier* resembles that of a serjeant in the British Army, rather than that of a corporal. A *Sergeant* is a senior *Unteroffizier*.

8. **Recruitment of officers.**—The recruitment of the corps of officers is assured by the following methods:—

(*a*.) Appointment of cadets (*Kadetten*) from one of the 11 cadet schools.
(*b*.) Promotion of probationers (*Fahnenjunker*), who join the ranks as candidates for a commission.
(*c*.) Granting commissions in the Reserve of Officers to one-year volunteers.
(*d*.) Promotion of non-commissioned officers (in war only) to temporary rank.

The procedure in each of these cases is briefly described below.

(*a*) **Cadets.**—The Central Cadet Institution (*Haupt-Kadetten-Anstalt*) is at Gross-Lichterfelde, near Berlin. The other 10 cadet schools are at—

Köslin (II. Corps).
Potsdam (Guard Corps).
Wahlstatt (V. Corps).
Bensberg (VIII. Corps).
Plön (IX. Corps).
Naumburg a/S. (IV. Corps).
Karlsruhe (XIV. Corps).
Oranienstein (XVIII. Corps).
München (I. Bav. Corps).
Dresden (XII. Corps).

After a course of $2\frac{1}{2}$ years at a cadet school (*Kadettenhaus*), the cadet undergoes his ensign's examination (*Fähnrichsprüfung*). The cadets who pass out highest are posted at once to a regiment as 2nd Lieutenants. The remainder are given the rank of Ensign (*Fähnrich*) and undergo a 9 months' course of military training at a War School (*Kriegs-Schule*), of which there are at least eleven. They are then posted to a unit as 2nd Lieutenants "temporarily without a commission" (*vorläufig ohne Patent*), and after being approved of by their brother officers are finally granted a commission.

(*b*.) **Probationers.**—In peace, a young man who had passed through the senior class at school, or who had undergone the ensign's examination mentioned above, joined a unit as a candidate for a commission (*Fahnenjunker*). After 3 months' service he was usually promoted to the rank of corporal. After six months he obtained a certificate from the officers of his unit to the effect that he was suitable, and was then sent to a War School for a course of training lasting 8 or 9 months. After the War School course the candidate was promoted to the rank of *Fähnrich*, and was posted to his unit for a short period of training, during which time he performed the duties of an *Unteroffizier*, before finally receiving his commission.

(*c.*) **One-year volunteers.**—In peace, one-year volunteers, after passing a special examination during their year's service, were transferred to the Reserve as "*Offizier-Aspiranten.*" After undergoing two annual trainings, passing another examination, and being suitably reported on, they obtained a commission in the Reserve of Officers. While in the Reserve they were liable to be called out for three annual trainings of 4 to 8 weeks.

Besides the above, officers who have retired from the Active Army with less than 18 years' service pass into the Reserve or Landwehr according to their age.

In 1913 the Army Lists contained the names of 23,000 Reserve officers and 11,000 Landwehr officers.

Officers of the Reserve or Landwehr have the words "*der Reserve,*" "*der Landwehr,*" after their rank—thus : "*Hauptmann der Reserve,*" "*Oberleutnant der Landwehr.*"

(*d.*) **Promotion of non-commissioned officers.**—In peace, provision was made for the promotion of a certain number of senior non-commissioned officers as acting officers on mobilization, receiving the grade of *Feldwebelleutnant* (serjeant-major-lieutenant).

The orders issued during the war with regard to *Feldwebelleutnants* are as follows :—

"In all arms, vacancies in the establishment of 2nd Lieutenants may be filled by promoting *Feldwebel* or *Vizefeldwebel*, who had retired before the war after 12 years' service, to the rank of *Feldwebelleutnant*, provided they are of good character and have held a suitable position in civil life.

"Similarly, non-commissioned officers of good character who had retired with 8 years' service may be promoted to the rank of *Feldwebelleutnant* in Landsturm formations, provided they are not fit for active service."

Another type of acting officer has been created during the war, namely the *Offizier-Stellvertreter* (acting officer). Acting officers of this grade never obtain a higher command than that of a platoon. Although treated as officers in the field, they are not entitled to the privileges of permanent commissioned rank. On demobilization, or discharge during the war, *Offizier-Stellvertreter* revert at once to the rank of *Feldwebel* or *Vizefeldwebel*. An *Offizier-Stellvertreter* can be promoted to the rank of *Feldwebelleutnant*.

**9. The training of aspirant officers in war.**—In war the methods of obtaining a commission in the Regular Army or in the Reserve of Officers are similar to those described above in paragraph 8, but the prescribed courses of instruction are of shorter duration.

Owing to the war, the number of commissions in the Reserve of Officers has been greatly increased. From two to ten *Offizier-Aspiranten* may be nominated at a time from each regiment at the front. After attending a special "*Offizier-Aspiranten-Kursus*" for 2 or 3 months the candidate returns to his unit for a short time as *Vizefeldwebel* or *Feldwebel*, after which he is promoted to the rank of *Leutnant der Reserve*.

Courses of instruction for *Offizier-Aspiranten* are held at all the big training centres in Germany and behind the front (*see* page 18).

The course lasts for 2 or 3 months. Each School of Instruction has from 1,600 to 2,000 pupils, who are formed into a regiment of four battalions, each of four companies. Each company, which comprises about 100 pupils, is divided into three platoons.

The school is commanded by a lieutenant-colonel, who is usually a Staff College graduate (*Kriegs-Akademiker*). The battalions are commanded by majors of the Regular Army; the companies are commanded by wounded or convalescent captains and subalterns.

The discipline at these schools is very strict; pupils are frequently returned to their units for misdemeanours or incompetence.

The instruction given is both theoretical and practical. The following programme is typical of the subjects taught :—

(*A.*) *Theoretical.*—Lectures on tactics by an Active officer serving with a unit. Twice a week the pupils are given a tactical problem to solve on the ground, using the 1/100,000 map, and executing sketches to illustrate their work.

The duties of an officer ; his relations to his men, to his comrades, to his superiors, to civilians, &c., code of honour. Discipline.

Short examination daily in duties in the field. Musketry and drill.

(*B.*) *Practical.*—Every morning the pupils carry out a tactical exercise on different ground with a skeleton enemy formed by one or two platoons. Nearly every pupil is called upon to command a platoon or a company. Casualties are practised.

Handling and practice with grenades and trench mortars.
Construction of shelters and dug-outs. Bridging exercise.
Physical training.

At the conclusion of the course an examination is held consisting of—

Battalion drill.
Oral test. Inspection by the Commandant.
Written test. Writing reports.

10. **Retirement of officers.**—Officers who are definitely retired are described as "*ausser Dienst*" (*a.D.*). Officers who have retired after 18 years' service may at their own request be placed *zur Disposition* (*z.D.*), that is, on the unemployed list; they are then liable to be called up for service on mobilization.

During war-time, officers who are removed from their commands or appointments are placed *zur Disposition*.

11. **Recruitment and training of non-commissioned officers.**—In peace, non-commissioned officers were given a thorough general and military education, and their prospects in civil life after leaving the Army were assured. Under the German system of peace training, the duties and responsibilities of non-commissioned officers conduced to develop their initiative and self-reliance.

Non-commissioned officers are drawn from two sources—

(*a.*) Training schools for non-commissioned officers.
(*b.*) The ranks.

In peace, about 25 per cent. were drawn from training schools and the remainder were promoted directly from the ranks.

(*a.*) **The training schools.**—The training schools are of two kinds—

(1.) N.C.O.'s Preparatory Schools (*Unteroffizier-Vorschulen*).
(2.) N.C.O.'s Schools (*Unteroffizier-Schulen*).

In the **N.C.O.'s Preparatory Schools** the education is of a general character and great attention is paid to physical development. The age of admission is from 14½ to 17. The course lasts for 2 years.

There are nine N.C.O.'s Preparatory Schools, at Annaburg (IV), Bartenstein (I), Frankenstein (VI), Jülich (VIII), Mölln (IX), Sigmaringen (XIV), Weilburg (XVIII), Wohlau (VI) and Marienberg (Saxony).

On leaving the preparatory schools, the pupils join the **N.C.O.'s Schools,** of which there are eight, at Marienwerder (XVII), Northeim (X), Potsdam (Guard), Treptow a/R. (II), Weissenfels (IV), Wetzlar (XVIII), Fürstenfeldbrück (Bavaria) and Marienberg (Saxony).

The age of admission to these schools is between 17 and 20. The training is free and the course is a purely military one. In peace the course lasted 2 years.

On leaving the schools the pupils are posted to regiments as *Unteroffiziere.*

(*b.*) **From the ranks.**—The majority of non-commissioned officers are drawn from the ranks. In peace they were selected during their Active colour service, and induced to re-engage (*kapitulieren*) by the offer of a bounty (*Kapitulations-Handgeld*). Re-engaged men (*Kapitulanten*) were given special instruction and a special rate of pay; they were promoted, generally, after 2 years' further service.

In war, likely men are picked out by their commanding officers and sent for a course of training, either in the divisional or Corps field recruit depôts, or in special non-commissioned officers' training courses (*Unteroffizier-Lehr-Kurse*), which are held in each Army.

In some Corps, each regiment has an instructional company (*Lehr-Kompagnie*) in which suitable candidates for promotion are trained.

A considerable number of men from the cavalry have been promoted during the war to non-commissioned rank in infantry units.

12. **Pay and allowances.**—Pay is termed *Gehalt* in the case of officers, and *Löhnung* in the case of non-commissioned officers and men. In peace time there were various allowances (*Gebührnisse*), such as *Kommandogeld, Stellenzulage* and *Tischgeld.*

Officers' pay is credited monthly in advance on the first day of each month; the pay of non-commissioned officers and men is credited on the 1st, 11th and 21st of each month (*i.e.*, every 10 days), and the month is reckoned at 30 days. On joining, recruits receive an allowance for cleaning materials (*Putzzeuggeld*), amounting to 7·10 marks for dismounted, and 8·80 marks for mounted men.

Special allowances and rates of pay were granted to officers and other ranks of the *Beurlaubtenstand, i.e.*, non-Active army, when called up for training or manoeuvres.

Prior to the war, the daily rates of pay for officers were as follows :—

| | |
|---|---|
| Corps commander .. .. .. .. .. .. | 87·60 marks. |
| Divisional commander .. .. .. .. .. | 49·50 ,, |
| Brigade commander .. .. .. .. .. .. | 30·50 ,, |
| Colonel (commanding a regiment) .. .. .. .. | 24·00 ,, |
| Major or Lieut.-Colonel .. .. .. .. .. | 18·00 ,, |
| Captain, over 9 years' service .. .. .. .. | 14·00 ,, |
| Captain, 5th to 9th year .. .. .. .. .. | 12·60 ,, |
| Captain, 1st to 4th year .. .. .. .. .. | 9·33 ,, |

Lieutenant or 2nd Lieutenant—

| | | | | | | |
|---|---|---|---|---|---|---|
| Over 13 year's service | .. | .. | .. | .. | .. | 6·6 marks. |
| 10th to 13th year | .. | .. | .. | .. | .. | 5·7 ,, |
| 7th to 9th year | .. | .. | .. | .. | .. | 5·2 ,, |
| 4th to 6th year | .. | .. | .. | .. | .. | 4·6 ,, |
| 1st to 3rd year | .. | .. | .. | .. | .. | 4·1 ,, |

The above rates include command pay (*Dienstzulage*) for officers of the rank of brigade commander and upwards.

During the war, the pay of the junior ranks has been considerably increased. A subaltern on joining receives 8·33 marks a day, which is increased to 10·33 marks after a year's service. A subaltern commanding a company receives 12·33 marks. A captain receives 21·83 marks while commanding a company, and 24·33 marks when commanding a battalion.

A flying officer or non-commissioned officer receives flying pay at the rate of 5 marks a day in addition to the above rates.

Since the 21st December, 1917, the rates of pay for non-commissioned officers have been raised by 20 per cent., and for men by 33 per cent.

The following table shows the daily rates of pay (in marks) of the various non-commissioned ranks (1 mark is nominally equivalent to 1 shilling) :—

| Rank. | Old scale. | | New scale. | |
|---|---|---|---|---|
| | At home. | In the field. | At home. | In the field. |
| *Feldwebel* or *Wachtmeister* (company-serjeant-major, &c.) | 3·20 | 4·20 | 3·80 | 5·00 |
| *Vizefeldwebel* or *Vizewachtmeister* .. .. .. | 1·90 | 2·10 | 2·30 | 2·53 |
| *Sergeant* or *Unteroffizier* after 5½ years' service .. | 1·65 | 1·90 | 2·00 | 2·25 |
| *Unteroffizier* or *Fähnrich* .. .. .. .. .. | 1·12 | 1·33 | 1·40 | 1·60 |
| *Gefreiter* (lance-corporal) mounted services .. | ·43 } ·63 | | ·57 } ·75 | |
| ,, ,, dismounted services .. .. | ·38 } | ·63 | ·50 } | ·75 |
| *Gemeiner* (private) mounted services.. .. .. | ·38 } ·53 | | ·50 } ·70 | |
| ,, ,, dismounted services .. .. .. | ·33 } | ·53 | ·44 } | ·70 |

The daily rates of separation allowance for non-commissioned officers were raised in July, 1917, and are now as follows :—

| | | | | | |
|---|---|---|---|---|---|
| Wife | .. | .. | .. | .. | 1·60 marks. |
| Wife and 1 child | .. | .. | .. | .. | 2·10 ,, |
| Wife and 2 children | .. | .. | .. | .. | 2·60 ,, |
| For each additional child | .. | .. | .. | 0·60 ,, |

# CHAPTER III.

## THE MOBILIZATION AND EXPANSION OF THE GERMAN ARMY.

### PEACE ORGANIZATION OF AN ARMY CORPS.

#### ARMY CORPS.

Inf. Division. — Inf. Division. — Pioneer Battalion.

Pioneer Battalion: 1st Fd. Coy. — 2nd Fd. Coy. — 3rd Fd. Coy. — 4th Fd. Coy.

Inf. Division: Inf. Bde. — Inf. Bde. — Field Art. Bde. — Jäger Bn.

Inf. Bde: Inf. Regt. — Inf. Regt.

Inf. Regt: I. Bn. — II. Bn. — III. Bn. — M.G. Coy.

Bn: 5th Coy. — 6th Coy. — 7th Coy. — 8th Coy.

Field Art. Bde: F.A. Regt. — F.A. Regt.

F.A. Regt: I. Abteilung. — II. Abteilung.

Abteilung: 1st Bty. — 2nd Bty. — 3rd Bty. — 4th Bty. — 5th Bty. — 6th Bty.

Cavalry Brigade.* — Cavalry Brigade.

Cavalry Brigade: Cav. Regt. — Cav. Regt.

Cav. Regt: 1st Sqn. — 2nd Sqn. — 3rd Sqn. — 4th Sqn. — 5th Sqn.

Foot Art. Regt: I. Bn. — II. Bn.

Foot Art. Bn: 1st Bty. — 2nd Bty. — 3rd Bty. — 4th Bty. — 5th Bty. — 6th Bty. — 7th Bty. — 8th Bty.

\* The cavalry brigades were administered by the Army Corps in the district of which they were formed, though not forming an integral part of the Army Corps.

In addition to the above combatant arms, the Army Corps comprised a Train Detachment (*Train-Abteilung*), an Administrative Department (*Militär-Intendantur*), a Clothing Office (*Bekleidungs-Amt*), and a Medical Office (*Sanitäts-Amt*).

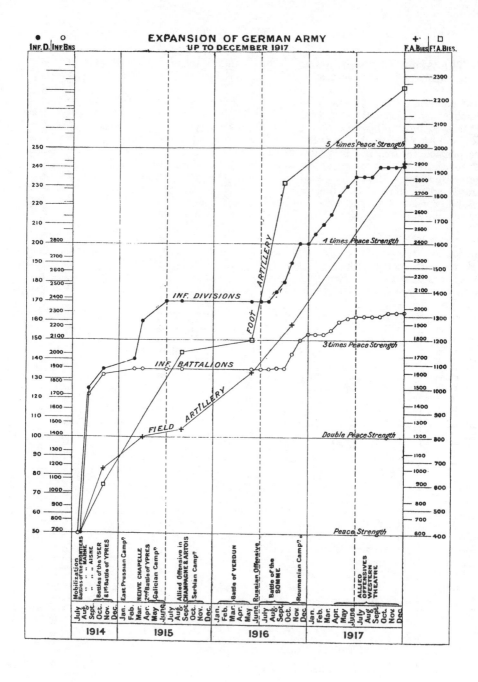

EXPANSION OF GERMAN ARMY
UP TO DECEMBER 1917

1. **The Army Corps in peace.**—The 25 Army Corps, which have served as the basis for expansion in war, formed the framework of the German Army organization in peace.

The diagram on page 28 shows in outline the peace organization of an Army Corps.

Each Army Corps formed a complete and self-supporting entity in the German Army. As regards command, the Army Corps Commander was absolutely independent in his own district, and took his orders direct from the Emperor (or King in the Bavarian Army). He was responsible for the *tactical* training of all troops in his command, although the responsibility for the *technical* training of the individual arms and branches rested with the various Inspector-Generals. The Army Corps Commander was also allowed considerable latitude as regards administrative and financial matters. This decentralization of command and responsibility was one of the main factors in the rapidity with which the German Army mobilized, and greatly facilitated its expansion during the war.

2. **The expansion of the German Army.**—The peace strength of the standing or Active German Army in 1914 amounted in round numbers to 840,000 of all ranks.

At the end of 1917, the total strength of the German Army had risen to at least 6,000,000 men, excluding recruits training in Germany.

The various arms comprised the following number of units in July, 1914, and January, 1918, respectively :—

| — | July, 1914. | January, 1918. |
|---|---|---|
| Infantry battalions .. .. .. .. .. | 669 | 2,300 |
| Cavalry squadrons .. .. .. .. .. | 550 | 570 |
| Field artillery batteries .. .. .. .. | 642 | 2,900 |
| Foot artillery batteries .. .. .. .. | 400 | 2,250 |
| Pioneer companies .. .. .. .. .. | 150 | 650 |

Thus in $3\frac{1}{2}$ years of war the various arms had increased in the following proportions :—

| | |
|---|---|
| Infantry.. .. .. .. .. .. .. | $3\frac{1}{4}$ times. |
| Field artillery .. .. .. .. .. .. | $4\frac{3}{4}$ ,, |
| Heavy artillery .. .. .. .. .. | $5\frac{1}{2}$ ,, |
| Pioneers .. .. .. .. .. .. | $4\frac{1}{3}$ ,, |

The strength of the cavalry has remained practically stationary, as many of the cavalry units formed since mobilization have been dismounted.

The accompanying diagram shows graphically the progress of this expansion as regards the infantry and artillery.

It is noteworthy that, although the number of infantry divisions has increased nearly five times, the number of battalions has only increased $3\frac{1}{4}$ times. This disparity originated in the spring of 1915, when the establishment of divisions began to be reduced from four to three regiments.

3. **The machinery of expansion.**—As seen in Chapter I., paragraph 13, the depôts (Ersatz battalions, &c.) fulfil a twofold rôle :—

(*a.*) The supply of drafts to the field units, and
(*b.*) The creation of new formations.

As each **Ersatz battalion** (squadron or *Abteilung*) is provided with one or two "recruit depôts" for the elementary training of recruits, the Ersatz battalion itself consists largely of trained, or at any rate partially trained, men. Every Ersatz battalion is, therefore, a potential new unit which may eventually take the field, and has in many cases done so.

At the beginning of the war, in the majority of infantry brigades, two companies were formed in each depôt of each Active regiment from the best elements that were surplus to the immediate needs of mobilization. These companies were combined to form a **brigade Ersatz battalion** which bore the number of the brigade in which it was formed. In the same way a number of **Reserve** and **Landwehr brigade Ersatz battalions** were formed later on in the depôts of Reserve and Landwehr regiments. These brigade Ersatz battalions were grouped together to form Ersatz brigades which were eventually (in the summer of 1915) regrouped as infantry regiments. The Ersatz brigades formed in this way were incorporated in the Ersatz divisions which took the field during the autumn of 1914.

Instead of merely acting as the parent stock of new formations, as described above, the Ersatz battalions themselves in many cases took the field as mobile units. These "mobile Ersatz battalions" were combined to complete the series of infantry regiments, numbered from 349 to 382.

The new infantry regiments, raised in the autumn of 1916, and numbered between 383 and 480, were formed in various ways :—*

(*a*.) In a number of Army Corps Districts each Ersatz battalion raised a company at war establishment, composed of men fit for field service. These companies were combined to form new infantry regiments (*e.g.*, the 411th and 412th Infantry Regiments, formed in the X. Corps District).

(*b*.) In a number of divisions in the field a complete company was withdrawn from every infantry regiment. The vacancies in the regiments drawn upon were filled by drafts from the depôts, and the companies withdrawn were combined to form new regiments (*e.g.*, the 392nd Infantry Regiment was formed from the regiments of the XIX. Corps and XII. Res. Corps, and the 393rd was formed from the 7th Div., 8th Div., 12th Div., and 50th Res. Div.).

(*c*.) In certain field recruit depôts and training centres new regiments were organized from the fittest Landsturm and Landwehr men picked out of Landsturm battalions on the Lines of Communication, or from the garrison battalions in Germany. These new units were stiffened with a proportion of returned wounded, but their fighting value was not high, and they were sent to quiet sectors of the front (*e.g.*, the 384th and 386th Landwehr Infantry Regiments).

New units of the other arms were usually created by the first of these methods, *e.g.*, the 263rd F.A. Regiment was formed by combining the Ersatz batteries raised in the depôts of all the field artillery regiments in the I. and XX. Corps Districts.

### 4. Mobilization and the process of expansion in 1914.—On mobilization in August, 1914, the **50 Active divisions** were brought up to War Establishment with reservists, and the extra Guard Regiments formed a 3rd Guard Division.†

---

* It should be mentioned that the series of new regiments numbered from 383 to 441 were formed in the field, while those numbered from 442 to 478 were formed in the training centres in Germany and were combined in the new series of divisions raised at the beginning of 1917 (*see* page 33).

† The instructional battalion of the Guard Corps was expanded into the *Lehr-Regiment*.

In addition to these 51 Active divisions. **32 Reserve divisions** were formed from the surplus reservists in the depôts, and also from the Landwehr 1st Ban. Some Active Corps had in peace a surplus infantry brigade or regiment which served to stiffen the Reserve divisions. The Reserve Corps, which were numbered correspondingly to the Active Corps, took the field simultaneously with them. They were organized similarly to the Active Corps, except that a Reserve division was only provided with 9 field artillery batteries instead of with 12.

At the same time, a number of **Landwehr and Ersatz brigades** were formed from the Landwehr 2nd Ban and from the trained Ersatz reservists available. These formations were at first used only on the Lines of Communication of the advancing armies. They were, later, largely combined to form Landwehr and Ersatz divisions.

As the Ersatz Reserve, surplus reservists and Landwehr men, together with a constant stream of war volunteers, still provided a large surplus of man-power, it was decided soon after the outbreak of war to increase the number of Army Corps. About the middle of October, 1914, six fresh Corps and an extra Bavarian Reserve division (*i.e.*, 13 divisions), together with a Naval division, left the depôts for the front.

These 13 divisions formed the **first series of new formation Reserve divisions** formed *after* mobilization had been completed. These Reserve divisions were numbered between 43 and 54, and formed the Reserve Corps numbered between XXII and XXVII; the 6th Bavarian Reserve Division also belongs to this series. The new Corps consisted of Landwehr men, Ersatz reservists and a large number of volunteers from the classes not previously called up.

The depôts in Germany were then filled up with the 1914 Class, the remaining Ersatz reservists and additional volunteers. Owing to the large number of men put back from the classes of previous years, the incorporation of the 1914 Class afforded an opportunity for still further increasing the army in the field, and in February, 1915, four fresh Reserve Corps and another Bavarian Reserve division (*i.e.*, nine divisions) had been sent to the front. These nine divisions made up the **second series of new formation Reserve divisions,** numbered between 75 and 82, forming the Reserve Corps numbered between XXXVIII and XLI; the 8th Bavarian Reserve Division also belongs to this series. At the same time, the Naval Division had been expanded to a Corps, and some additional Landwehr brigades had been formed.

Thus in February, 1915, the German forces in the field had risen to:—

51 Active divisions.  
32 Reserve divisions formed on mobilization.  
13   „      „      „    in October, 1914.  
 9   „      „      „    in February, 1915,

a total of 105 Active and Reserve divisions, and the equivalent of 38 Landwehr, Ersatz and additional divisions.

### 5. Formation of the reconstituted divisions in 1915.

—In the spring of 1915, the prospect of offensive operations in Russia during the summer necessitated a further increase in the number of mobile field units.

The winter campaign had, however, exhausted the 1914 Class and practically the whole of the trained Landsturm, so that there were not sufficient trained men in the depôts to form new regiments.

The increasing importance of artillery, and the frequent divisional reliefs occasioned by the conditions of trench warfare, made possible a reduction in the infantry strength of the division.

Thus, 19 new divisions* were raised in March and April, 1915, which were organized on a 3-regiment instead of a 4-regiment basis. Their formation involved the creation of no new infantry units, but was effected by grouping together three existing infantry regiments withdrawn from three Active or Reserve divisions. In this way a certain number of Active and Reserve divisions were also reduced from 4 to 3 infantry regiments.

In June, 1915, four new independent infantry brigades were formed on the Western Front by the creation of new infantry regiments. These brigades were numbered 183, 185, 187 and 192; they consisted of three infantry regiments and were as strong in infantry as the reconstituted divisions. The regiments of these divisions were formed by withdrawing trained men from units fighting on the Western Front. When first formed, presumably because only three field batteries were available for each, these units were classified as brigades; a year later they received their full artillery complement and were raised to the status of divisions. In August, 1915, the number of divisions in the field had risen to 170.

## 6. New formations raised in 1916.—Beyond a steady increase in the formation of artillery and technical units, no noteworthy expansion of the German Army took place between June, 1915, and June, 1916, but the trench mortar and machine gun units were completely reorganized.

At the latter date the strain on the Eastern Front caused by the Russian offensive, together with the prospective lengthening of the line involved by the imminent entry into the war of Roumania, necessitated a further increase in the number of mobile field units.

Between 1st June and 31st December, 1916, a further series of 34 new divisions was raised. Some of these (series 195–200) were formed by grouping together *Jäger* battalions and odd battalions withdrawn from existing divisions, but the great majority of them (series numbered over 200) were reconstituted with the fourth regiments of Active and Reserve divisions, similarly to the reconstituted divisions formed in the spring of 1915.

Among the divisions formed on the Eastern Front during 1916 were the 91st, 92nd and 93rd, which were of poor quality.

At the same time, the number of battalions in the German Army was increased by the formation of between 60 and 70 new infantry regiments in the manner described on page 30. In a few cases the new divisions (201st to 205th Divisions, 19th and 20th Landwehr Divisions and 12th Bavarian Division) were composed entirely of these new infantry regiments. In general, however, the new infantry regiments were sent to Active or Reserve divisions to replace the old regiments withdrawn to make up the new divisions. By the end of 1916 the number of divisions in the field had risen to 203.

The reduction in the divisional establishment had the additional advantage of setting free an infantry brigade staff in each division so reduced; in this manner a number of trained staffs were obtained for the 19 new divisions reconstituted by the process described above.

The field artillery of the series of reconstituted divisions was obtained by a general reduction of all the existing field batteries from 6 to 4 guns. The divisional artillery of these divisions consisted of from 9 to 12 field batteries, the establishment being eventually fixed at 9 batteries.

---

* In addition to these 19 divisions, the 108th and 109th Divisions were formed on the Russian Front in November, 1915.

**7. New formations raised in 1917.**—At the beginning of 1917, a new series of divisions, 13 in number, was formed in Germany. These divisions were numbered from 231 to 242, together with the 15th Bavarian Division. The rank and file of these divisions were composed as follows :—

| | |
|---|---|
| 50 per cent. ... ... | recruits of the 1918 Class. |
| 25 per cent. ... ... | recovered wounded from the depôts in Germany. |
| 25 per cent. ... ... | trained men withdrawn from the front. |

The requisite number of trained men was provided by withdrawing about 10 seasoned men per company from the majority of the divisions on the Western Front. The cavalry and artillery for these new formations were provided by the squadrons and batteries set free owing to the general reduction in the divisional establishment.

These 13 divisions took the field during February, March and April, 1917, three of them being sent to Russia, the remaining 10 to the Western Front. They did not prove a success, owing to the high percentage of the immature 1918 Class which they included.

In addition to these 13 entirely new formations, a further number of new divisions was raised by regrouping the fourth regiments which still existed in a number of divisions, Active, Reserve and Landwehr. Most of the independent Landwehr brigades were thus raised to the status of divisions. In this way all divisions were brought on to the uniform 3-regiment basis, the following new divisions being formed :—

> 5th Guard, 94th, 95th, 96th, 219th, 220th, 227th, 228th, 301st, 302nd, 16th Bavarian, 3rd Naval, 21st Landwehr, 22nd Landwehr, 23rd Landwehr, 24th Landwehr, 26th Landwehr, 29th Landwehr, 38th Landwehr, 44th Landwehr, 45th Landwehr, 46th Landwehr, 48th Landwehr.

By the end of 1917, the number of divisions in the field had risen to 241, excluding the German contingent with the Turkish armies and 3 semi-instructional divisions employed inside Germany for frontier defence.

**8. Organization of an infantry division in war.**—Before the war the Army Corps was the tactical as well as the administrative unit of the German Army. Under the conditions of the present war, where divisions are constantly being relieved and interchanged, the Corps has not proved a suitable tactical unit, and, in the German Army, as in other armies, the *Division* is now the unit of tactical manœuvre, *i.e.*, the smallest self-contained formation of all arms. At the same time, the mobility of the division has been increased by reducing the proportion of infantry (*see* paragraph 5 above).

From the spring of 1915 onwards, the new divisions raised have been independent of a Corps formation (*fliegende Divisionen*); the new Corps staffs which have since been formed have no permanent connection with any division. At the beginning of 1918 there was only one Corps staff for every 3½ divisions in the field, and in many cases even the Active divisions had been entirely dissociated from their original Corps staffs.

All German divisions are now organized on the 3-regiment basis, the three infantry regiments (9 battalions) being grouped under one infantry brigade staff.

The infantry and artillery of practically every division in the German Army are now organized in the following manner :—

# DIVISIONAL HEADQUARTERS.

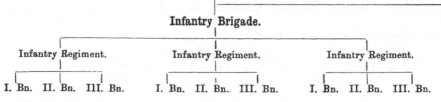

## Infantry Brigade.

| Infantry Regiment. | Infantry Regiment. | Infantry Regiment. |

I. Bn.   II. Bn.   III. Bn.      I. Bn.   II. Bn.   III. Bn.      I. Bn.   II. Bn.   III. Bn.

Each battalion is divided into 4 companies and a machine gun company.   Each company (including the machine gun company) is divided into 3 platoons (*Züge*).

## Artillery Command.*

### Field Artillery Regiment.

I. *Abteilung* (field gun).    II. *Abteilung* (field gun).    III. (*F.*) *Abteilung* (field howitzer).

1st Bty.   2nd Bty.   3rd Bty.      4th Bty.   5th Bty.   6th Bty.      7th Bty.   8th Bty.   9th Bty.

The approximate establishment of a German infantry division is given below :—

|  | Number. | Total Establishment. | |
|---|---|---|---|
| Divisional headquarters .. | 1 | 108 | |
|  | | —— | 108 |
| *Infantry—* | | | |
| Brigade headquarters | 1 | 13 | |
| Regimental headquarters .. | 3 | 177 | |
| Infantry battalions.. | 9 | 6,984 | |
| Machine gun companies .. | 9 | 1,233 | |
|  | | —— | 8,407 |
| *Cavalry—* | | | |
| Cavalry squadron .. | 1 | 170 | |
|  | | —— | 170 |
| *Artillery—* | | | |
| Artillery command.. | 1 | 25 | |
| Field artillery regiment headquarters .. | 1 | 18 | |
| Field artillery *Abteilungen* (headquarters and 3 batteries) .. | 3 | 1,320 | |
|  | | —— | 1,363 |
| *Pioneers—* | | | |
| Pioneer battalion headquarters | 1 | 5 | |
| Field companies .. | 2 | 536 | |
| Searchlight section.. | 1 | 47 | |
| Trench mortar company .. | 1 | 250 | |
|  | | —— | 838 |
| *Divisional Troops—* | | | |
| Telephone detachment | 1 | 200 | |
| Divisional M.T. column | 1 | 100 | |
| Bearer company .. | 1 | 260 | |
| Field hospitals .. | 2 | 122 | |
| Veterinary hospital.. | 1 | 75 | |
|  | | —— | 757 |
|  | | | 11,643 |

\* The artillery commander commands also all the heavy artillery allotted to the divisional sector.

As a general rule each division is accompanied by its field recruit depôt, amounting to about 100 men per infantry battalion.  Thus 900 men should  be added to the above figure, raising it to 12,543.

The above units are all " divisional troops," and move as integral portions of the division.   Other units, such as :—

> Heavy artillery,
> Survey units,
> Mining companies,
> Wireless detachments,
> Machine gun marksman detachments,
> *Minenwerfer* battalions,
> Echelon staffs (comprising columns and train), and
> Labour units,

are allotted by the Higher Command to divisional sectors as required, and are temporarily placed under the orders of the division in whose sector they happen to be.  They do not, however, move with the division when the latter is relieved.

# CHAPTER IV.

## COMMAND AND STAFFS.

1. **The German Military System.**—The general military system of the German Army falls broadly under three headings, which are kept quite separate :—

**Appointments,** under the Chief of the Military Cabinet.
**Administration,** under the Minister of War.
**General Staff,** under the Chief of the General Staff.

The three officers* above mentioned are the highest military authorities and act as personal advisers to the Emperor, who is the supreme head of the Army.

2. **The Military Cabinet** (*Militär-Kabinett*) issues the Official Gazette and Cabinet Orders, and controls all appointments, promotions, transfers, exchanges, retirements, honours and rewards, except for the posting of General Staff officers.

The Chief of the Military Cabinet is senior personal aide-de-camp and military secretary to the Emperor, and is practically his ear and mouthpiece.

3. **Ministry of War** (*Kriegs-Ministerium*).—Each of the four Sovereign States of the Empire has its own Ministry of War, but, in war, authority is entirely centred in the Prussian Ministry of War, while those of the other States merely arrange local details. Only the Prussian Ministry of War will therefore be dealt with in this chapter.

The Minister of War is appointed by the Emperor, and is the highest *administrative* authority in the German Army, but exercises no *military command* over the troops in the field.†

Lieut.-General Wild von Hohenborn, who held this appointment during the first part of the war, was replaced in October, 1916, by General von Stein, who commanded the XIV. Reserve Corps on the Somme. The Minister of War is assisted by a Chief of the Acting General Staff (*Chef des stellvertretenden Generalstabes der Armee*).

**The Ministry of War,** which in peace comprised six departments, now consists of eight :—

I.—**Central Department.** (*Zentral-Departement, ZD.*)

    (*a.*) Ministerial Section. (*Z1.*)
    (*b.*) Estimates and Establishments Section. (*Z2.*)
    (*c.*) Publicity Section. (*Z3.*)
    (*d.*) Central Information Bureau. (*NB.*)

II.—**General War Department.** (*Allgemeines Kriegs-Departement, AD.*)

    (*a.*) Army Section (*A*1.) and Mobilization Section (*Mob. A.*)
    (*b.*) Supply of Officers and Non-commissioned Officers Section (*C* 1*a*).
    (*c.*) Infantry Section. (*A*2.)
    (*d.*) Cavalry Section. (*A*3.)

---

* The names of the officers holding these appointments are given in the Index to "The German Forces in the Field," as are also the names of the higher commanders mentioned on page 39.

† The Minister of War, however, directly controls the Home Army (*Heimatsheer*).

(e). Field Artillery Section.  (*A*4.)
(f.) Foot Artillery Section.  (*A*5.)
(g.) Engineer and Pioneer Section.  (*A*6.)
(h.) Communication Section.  (*A*7*V*.)
(i.) Air Section.  (*A*7*L*.)
(k.) Chemical Section.  (*A*10 )
(l.) Signals Section.  (*A. Nch.*)
(m.) Railway Section.  (*A E.*)*

## III.—Army Administration Department.  (*Armee-Verwaltungs-Departement, BD.*)
(a.) War Supply Section.  (*B*1.)
(b.) Peace Supply Section.  (*B*2.)
(c.) Clothing Section.  (*B*3.)
(d.) Finance Section.  (*B*4.)
(e.) Central Depôt for captured War Material.  (*ZK.*)

## IV.—Quartering Department.  (*Unterkunfts-Departement, UD.*)
(a.) Quartering Section, Western Front.  (*U*1.)
(b ) Quartering Section, Eastern Front.  (*U*2.)
(c.) Training Grounds Section.  (*U*3.)
(d.) Works Section.  (*U*4.)
(e.) Section for the Protection of German Prisoners of War and for Breaches of International Law.  (*U*5.)
(f.) Section for Rationing Prisoners of War.  (*U*6.)
(g.) War Quartering Section.  (*UK.*)

## V.—Pensions and Law Department.  (*Versorgungs- und Justiz-Departement, CD.*)
(a.) Pensions Section.  (*C*2*P*.)
(b.) Annuity Section.  (*C*2*R*.)
(c.) Assistance Section for Officers and Men.  (*C*3*F*.)
(d.) Assistance Section for Soldiers' Dependents.  (*C*3*V*.)
(e.) Law Section.  (*C*4.)

## VI.—Remount Inspection.  (*Remonte-Inspektion, RI.*)

## VII.—Medical Department.  (*Sanitäts-Departement, SD.*)
(a.) Personnel Section  (*S*1.)
(b.) Medical Section.  (*S*2.)
(c.) Assistance Section.  (*S*3.)

## VIII.—War Bureau.  (*Kriegs-Amt, K.*)
(a.) War Recruiting and Labour Department.  (*ED*)—

(1.) War Recruiting Office.  (*C* 1*b*.)
(2.) War Labour Office.  (*AZS.*)

(b.) Munitions Department (*Wumba*†), which has absorbed the Department of the Master of Ordnance (*F*2), and the Manufactories Section of the Ministry of War (*B*5).

---

* For the duration of the war only.      † *Waffen-und Munitions-Beschaffungs-Amt.*

(*c.*) War Raw Materials Section (*KRA*), combined with a Purchase Section for Requisitioned Textiles (*Ab.W*).

(*d.*) Exports and Imports Section. (*A*8.)

(*e.*) National Food Supply Section. (*B*6.)

The new departments formed in the War Ministry during the war are No. IV. (Quartering) and No. VIII. (War Bureau).

The **War Bureau** is the department which is charged with utilizing to the full the resources of the country for war. It was created in October, 1916, when the Ministry of War and General Staff were reorganized, and its five branches, mentioned above, deal with the subjects enumerated below :—

(*a.*) The *War Recruiting and Labour Department* has three reporting offices (*Referate*) connected with parliamentary business and Press propaganda.

There are also six reporting offices for agriculture, mining, steel and machinery, chemistry, armament firms, and exemptions. Besides these there are five sections dealing with the various sources of labour, namely women, prisoners of war and enemy aliens, allied and neutral aliens, civilians between 17 and 60 available under the Auxiliary Service Act, skilled mechanics withdrawn from the army, and soldiers not yet called up.

(*b.*) *The Munitions Department* is divided into four main sections :—

Central Section.
Inspection of Technical Artillery Establishments and Pioneer Depôts.
Inspection of Artillery Depôts. Depôt Inspection (divided into four sub-sections).
Inspection of Technical Infantry Establishments. This branch also inspects the engineer and other depôts.

(*c.*) *The War Raw Materials Section* is divided into 19 sections and deals with explosives, leather, metals, wood, wool, fibre, silk, rags, textiles, rubber, cotton and other raw materials.

(*d.*) *The Exports and Imports Section* deals with statistical questions, and the policy connected with imports, exports and special contracts.

(*e.*) *The National Food Supply Section* operates in conjunction with the War Food Department.

Connected with the War Bureau is a " scientific commission " of 20 leading scientists who form a technical advisory board ; there are also legal and financial experts, and special sections for economic propaganda work in neutral countries and among the troops, and for distributing information among the manufacturers of war supplies.

## 4. The General Staff.—The Staff consists of :—

(*a.*) The General Staff (*Generalstab*), including the *Adjutantur*.
(*b.*) The Great General Staff (*Grosser Generalstab*).

**The General Staff** supplies officers for the whole Army.

With few exceptions, every staff officer has undergone a course of three years' training at the Staff College (*Kriegs-Akademie*), and has been attached to the Great General Staff before taking up an appointment on the staff of a Corps or division.

The *Adjutantur*, *i.e.*, the Administrative or Routine Staff, consisted in peace mainly of Staff College graduates who had not been selected for appointment to the General Staff. *Adjutantur* officers hold 2nd Grade appointments on the staffs of Corps, divisions, and brigades.

**The Great General Staff** is an inner ring of selected staff officers working in Berlin and at General Headquarters, directly under the Chief of the General Staff. Its work comprises everything which comes under the heading of Operations, Movements and Intelligence.

5. **General Headquarters.**—Up to March, 1917, General Headquarters (*Grosses Hauptquartier*) was at Charleville. The Emperor's General Headquarters was then moved back to Kreuznach,* while General Headquarters for the Western Front remained at Charleville. All orders and gazettes concerning the Field Army are issued from General Headquarters, with the exception of administrative and technical orders, which emanate from the Ministry of War.

The General Staff at General Headquarters is presided over by the Chief of the General Staff of the Field Army, who has a special branch under him, concerned with operations and ammunition allotment. The Quartermaster-General (*Generalquartiermeister*) and a branch of the Ministry of War are also at General Headquarters. In addition, there are the following Directors and heads of departments:—

General of Foot Artillery (*General von der Fussartillerie*).
Director of Railways (*Chef des Feldeisenbahnwesens*).
General Commanding the Air Forces (*Kommandierender Gen. der Luftstreitkräfte*).
Director of Signals (*Chef des Nachrichtenwesens*).
Director of Mechanical Transport (*Chef des Feldkraftfahrwesens*).
Director of Survey (*Chef des Kriegsvermessungswesens*).
Director of Medical Services (*Chef des Feldsanitätswesens*).
Intendant-General of the Field Army (*General-Intendant des Feldheeres*).
Director of Anti-Aircraft Guns (*Chef der Flug-Abwehr-Kanonen*)
Inspector of Gas Regiments (*Inspekteur der Gasregimenter*).

The General of the Engineer and Pioneer Corps is at General Headquarters on the Western Front.

The War Ministry is represented by a staff at General Headquarters.

6. **The Higher Command.**—The supreme command of the Field Army (*Oberste Heeresleitung*) is vested in the Emperor as *Oberkommandierender Kriegsherr*. The Emperor's principal adviser with regard to all military operations is the Chief of the General Staff of the Field Army (*Chef des Generalstabes des Feldheeres*), who has under him a special department dealing with operations and ammunition allotment.

Early in 1915, General v. Moltke was succeeded as Chief of the General Staff by Lieut.-General Erich von Falkenhayn. He was, in turn, succeeded by Field-Marshal von Hindenburg in August, 1916. Under the Chief of the General Staff is the *Erster Oberquartiermeister* or Deputy Chief of the General Staff (Ludendorff).

The Emperor nominally retains the personal command of the main Groups of Armies operating on the Western Front.

The higher command in the Eastern Theatre is delegated to the Commander-in-Chief on the Eastern Front (*Oberbefehlshaber Ost*), and to the Commander-in-Chief in the South-Eastern Theatre.

---

* The Emperor's General Headquarters was moved to Spa in February, 1918.

The Commander-in-Chief on the Eastern Front (*Obost*) has practically a separate General Headquarters, with the following independent directors :—

Director of Ammunition Supply (*Chef des Feldmunitionswesens beim Obost*).
Director of Medical Services (*Feldsanitätschef beim Obost*).
Army-Intendant (*Armee-Intendant beim Obost*).

The forces operating on the Russo-Roumanian Front were formed in two German Groups of Armies and one Austrian Group of Armies. There is, however, a German Chief of the General Staff for the Army front of the Archduke Joseph.

The South-Eastern Group of Armies includes the Army Group operating on the Macedonian Front.

The German Army operating on the Italian Front in 1917/1918 was nominally under the Austro-Hungarian General Headquarters.

A Group of Armies (*Heeresgruppe*) consists of two to five Armies, and is commanded by a Field-Marshal or *General-Oberst*.

7. **Composition and Staff of an Army.**—An Army (*Armee*) consists of three to six Corps, but this varies considerably on different sectors of the front. The average number of divisions in an Army on the Western Front is 15. An Army is usually commanded by a *General-Oberst*.

The forces operating in Lorraine and Alsace are grouped in Army Detachments (*Armee-Abteilungen*), each of six to ten divisions.

The Staff of an Army in the field is divided into four sections, under the Chief of the General Staff of the Army, as follows :—

**Section I.—General Staff** (*Generalstab*).—Consisting of General Staff Officers. It is divided into the following sub-sections :—

I(*a*).—Operations, orders, order of battle, tactics, training.

I(*b*).—Areas, movements, traffic regulations, road control, salvage.

I(*c*).—Intelligence, air service, signals.

*I(*d*).—Ammunition supply (artillery and infantry).

**Section II.—Administrative Staff** (*Adjutantur*).—Consisting of one General Staff officer and several *Adjutantur* officers. It is divided into—

II(*a*).—Personnel, promotions, honours and rewards, leave, chaplains, lectures, regimental newspapers, supply, transport, clothing, boots, captured material.

II(*b*).—Organization, establishments, strengths, returns, billeting, replacing of guns, ammunition and horses, contre-espionage and censorship, graves registration, railway service.

II(*c*).—Interior economy, routine orders, returns.

**Section III.—Military Law** (*Feldjustizamt*), under the Judge-Advocate (*Kriegsgerichtsrat*).
Provost-Marshal's duties, discipline, courts martial.

---

* This section is also controlled by the *Oberquartiermeister*, but it is sometimes known as I(*c*).

**Section IV.**—**Intendance** (*Intendantur*), medical and veterinary services, staffed by military officials, medical and veterinary officers.

IV(*a*) —Administrative details, rations, clothing, pay, allowances, requisitions, food-prices, local contributions, postal service, dealings with civilians.

IV(*b*).—Medical services, anti-gas measures.

IV(*c*) or IV(*d*).—Veterinary services.*

Sections I(*d*), II, III and IV are directly subordinate to the *Oberquartiermeister* of the Army, but the work of all the sections is co-ordinated under the Chief of the General Staff.

The *Generalstabschef* of an Army corresponds to our Major-General, General Staff. The *Oberquartiermeister* corresponds to the Deputy Adjutant and Quartermaster-General of a British Army, but is an officer of the General Staff, and is subordinate to the *Generalstabschef.* Administrative and routine orders are issued over the signature of the *Oberquartiermeister.*

In addition to the General and Administrative Staffs, there are various other technical advisers and directors at the Headquarters of each Army :—

General of Artillery (*General von der Artillerie*).

General of Pioneers (*General der Pioniere*).

Army Signal Commander (*Akonach*).†

Army Aviation Commander (*Kofl.*).

Army Balloon Commander (*Koluft*).

Commander of Anti-Aircraft Guns (*Koflak*).

Staff Officer for Machine Gun Troops (*Stomag*).

Intelligence Officer (*Nachrichten-Offizier*)—sometimes included in I(*c*).

Gas Officer (*Stabs-Offizier-Gas*)—sometimes included in IV(*b*).

Staff Officer for Survey (*Stoverm*).

Mechanical Transport Commander (*Kdeur. d. Krftr.*).

Commander of Ammunition Columns and Trains (*Kdeur. d. Mun. Kol. u. Tr.*).

Camp Commandant (*Kdt. d. H. Qu.*).

There are also a number of attached officers, such as chaplains, &c.

The above gives a typical distribution of duties at the Headquarters of a German Army, but the details differ somewhat in the different Armies, and the functions of some of the sections have not yet been clearly established.

*Organization of the Staff of a German Army.*

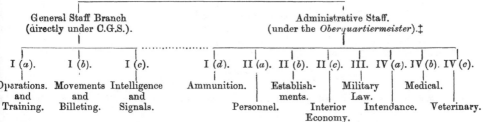

ARMY COMMANDER.

Chief of the General Staff.

| General Staff Branch (directly under C.G.S.). | | | Administrative Staff. (under the *Oberquartiermeister*).‡ | | | | | | |
|---|---|---|---|---|---|---|---|---|---|
| I (*a*). | I (*b*). | I (*c*). | I (*d*). | II (*a*). | II (*b*). | II (*c*). | III. | IV (*a*). | IV (*b*). IV (*c*). |
| Operations. and Training. | Movements and Billeting. | Intelligence and Signals. | Ammunition. Personnel. | Establishments. Interior Economy. | | | Military Law. Intendance. | | Medical. Veterinary. |

The headquarters staff of an Army comprises about 50 staff officers and 40 officials.

* Sometimes known as Section V.

† Has under him the Army Telephone Commander (*Akofern*) and the Army Wireless Commander *Akofunk*).

‡ The *Oberquartiermeister* is a senior General Staff Officer.

**8. The Staff of a Corps and division.**—The organization of a Corps staff is similar to that of an Army staff as given above, and is divided into the same sections, I, II, III and IV. A Corps staff comprises about 30 staff officers and 25 officials.

The staff of a division is, naturally, much smaller than that of an Army or Corps; the system is similar in principle but less complicated in detail. The divisional staff consists of two General Staff officers (majors or captains), two *Adjutantur* officers (captains or lieutenants), and two orderly officers (*Ordonnanz-Offiziere*).

Besides the General Staff, artillery commander and pioneer commander, a divisional headquarters comprises the following :—

> Divisional signal commander (*Divkonach*).
> Camp Commandant (*Kommandant des Hauptquartiers*).
> Administration (*Feldintendantur*).
> Supply office (*Feldproviantamt*).
> Supply officer (*Verpflegungsoffizier*).
> Transport officer (*Führer der grossen Bagage*).
> Judge-Advocate's office (*Kriegsgericht*).
> Medical officer (*Divisionsarzt*) and assistant.
> Anti-gas officer (*Gas-Schutz-Offizier*).
> Veterinary officer (*Divisionsveterinär*).
> Protestant and Roman Catholic Chaplains (*Divisionspfarrer*).
> Field Post Office (*Feldpostexpedition*).

A total of 20—25 officers and officials.

The divisional artillery commander has 1 staff officer (*Adjutant*) and 3 orderly officers.

An infantry brigade headquarters comprises the brigade commander, 1 staff officer (*Adjutant*), 2 orderly officers and 2 chaplains.

**9. The chain of command in the field.**—The Army Corps, of two divisions, which, in peace, formed the unit of higher command, has not proved a suitable formation under war conditions. The unit of strategic manœuvre has become the division, and the divisions have in practically all cases become entirely independent of their original Corps grouping. Corps staffs normally remain semi-permanently in a sector after the divisions composing the Corps have been transferred elsewhere. In the field, three or four divisions are usually grouped under one Corps staff.

During the Somme battle, when divisions had to be relieved frequently, semi-permanent "Groups" were formed in the First and Second Armies. Each Group held a definite sector of the front with two, three or four divisions in line. These Groups were similar to our Corps, and this system has now become general on all sectors of the front.

In an infantry division, the chain of command has been considerably simplified by the reorganization of all divisions on a three-regiment basis.

The divisional commander issues his orders to :—

> (*a.*) the infantry brigade commander,
> (*b.*) the divisional artillery commander,

who respectively command all the infantry and artillery units (including heavy artillery operating in the divisional sector.

# CHAPTER V.

## INFANTRY.

**1. Infantry organization.**—The German infantry is organized in regiments of three battalions. As stated in Chapter III., a division comprises three infantry regiments grouped under an infantry brigade staff.

There are still some independent battalions, such as *Jäger, Schützen*, ski and mountain battalions, but the tendency has been to combine all independent battalions into regiments. The *Jäger* (Rifle) battalions, one of which was originally attached to each Corps, consisted of specially picked men, who wear a distinctive grey-green uniform and shako.

During 1916, most of the *Jäger* battalions were combined to form *Jäger* regiments, and in 1917, a *Jäger* division was formed to take part in the Italian campaign.

## 2. Organization of an infantry regiment.—

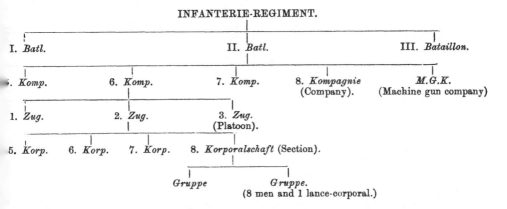

INFANTERIE-REGIMENT.

The above diagram shows the chain of command in an infantry regiment. The three battalions of the regiment are numbered I., II. and III. Each battalion consists of four companies and a machine gun company; the companies are numbered from 1 to 12 throughout the regiment; the machine gun companies are numbered 1, 2 and 3. A company is organized in three platoons, numbered 1, 2, 3 in each company. Each platoon (*Zug*) is divided into four sections,* numbered from 1 to 12 throughout the company. The smallest subdivision is the group (*Gruppe*) of 8 men and a lance-corporal.

Each company has four stretcher bearers (*Krankenträger*).

The organization of a machine gun company is given on page 56.

---

* The *Korporalschaft* is an administrative, not a tactical unit; there are now usually only three *Korporalschaften* in a platoon owing to the reduction in company strengths.

The various units are nominally commanded as follows:—

Regiment by a colonel (*Oberst*), with a Lieut.-Col. (*Oberstleutnant*) as second-in-command.

Battalion by a major (*Major*).

Company    „    captain (*Hauptmann*).

Platoon    „    lieutenant (*Oberleutnant*) or 2nd Lieut. (*Leutnant*).

Section    „    corporal (*Unteroffizier*).

Squad    „    lance-corporal (*Gefreiter*).

In practice, a regiment is now usually commanded by a major, a battalion by a captain, a company by a subaltern, and a platoon by an *Offizierstellvertreter* or *Vizefeldwebel*.

The war establishments (excluding machine gun companies) are shown in the following table:—

| — | Officers. | Medical officers and paymasters. | Other ranks. | Horses. | Vehicles. |
|---|---|---|---|---|---|
| Company .. .. .. .. | 5 | .. | 259 | 10 | 4 |
| Battalion .. .. .. .. | 23* | 3 | 1,050 | 59 | 19 |
| Regiment .. .. .. .. | 73 | 10 | 3,204 | 193 | 59 |
| Regimental Staff .. .. .. | 4† | 1 | 54 | 16 | 2 |

According to a Prussian War Ministry Order of the 12th March, 1917, it was intended to reduce the strength of a battalion to 750 other ranks, of whom 100 were to be *g.v.* or *a.v.* men. This reduction in establishment was to be carried into effect consequent on the issue of 3 light machine guns ('08/'15 pattern) to each infantry company.

At the end of 1917 the approximate strength of a German infantry battalion was estimated at 800 other ranks, but in 1918 the strength was raised to 850 rifles, excluding the machine gun company.

3. **Transport.**—The transport of a regiment of 3 battalions at war establishment, exclusive of the machine gun companies, consists of 16 led horses, 58 two-horsed vehicles, and 1 four-horsed vehicle, and is organized thus :—

### Transport of a regiment.

**1st Line Transport** (*Gefechts-Bagage*)—

16 led horses (1 per company and 4 for regimental staff).

12 small-arm ammunition wagons (1 per company).

12 travelling kitchens (1 per company).

3 infantry medical store wagons (1 per battalion).

**Train** ‡ (*Grosse Bagage*)—

16 baggage wagons (1 per company, 1 per battalion staff and 1 for regimental staff).

12 supply wagons (1 per company).

3 sutlers' wagons (1 per battalion).

1 tool wagon (four-horsed).

* Includes a supply officer (*Verpflegungs-Offizier*).    † Includes a transport officer (*Bagage-Führer*).
‡ According to a captured document, a light 2-wheeled telephone cart has been added to the transport of an infantry regiment. It is not certain whether this is an authorized war establishment.

All infantry transport wagons are four-wheeled, drawn by two horses (except the tool wagon) and painted grey. They are driven from the box and, with the exception of the small-arm ammunition wagons and travelling kitchens, are made up of a body only, with a fore-carriage which locks under. The small-arm ammunition wagon is composed of two boxes, rigidly connected by futchells, and carries 14,400 rounds, or about 70 per rifle.

## Transport of a battalion.

(Without machine gun company).

### 1st Line Transport (*Gefechts-Bagage*)—

4 led horses.
4 company small-arm ammunition wagons.
4 travelling kitchens.
1 infantry medical store wagon.

### Train (*Grosse Bagage*)—

1 baggage wagon for battalion headquarters.
4 company baggage wagons.
5 supply wagons (including 1 sutler's wagon).

## Transport of a Company.

### 1st Line Transport (*Gefechts-Bagage*)—

1 led horse.
1 company small-arm ammunition wagon.
1 travelling kitchen.

### Train (*Grosse Bagage*)—

1 company baggage wagon.
1 company supply wagon.

4. **Regimental specialists.**—During 1915 and 1916, the requirements of trench warfare caused a number of specialist companies, detachments and sections to be attached to infantry regiments. Artificers and men with special trade qualifications were selected from the battalions of the regiment and formed into regimental pioneer companies, entrenching and tunnelling companies, concrete construction sections, &c.

As the formation of these unauthorized units reduced the company rifle strength considerably, the practice was discouraged, and regular units were formed for carrying out special duties of this nature. The experiences of the 1916 campaign, however, led the Germans to organize, internally within each infantry regiment, three special units, viz.:—

(a.) Light machine gun sections, two* per company, each consisting of 3 light machine guns ('08/'15 pattern) (*see* page 61).

(b.) *Minenwerfer* detachments, one per battalion, each consisting of 4 light *Minenwerfer* (*see* page 102).

(c.) Signalling detachments (*Nachrichtenmittelabteilungen*) of varying strengths (*see* page 117).

The men forming these units are not supernumerary to the regimental establishment, but remain on the nominal rolls of the companies from which they are drawn.

---

\* At the beginning of 1918, the majority of infantry companies probably had only one light machine gun section, but the full establishment is two.

5. **Cyclist units.**—Prior to mobilization, the only cyclist units in the German Army were the cyclist companies of *Jäger* battalions. Each of these battalions had one, and in some cases two, cyclist companies.

During the war, a number of new cyclist companies have been formed, and, by the end of 1917, about 150 were in existence. Some of the new divisions formed during the war have been provided with divisional cyclist companies, and a few of the cavalry divisions are also provided with cyclist companies.

A number of cyclist companies have been grouped into cyclist battalions, of four companies each. These units first appeared in September, 1916, when five cyclist battalions were formed, and a sixth in July, 1917. Two of these battalions were formed on the Western Front, and took part in the Somme battle, but they were all transferred to Roumania in November, 1916, where the 1st, 2nd and 3rd Cyclist Battalions were grouped to form the Cyclist Brigade.

Cyclist battalions appear to be used as a mobile reserve, and are concentrated at points from which they can be moved up rapidly as reinforcements.

The Cyclist Brigade, in conjunction with a composite cavalry division, covered the German retirement to the "Hindenburg Line" in March, 1917, and took part in the operations at Oesel in October, 1917. It has also been employed to relieve temporarily divisions in line in Flanders, and in guarding the Dutch-Belgian frontier.

The war establishment of a cyclist company is as follows :—

*War establishment of a cyclist company.*

| —— | Officers. | Other ranks. | Vehicles. |
|---|---|---|---|
| Company commander .. .. .. | 1 | .. | .. |
| Lieutenants .. .. .. .. .. | 2 | .. | .. |
| *Feldwebel* .. .. .. .. .. | .. | 1 | .. |
| *Vizefeldwebel*.. .. .. .. .. | .. | 2 | .. |
| *Unteroffiziere* or *Oberjäger* .. .. | .. | 12 | .. |
| Armourer, non-commissioned officer .. | .. | 1 | .. |
| Lance-corporals .. .. .. .. | .. | 11 | .. |
| Privates .. .. .. .. .. | .. | 111 | .. |
| Cavalry or Train non-commissioned officer.. | .. | 1 | .. |
| Medical corporal .. .. .. .. | .. | 1 | .. |
| Train privates.. .. .. .. .. | .. | 7 | .. |
| Mechanical transport drivers .. .. | .. | 3 | .. |
| Touring car .. .. .. .. .. | .. | .. | 1 |
| Lorries . .. .. .. .. .. | .. | .. | 2 |
| 4-horsed small-arm ammunition wagon .. | .. | .. | 1 |
| 4-horsed large travelling kitchen .. .. | .. | .. | 1 |
| 4-horsed supply wagon .. .. .. | .. | .. | 1 |

6. **Mountain units.**—In peace, a few *Jäger* battalions were trained annually in mountain and winter warfare. During the war, four ski battalions were formed in Bavaria, and one ski battalion in Württemberg.

The 1st, 2nd, 3rd and 4th Ski Battalions form the 3rd *Jäger* Regiment in the Alpine Corps. These battalions were formed in the spring of 1915, and were sent to the Trentino. They were afterwards employed in Serbia, and in the spring of 1916 were transferred to the Western Front, where they took part in the battle of Verdun. In August, 1916, they went to the Carpathians, where they were attached to the 200th Division.

The Württemberg Ski Battalion (*Württembergisches Gebirgs- und Schneeschuh-Bataillon*) fought in the Vosges until October, 1916, when it was transferred to Transylvania. In the spring of 1917 the battalion returned to the Vosges. Later, it was sent to Roumania, and arrived on the Italian Front in November, 1917. It consists of nine companies.

Mountain units wear a grey uniform with green facings and twisted cord on the shoulders, similar to that worn by foresters. The stand and fall collar bears the letter " S " on either side. A mountaineering cap, similar to the Austrian, is worn, with two cockades in front and an Edelweiss badge at the side. Ankle boots and puttees are worn.

7. **Assault detachments.**—A noteworthy feature of infantry organization has been the introduction of " Assault Detachments " (*Sturmtrupps*). These units consist of picked men whose initiative and skill in attack are developed by special training. Assault detachments were first used in the Verdun fighting, and the idea has since been extensively developed.

During the latter part of 1916 an assault company (*Sturmkompagnie*) was formed in a number of divisions. An assault company usually consists of 1 officer and 120 men ; the company is organized in 3 platoons, one of which is often attached to each regiment of the division. These units are mainly employed in patrolling, and in carrying out trench raids and offensive operations.

In most of the Armies on the Western Front an assault battalion (*Sturmbataillon*) has been formed. An assault battalion usually comprises—

> 4 assault companies.
> Infantry gun battery.
> Light trench mortar detachment.
> Light flame-projector detachment (*Kleif-Trupp*).
> Machine gun company.
> Park company.

Assault battalions are sent up to the front to take part in special operations and raids. When not so employed they act as schools for training divisional assault detachments.

Assault battalions wear puttees. The men of assault battalions are known as " Grenadiers " and wear *Litzen* (*see* page 152).

8. **Armament.**—(*a.*) **General.**—The following table shows how infantry personnel are armed :—

| | |
|---|---|
| Sword and '08 automatic pistol    .. .. | Officers, medical officers, officials, serjeant-majors, ensigns, and vice-serjeant-majors. |
| Short side-arm ..    ..    ..    ..    .. | Drummers, buglers, bandsmen, officers' servants, and medical personnel. |
| Short side-arm and '98 carbine    ..    .. | Transport drivers. |
| '98 rifle and short side-arm    ..    ..    .. | Other ranks. |

The four company stretcher bearers are armed with rifles, but do not take them into action. Machine gun troops are armed with pistols and short bayonets.

(*b.*) **The rifle.**—The '98 pattern of rifle is on the Mauser system: calibre, ·311-inch (7·9-mm.); weight, empty, without bayonet, 9 lbs. 3 ozs.; length, 48·6 inches; length of barrel, 29·05 inches; number of grooves, 4; width of groove, ·153 inch; depth of groove, ·0049 inch; twist of rifle, right-handed, 1 in 30·2 calibres (1 turn in 9·39 inches); maximum rate of fire obtainable, 35 to 40 rounds per minute.

The left side of the body is cut down flush with the bottom of the bolt recess and, therefore, level with the top of the magazine. This enables all the cartridges to be pushed into the magazine with the flat of the thumb, and avoids the necessity of pressing the last cartridge in the charger home with the point of the thumb.

The cartridges are held together by a grooved charger or strip (*falzartiger Halter oder Ladestreifen*), which grips the bases only, and falls out when the breech is closed after the five cartridges have been put in. They, therefore, lie free in the magazine, and single cartridges can be put in at any time. There is no cut-off.

The cartridges are arranged in two vertical rows, one of three, the other of two rounds, close against each other, so that the magazine is small and entirely in the stock.

A certain number of detachable magazines (*Ansteckmagazin*) holding 25 cartridges have been issued with the object of providing an increased volume of fire. Rifles fitted with these magazines are awkward to handle, and are only suited for certain phases of trench warfare.

The extractor consists of a piece of spring steel extending a little more than half the length of the bolt. It is dovetailed on to a ring of steel which works in a cannelure near the fore-part of the bolt.

The platform is actuated by a W-shaped spring of ribbon steel. The bottom of the magazine dovetails into its seat and is secured by a stud and spring. It is easily removed for cleaning purposes.

The bolt is a single steel forging with no separate bolt-head. It is retained in the body by a stud on the left, and is removed by pulling out a hinged spring shutter to which the ejector is attached. The bolt is provided with an extra lug engaging in a recess in the cylindrical part of the rear end of the body. On the bolt is a small rib which acts as a guide in withdrawing it. The rib lies underneath the extractor and supports it when the bolt is closed. The bolt can be stripped without tools.

The bands are secured by means of spring catches.

The rear end of the bolt is provided with a safety catch, which is manipulated by the thumb and forefinger from left to right, and can only be used when the mainspring is compressed.

The backsight consists of—

(i.) The bed, which is graduated for 200 metres* and for every 50 metres from 300 to 2,000, and has a series of notches cut on either side. Those on the left side give the elevation for hundreds of metres, and those on the right for the intermediate fifties.

(ii.) The sliding-piece, which is provided with spring clutches to engage in the notches, and a pointer.

(iii.) The girder-shaped leaf, which is of unusual strength, and is supported by the sliding-piece.

The foresight is a barleycorn, dovetailed into its block at right angles to the axis of the barrel.

---

\* 10 metres equal 11 yards, nearly.

Three rifles fitted with telescopic sights are issued to every infantry company.
'arious patterns of periscopic sights have also been tried.

Detachable luminous sights (backsight and foresight) are issued for use with the
ervice rifle. They consist of a "bead" of luminous paint and a V-shaped backsight
lefined by a line of luminous paint.

(c.) **Automatic pistol.**—The '83 pattern revolver has been replaced by the '08
utomatic pistol.

This pistol takes eight cartridges, has a calibre of ·354 inch (9 mm.) and weighs
·8 lbs. (835 grammes). The length of its bore is 122 mm.

The length of the cartridge is 29 mm., weight 12·5 grammes, and weight of charge
35 grammes. The bullet has a blunted point and weighs 8 grammes.

The maximum range is 1,640 yards, and the velocity at 40 feet from the muzzle is
84 f.s.

(d.) **Bayonet.**—The latest pattern bayonet used with the '98 rifle is about 18 inches
46 cm.) long.

The weight of the bayonet and scabbard is 1¼ lbs.

9. **Ammunition.**—The following types of ammunition (calibre ·311-inch) are used
vith the German '98 pattern rifle, the '08 and '08/15 (heavy and light) machine guns, and
he Bergmann, Madsen and Parabellum machine guns :—

(a.) **" S " Ammunition** (*Spitz-Munition ; Spitze*=point).

The bullet is pointed in shape. It is 1·10 inches (28 mm.) in length, and tapers down
ɔ a diameter of only ·05 inch (1·25 mm.) at the point, so that only ·3 inch of the bullet
ɔuches the bore of the rifle.

The bullet is made of lead, with an envelope of steel coated with cupro-nickel, and is
lightly cupped at the base. It weighs 154·32 grains (10 grammes). The cap of the
rass cartridge-case is edged with *black* lacquer.

The powder consists of graphited nitro-cellulose in flakes. The weight of the charge
48·4 grains (3·15 grammes).

The muzzle velocity is stated to be 2,821 f.s. as against 2,034 f.s. with the '88 pattern
mmunition formerly in use.

(b.) **" R " Ammunition** (*Rillen-Munition ; Rille*=groove). This ammunition differs
om the ordinary " S " ammunition in the following particular :—

A shallow groove about 1 mm. wide, into which the cartridge-case is crimped, is cut
ɔund the lower end of the bullet. The object of this groove is to obviate stoppages
ιused by loose cases. According to an official document, all bullets of the " S " type will
future have this groove.

(c.) **Armour-piercing ammunition** (*K-Munition* or *S.m.K.; Spitz mit Kern;
ern=core*).

The envelope, instead of being filled with lead, contains a hardened steel core set
lead.

Externally this ammunition is almost exactly similar to the " S " ammunition, the
ιly distinguishing features being a somewhat blunter point, a *red* lacquer edging round

the cap of the cartridge, and usually the letter "K" on the base instead of "S." The actual bullet is, however, considerably longer, though the portion projecting beyond the cartridge is the same length. This "K" ammunition is used against aircraft, loophole plates, &c., and particularly against tanks.

(*d.*) **Armour-piercing tracer ammunition** (*L.S. Munition; L.S. = Leucht-Spur* or *Licht-Spur* = luminous trace).—Indistinguishable externally from the above, though in some cases the bullet is darkened near the point. The rim of the cap is painted red. The forward half of the envelope of the bullet contains a steel core set in lead, the rest being filled with tracer composition. The base is closed by a brass washer, through which appears the igniting mixture. This bullet traces up to about 600 yards.

(*e.*) **Explosive ammunition** (*L.E. Munition; L.E. = Luft-Einschiess* = aerial ranging.)—The bullet is similar in appearance to the old-fashioned round-nosed bullet, except that it is longer and the nose is pierced by a small hole to act as a gas escape The explosion is caused by an igniting device actuated by the shock of discharge, and takes place in less than one second after firing, at a range of about 300 yards. The bullet produces a puff of white smoke on bursting and is intended for ranging purposes. It has been discarded.

(*f.*) **Incendiary tracer ammunition** (*Brand-Munition*).—The bullet is flatter or the shoulder than the armour-piercing bullet. The bullet consists of a steel envelope coppered inside and outside, the forward portion of which is filled with yellow phosphorus It is closed by a lead plug. The base of the bullet is painted red, and at the side of the bullet is a filling hole closed with solder. In a complete round this hole is not visible As regards the cartridge-case, the rim of the cap is painted black.

It would appear that this bullet has been designed primarily for incendiary effect, but it traces after about 30 yards and remains tracing for about 500 yards.

(*g.*) The old round-nosed bullet is still sometimes met with.

Loading clips are made of iron coated with zinc. A clip holds five rounds.

(*h.*) **Cartridge-cases.**—Brass cases appear to be still in general use, but, for reasons o economy, attempts have been made to produce a suitable coppered steel case. In April 1917, notice was given that, in future, one third of the "S" ammunition would be issued with steel cases for use with rifles only.

10. **Distribution of ammunition.**—The following is the distribution of ammunition in the field :—

|  | Number of rounds per man. |
|---|---|
| Carried on the soldier .. .. .. .. .. .. .. | 150 |
| In the company ammunition wagon (holding 14,400 rounds) .. | 70 |
| *In the infantry ammunition columns (28,800 in each wagon), some | 155 |
| *In the heavy ammunition column, some .. .. .. .. | 20 |
| Total .. .. .. .. .. | 395 |

Cartridges are made up in clips of five, three of which form a packet (*Schachtel*); packets (225 rounds) are put up into a box weighing, packed, 16·97 lbs., and 64 of these are carried in each company ammunition wagon, which thus holds 14,400 rounds, weighing 1,069 lbs.

---

* The infantry and heavy ammunition columns have now been reorganized.

11. **Grenades.**\*—(*a.*) **Rifle grenades.**—The older patterns of rifle grenades were fitted with a rod or tail. Their manufacture was abandoned owing to their want of accuracy.

The new pattern closely resembles the *Vivens-Bessières* grenade in use in the French Army. It is fired out of a cylindrical cup or discharger attached to the service rifle, using ordinary ball ammunition.

The grenade is cylindrical in shape and is bored centrally to permit the passage of the bullet. It weighs 1 lb.

The cup is $11\frac{1}{8}$ inches in length, the cylindrical portion being $5\frac{1}{8}$ inches long, with an interior diameter of $2\frac{3}{8}$ inches. Near the bottom is a ledge to carry the grenade. The stem of the cup, $5\frac{1}{8}$ inches long, slips over the muzzle of the rifle, and is secured by a collar.

The maximum range of this new rifle grenade has been found by trial to be about 210 yards.

(*b.*) **Hand grenades.**—The following are the types in general use :—

The "**Cylindrical grenade with handle**" (*Stielhandgranate*), sometimes known as the "jam-pot and stick grenade"). This is a time grenade ($5\frac{1}{2}$ secs.). It would appear from captured orders that this grenade with a short-burning fuze (2-3 secs.) is issued to "assault" troops.

The "**Egg grenade**" (*Eierhandgranate*). This is a small time grenade of the shape, and about the size, of a hen's egg. It weighs only 11 oz. and can be thrown about 50 yards. The bursting charge, consisting of a mixture of black powder, potassium perchlorate, barium nitrate and aluminium powder, is exploded by a time fuze fitted with a friction lighter. The effect of this bomb is small and very local. Duration of burning, 8 secs. when fired from a thrower, 5 secs. when intended to be thrown by hand.

(*c.*) **Gas and smoke grenades.**—Gas and smoke grenades have never been employed by the Germans to any great extent. The type now in use consists of a spherical iron container about 4 inches in diameter, made of thin sheet iron and containing about two-thirds of a pint of liquid, which is scattered by the explosion of a small charge of black powder. The liquid is sometimes in a porcelain container. The usual friction igniter (time) is used. The following types are known; these differ merely by the nature of the liquid filling :—

*Handgasbombe* "*B*," marked "**B**" in red lettering ; contents, mono- and di-bromethyl-ketones ; nature, lachrymatory.

*Handgasbombe* "*C*," marked "**Gas C**" in red lettering ; contents, methylsulphuric chloride ; nature, lethal and lachrymatory.

*Reizgasbombe* "*R*," marked "**R**" in red lettering.

*Nebelbombe* "*N*," marked "**Nebel**"; contents, "*N*" *Stoff*, *i.e.*, chlorsulphonic acid ; produces an opaque white cloud of very heavy smoke, which clings to the ground. The smoke is an irritant, but is not poisonous.

(*d.*) **Portable flares.**—The infantry are issued with a ground flare (*Flammenfeuer*) and torch flare (*Magnesiumfackel*). The latter is a long white metal tube, filled with flare composition, and provided with a wooden handle.

---

\* *See* "Instructions on Bombing," Part I. (S.S. 182).

**12. Equipment.—**(*a.*) **Personal.—**The man's kit, consisting of—

| | |
|---|---|
| 1 pair " slacks," | 1 pair drawers, |
| 1 forage cap, | 1 pair lace shoes, |
| 2 shirts, | 1 set boot brushes, |
| 1 pair of socks, | 1 grease tin, |
| 2 handkerchiefs, | 1 copper tin, |
| 1 rice bag, | 1 salt bag, |
| 1 housewife, | |

is carried in a cowhide pack, supported by braces attached to the waistbelt. Inside the pack is a bag for preserved meat rations (iron rations), which can be carried separately if the packs are left behind. An aluminium (blackened) canteen, containing a cup which can be used as a frying pan with detachable handle, is carried on the back of the pack; the canteen holds $4\frac{1}{4}$ pints. On the waistbelt, on each side of the buckle in front, is a leather pouch for 45 rounds, and 30 more are carried in the haversack, and the other 30 in pockets placed in the corners of the flap of the pack (150 rounds in all), The haversack (containing an aluminium drinking-cup) is carried looped on to the belt on the right side, and hooked on in rear of it is the water-bottle, of aluminium, felt-covered, with aluminium screw-stopper and a capacity of $1\frac{3}{4}$ pints. On the left side are carried the sword-bayonet and the entrenching tool. The tools (spade, pick or hatchet), the metal portions of which are enclosed in leather cases, are hung (by means of a leather loop on the cases) from the belt handle downwards, immediately behind the bayonet. Each man also carries a portion of a tent, consisting of a square of canvas, a pole in three pieces, three tent pegs and a cord two men, therefore, carry the equipment (*Zeltausrüstung*) for one tent which can accommodate both. The whole equipment, put together, can be taken off and put on like a coat The total weight, including arms, carried in field service marching order by an infantry soldier of medium height, is about 55 lbs. (*See* Plate 5.)

Field glasses are issued in the proportion of five per company.

Steel helmets are issued for trench warfare. The German steel helmet is made of hard, magnetic nickel-steel, and is rather heavier than our own, weighing complete about 2 lb. 8 oz. The helmet has a large lug projecting from either side to which a thick, bullet-proof, protective face-shield can be attached. This shield is very heavy, and is probably intended only for use by snipers and sentries. The Germans have a high opinion of the value of the steel helmet.

(*b.*) **Telephone.—**Prior to mobilization, it was laid down that each infantry regiment should provide 6 telephone squads (*Fernsprech-Trupps*), each consisting of 1 corporal or lance-corporal and 3 men. Each of these squads carried 3,300 yards of cable and 1 army telephone; two squads were necessary to construct a line, the maximum length of which was 6,600 yards. This allotment of stores provided for communication between the regiment and each of its 3 battalions.

It would appear from captured documents that the above allotment has been considerably increased; the present organization for open warfare varies, but appears to be roughly as follows:—

Each battalion has a telephone detachment (*Fernsprech-Abteilung*), consisting of an officer and 4 company squads (*Trupps*) each of 1 non-commissioned officer and 3 men. The detachment is provided with 4 army telephones and sufficient cable to erect 13,000 yards of line.

The 3 battalion detachments of an infantry regiment are responsible for all telephone communications from the infantry brigade downwards. Under the new organization, neither brigade nor regimental staffs appear to be provided with telephone equipment.

(c.) **Tools.**—The tools carried by an infantry regiment are as shown in the following table :—

| How carried. | For earth works. | | | | For timber work, &c. | | | | |
|---|---|---|---|---|---|---|---|---|---|
| | Spades and shovels. | | Picks. | Pickaxes. | Hatchets. | Axes. | Saws. | | Wire-cutters.* |
| | Small. | Large. | | | | | Hand. | Cross-cut. | |
| By the men† .. | 1,200 | .. | .. | 120 | 60 | .. | .. | .. | .. |
| 1st line transport | .. | 30 | 15 | .. | 15 | 24 | .. | 12 | .. |
| Train .. .. | .. | 230 | 65 | .. | 30 | 30 | 6 | 2 | .. |
| Total.. .. | 1,200 | 260 | 80 | 120 | 105 | 54 | 6 | 14 | .. |

**13. Designation of infantry regiments.**—Although all infantry regiments are similarly armed and equipped, a number of them bear special designations which serve to foster *esprit de corps.* Guard regiments are designated as follows :—

Foot Guards Regiment (*Garde-Regiment zu Fuss*).
Guard Fusilier Regiment (*Garde-Füsilier-Regiment*).
Guard Grenadier Regiment (*Garde-Grenadier-Regiment*).

Line regiments also in some cases have special designations, such as :—

Grenadier Regiment (*Grenadier-Regiment*).
Body Grenadier Regiment (*Leib-Grenadier-Regiment*).
Body Regiment (*Infanterie-Leib-Regiment*).
Fusilier Regiment (*Füsilier-Regiment*).

Grenadier regiments wear the *Litzen* ‡ on collar and cuffs, which also distinguish all Guard regiments. In most cases, the 3rd battalion of a grenadier regiment is known as a fusilier battalion.

All Active infantry regiments of the line have, besides their number, a territorial title, *e.g.*, 120th Inf. Regt. (*2nd Württemberg*). The Active regiments of old standing have often an honorary title in addition, thus the 120th Inf. Regt. (*2nd Württ.*) also bears the title *Kaiser Wilhelm, König von Preussen.*

---

* Numbers not known.

† In every company half the men carry entrenching tools (viz., 100 small spades, 10 pickaxes and 5 hatchets).

‡ *See* page 147.

# CHAPTER VI.

## MACHINE GUNS.

**1. Peace organization.**—Machine guns form a factor of ever increasing importance in the organization of the German Army. In peace, every infantry regiment and *Jäger* battalion was provided with a machine gun company of 6 guns and 1 spare gun. In addition, there were a number of independent field and fortress machine gun detachments (*Abteilungen*), which were rapidly absorbed in the early stages of the war to provide machine gun units for new formations.

**2. Expansion during 1915 and 1916.**—As the demand for more machine guns grew, and as the output increased, a number of new machine gun sections were formed. These sections, known as *Feldmaschinengewehrzüge* and *Maschinengewehr-Ergänzungszüge* (supplementary machine gun sections), consisted of 30—40 men under an officer, with three or four machine guns. One or two of these sections were attached to infantry regiments as required, and, in some cases, were absorbed to form a second machine gun company for the regiment to which they were attached. By the end of 1915 several infantry regiments possessed two machine gun companies.

During the winter of 1915-1916, a new series of machine gun units was formed and trained with the purpose of developing to the full the power of the arm.

These units were known as machine gun marksman sections (*M.G. Scharfschützen-Trupps*). They were formed from picked machine gunners who underwent a course of four or five weeks' instruction at the training centres at Döberitz (Brandenburg), Hammelburg (Bavaria) and Beverloo (Belgium). Their training was specially directed towards the employment of machine guns in the attack.

In February and March, these units began to arrive at the front and were first employed in the battle of Verdun during March, 1916. They were allotted to infantry regiments engaged in offensive operations or holding difficult sectors. The total number of marksman sections formed was 200, *i.e.*, approximately one per division.

The establishment of a machine gun marksman section was as follows:—

1 captain or lieutenant,
2 *Feldwebel* or *Vizefeldwebel*,
6 gun commanders (*Unteroffiziere*),
20 lance-corporals,
40 machine gunners.
1 cyclist orderly,
1 armourer,
1 medical corporal,
1 transport driver,
6 spare men,

making a total of 1 officer and 78 other ranks.

At the beginning of 1916 the number of machine guns in the German Army had increased from 1,600, the peace strength, to something over 8,000. The output was steadily increasing and the experiences of the campaign had established the extreme importance of the machine gun both in attack and defence. A separate inspectorate was formed for the machine gun service.

_3. **Reorganization in 1916.**—By July, 1916, the total number of machine guns, including captured guns, in use, had risen to 11,000. No standard organization had, however, been adopted, so that the successive creation of variously organized machine gun units led to a very irregular allotment of machine guns to infantry formations. Thus, in the spring of 1916, some infantry regiments had only 6 machine guns, while others had more than 25. In August, 1916, the machine gun formations were reorganized, and the machine gun company of 6 guns was adopted as the standard unit. A staff officer for machine guns was added to the Headquarters of each Army. By the end of 1916, the number of machine guns in the German Army had risen to nearly 16,000.

The organization introduced in September, 1916, is as follows :—

A.—**Regimental machine gun companies.**—Every infantry regiment has three machine gun companies, numbered 1st, 2nd and 3rd. One of these companies is attached to each battalion of the regiment. At the headquarters of each infantry regiment there is a regimental machine gun officer who supervises the work of the three machine gun companies.

The second and third machine gun companies in each regiment were formed by absorbing the existing " sections," " supplementary sections " and " detachments " attached to infantry units. The reorganization had been completed by the end of 1916.

B.—**Machine gun marksman companies.**—The machine gun marksman sections already existing prior to August, 1916, were converted into companies, with an establishment identical to that of the regimental machine gun companies. These machine gun marksman companies are not attached to infantry regiments, but are combined in groups of three to form "machine gun marksman detachments" (*Maschinen-Gewehr-Scharfschützen-Abteilungen*), which act as a reserve of machine guns at the disposal of G.H.Q. One of these machine gun marksman detachments is normally attached to each division engaged in active operations. About 90 have been identified.

These units are more highly trained than the regimental machine gun companies ; all ranks wear a metal badge, representing a machine gun, on the left arm.

The Machine Gun Marksman Headquarters Staff West, which was formerly at Rozoy (south of Hirson), has been transferred to Tongres (north of Liége).

To summarize :—The basis of the machine gun organization in the German Army is the machine gun company. These units are employed either :—

(a.) Singly, attached to infantry battalions, or
(b.) Combined in groups of three " marksman companies " in " marksman detachments," which are attached as a reserve to divisions on active fronts.

4. **Development in 1917.**—During 1917, the number of machine guns in the German Army was very largely increased. Although the number of machine gun units allotted to a division was not raised, the formation of new divisions involved the creation of a number of new machine gun companies. But the greatest change consisted in the increase of the number of guns in a machine gun company, which was successively raised from 6 to 8, then to 10, and finally to 12.

At the same time, the various types of light machine guns (*see* page 60), which had been introduced by way of experiment in 1916 as an answer to the Lewis gun, were superseded by the issue of the light ('08/'15 pattern) machine gun to all infantry battalions. By the end of 1917 every infantry company on the Western Front had received 3 light machine guns, and some companies had already been equipped with 6 light machine guns—the maximum contemplated. The detachments for these machine guns were found by the units themselves, so that no additional personnel had to be provided.

At the beginning of 1918 each division on an active front might be expected to have the following allotment of machine guns :—

*Light machine guns.*—3 per infantry company ; total, 108.*

'08 *pattern machine guns.*—12 per battalion machine gun company ; total, 108.    Marksman detachment attached—36.

A total of 108 light and 144 heavy machine guns.

The following table gives an approximate idea of the increase in the number of machine guns in the German Army during the war :—

| | |
|---|---|
| August, 1914.. .. .. .. .. | 1,600 |
| December, 1915 .. .. .. .. | 8,000 |
| July, 1916 .. .. .. .. .. | 11,000 |
| January, 1917 .. .. .. .. | 16,000 |
| January, 1918 .. .. .. .. | 32,000 + 37,000 light machine guns. |

5. The **establishment of a machine gun company** (or a machine gun marksman company) is as follows :—

| Personnel. | | | Horses. | | Vehicles. |
|---|---|---|---|---|---|
| Officers. | N.C.Os. and men. | | Riding. | Draught. | (2-horsed). |
| 1 | .. | Company commander .. .. .. | 1 | .. | .. |
| 3 | .. | 2nd Lieutenants or *Offizierstellvertreter* | .. | .. | .. |
| .. | 1 | Serjt.-major ( *Feldwebel*) .. .. | .. | .. | .. |
| .. | 5 | *Vizefeldwebel* .. .. .. | .. | .. | .. |
| .. | 12 | Gun commanders (*Unteroffiziere*) .. | .. | .. | .. |
| .. | 1 | Armourer-serjeant .. .. .. | .. | .. | .. |
| .. | 1 | Quarter-master-serjeant.. .. .. | .. | .. | .. |
| .. | 1 | Corporal-cook .. .. .. .. | 1 | .. | .. |
| .. | 2 | Armourer's assistant .. .. .. | .. | .. | .. |
| .. | 1 | Medical corporal .. .. .. .. | .. | .. | .. |
| .. | 16 | Lance-corporals } † .. .. .. | .. | .. | .. |
| .. | 89 | Privates .. } | | | |
| .. | 4 | Train soldiers attached .. .. .. | .. | .. | . |
| .. | .. | 2-horsed machine gun wagons .. .. | .. | 12 | 6 |
| .. | .. | 2-horsed machine gun ammunition wagon. | .. | 2 | 1 |
| .. | .. | 2-horsed machine gun supply wagon for rations and forage. | .. | 2 | 1 |
| .. | .. | Small 2-horsed travelling kitchen .. | .. | 2 | 1 |
| 4 | 133 | Total .. .. .. | 2 | 18 | 9 |

There are also 6 hand-carts (M.G. 08), each drawn by 2 men.

* The full establishment is 6 per infantry company (*see* page 45).
† Made up as follows :—

| | | |
|---|---|---|
| 84 machine gunners. | 1 cyclist. | 1 shoemaker. |
| 3 orderlies. | 1 shoeing-smith. | 6 drivers. |
| 6 telephonists. | 1 tailor. | 2 cooks. |

**6. Special machine gun units.**—(*a.*) **mountain machine gun detachments.**—
In addition to the regimental machine gun companies and machine gun marksman companies described above, there exist 50 mountain machine gun detachments (*Gebirgs-Maschinen-Gewehr-Abteilungen*), which are specially equipped for mountain warfare. They were at one time employed in the Vosges, but in 1916 were all transferred to the Carpathians and the Balkans. The personnel wear the uniform of the mountain troops.

(*b.*) **Machine gun companies of cyclist battalions.**—These units were formed in July, 1916, for use with the cyclist battalions which later took part in the Roumanian campaign. The machine guns are mounted on motor lorries.

Each company has six machine guns; its establishment is as follows :—

> 3 officers,
> 1 serjeant-major (*Feldwebel*),
> 1 *Vizefeldwebel*,
> 6 gun commanders (*Unteroffiziere*),
> 1 armourer-serjeant,
> 1 medical corporal,
> 34 lance-corporals and privates,
> 2 corporals of the mechanical transport troops,
> 12 mechanical transport drivers,
> 1 motor-cyclist,
> 3 train soldiers attached.

The company is organized in 3 sections, each of 2 guns. Each section is transported in a motor lorry, with guns, detachment and ammunition, so that each lorry can act as an independent unit. The ammunition carried consists of 15,000 rounds per gun.

The transport consists of—

> 2 3-ton lorries for gun detachments,
> 1 3-ton lorry for baggage, tools and reserve ammunition,
> 1 4-horsed machine gun supply wagon ('08/'15 pattern).

The men are armed with revolvers and the non-commissioned officers are provided with field-glasses in addition.

(*c.*) **Cavalry machine gun units.**—In peace, no machine gun units were attached to cavalry formations. There existed, however, 11 independent machine gun batteries (*Abteilungen*), which, on mobilization, were allotted to the 11 cavalry divisions.

A *Jäger* battalion (with its machine gun company) was also attached to each cavalry division, which thus disposed of 12 to 14 machine guns.

During 1916, a machine gun section was attached to each cavalry regiment, and these sections were finally expanded into machine gun squadrons, each comprising 8 machine guns.

No details are yet available concerning the organization, armament or means of transport of machine gun squadrons.

(*d.*) **Anti-aircraft machine gun units** (*see* page 115). (*see* page 115)

**7. The '08 heavy machine gun.**—All the above-mentioned units are armed with the 1908 pattern (Maxim) machine gun, known as *M.G. 08* (*see* Plate 7). The '08 gun has the same calibre as the German rifle, namely, ·311 inch (7·9 mm.). The gun is mounted on a sledge with four legs. The height of the gun in action can be adjusted by altering the spread of the legs.

*Details of '08 machine gun.*

| | |
|---|---|
| Muzzle velocity | 2821 f.s. |
| Limit of sighting | 2,200 yards. |
| Extreme range (at 32° elevation) | 4,400 yards. |
| Rate of fire | 400–500 rounds per minute. |
| Number of rounds in belt | 250. |
| Weight of filled belt | 16 lbs. |
| Length of gun without muzzle attachment | 43 inches (overall). |
| Length of barrel | 28·35 inches. |
| Weight of gun | 55 lbs. |
| Weight of sledge mounting | 75 lbs. |
| Weight of gun complete with sledge (*Schlitten*) and barrel casing filled | 140 lbs. |
| Weight of water-filling (7 pints) | 8½ lbs. (7 pints). |
| Height of axis above ground | 11 inches. |

Machine guns were originally manufactured only at the Government factories at Berlin and Spandau, but factories now exist also at Nürnberg, Erfurt, Sommerda and Suhl. The three last appear to produce principally light machine guns. Each gun is stamped with the year of manufacture and the factory number.

There are factories for repairing captured machine guns at Brussels-Etterbeek and Warsaw.

A prismatic Goerz sight with a magnification of 2½ diameters is provided, which slides into a slot on the gun. One pair of field glasses is allowed for each '08 pattern machine gun.

**Anti-aircraft sights.**—A circular foresight (*Kreiskorn*) and special V-shaped backsight are employed with both the '08 and the '08/'15 pattern machine gun for anti-aircraft purposes.

The *circular foresight,* which is attached to the barrel casing, consists of two wires crossed at right angles in the centre of two concentric circles. According to the angle at which the aeroplane is either approaching or flying away, the requisite amount of "lead" is obtained by taking aim over the appropriate portion of the inner or outer circle. The *backsight* is clamped to the leaf of the ordinary backsight.

**8. Machine gun ammunition.**—The amount of ammunition carried per gun prior to the reorganization of the machine gun units was—

> 8,000 rounds per gun on the limbered gun wagons
> 4,000 rounds per gun on the 3 ammunition wagons.

Total    12,000 rounds.

The amount now carried appears to be—

> 8,000 rounds per gun on the limbered gun wagons.
> 1,300 rounds per gun on the ammunition wagons.

Total    9,300 rounds.

The ammunition used by machine gun units is of three kinds (for description, *see* page 49), namely—

(*a.*) Ordinary (*S* or *Rillenmunition*).
(*b.*) Armour-piercing (*S.m.K.*).
(*c.*) Tracer (*L.S.*).

Armour-piercing and tracer ammunition are employed against aircraft, the former being also used against tanks, loophole plates, &c.

The usual proportion of tracer to ordinary ammunition in a machine gun belt is one tracer in every 10 rounds.

Explosive bullet ammunition was formerly used against aircraft, but its use has apparently been discontinued.

9. **Training of machine gunners.**—Great care is devoted to the training of machine gunners, more particularly of the personnel of "marksman" units, but all machine gunners are picked men.

The principal machine gun schools in Germany are at Döberitz (for Prussian troops), Hammelburg (for Bavaria), and Zeithain (for Saxony). There are also large schools at Beverloo and Brasschaet in Belgium.

The principal training school for machine gun marksmen (*M.G. Scharfschützen Ausbildungs-Kommando West*) was at Rozoy-sur-Serre (south of Hirson), but was transferred to Tongres (north of Liége) at the beginning of 1918. Courses of instruction for machine gun officers are held at Waulsort in Belgium.

A machine gun course usually lasts a month, and the following are the main features of the instruction given :—

(*a.*) Expert knowledge of the German machine gun, which every man must be able to dismantle and assemble again.
(*b.*) Carrying out repairs, and dealing quickly with all kinds of "jams."
(*c.*) Handling of captured guns (especially the Lewis gun).
(*d.*) Range practice at fixed targets—beginning at 400 and ending at 800 metres.
(*e.*) Firing at moving dummies at various ranges up to 800 metres.
(*f.*) Sustained fire at the rate of 500 rounds per minute, including addition of fresh water to the jacket at the end of the fourth belt (*i.e.*, after 1,000 rounds).
(*g.*) Signalling and entrenching.
(*h.*) Lessons in the construction of alternative emplacements in the trenches.

10. **Light machine guns and automatic rifles.**—Two independent series of units armed with automatic rifles have appeared in the German Army during the war :—

(*a.*) *Musketen* battalions (*Musketen-Bataillone*).
(*b.*) Light machine gun sections (*Leichte M.G. Trupps*).

(*a.*) "**Musketen**" **battalions.**—*Musketen* battalions first appeared in the Champagne battle in September, 1915, when three were identified ;* their number has not since been increased. Two of these units took part in the Somme battle, but they did not prove a success.

A *Musketen* battalion consisted of about 500 men, and was organized in three companies. Each company was armed with 30 automatic rifles, and had an establishment of 4 officers and 160 other ranks. There was a squad of 4 men for each automatic rifle.

---

* The 1st *Musketen* Battalion was originally the 4th Battalion of the 117th Body Infantry Regiment.

According to official orders captured during the Somme battle, the automatic rifle was regarded purely as a defensive weapon and was not employed in the attack. Units armed with automatic rifles were to be kept as a reserve of fire-power, usually in second line positions, to defend threatened points.

The *Muskete* is similar in construction to the Danish Madsen automatic rifle. It has two pivoted supporting legs attached near the muzzle.

| | |
|---|---|
| Length of rifle .. .. .. . .. .. | 3 feet 8 inches, |
| Height at point of support .. .. .. .. | 1 foot 2 inches. |
| Weight unloaded .. .. .. .. .. .. | 21¾ lbs. |

The rifle is fed from a magazine holding 25 rounds. The barrel, range and ammunition are the same as for the '08 pattern machine gun.

(*b.*) **Light machine gun sections.**—These units were formed at the Döberitz machine gun school during July, August and September, 1916, doubtless as an answer to the British Lewis gun. They were armed with the 1915 pattern light machine gun (*l.M.G. 15*), manufactured by the firm of Bergmann at Suhl. The barrel of the Bergmann light machine gun is the same as that of the '08 pattern machine gun, and its range is the same ; but the Bergmann gun is only sighted up to 400 metres, as it is intended to be employed at close ranges. The barrel becomes overheated after firing 300 rounds rapid.

The establishment of a light machine gun section was as follows :—

1 officer (lieut., 2nd lieut., or *Offizierstellvertreter*).
1 *Vizefeldwebel.*
3 corporals (*Unteroffiziere*).
9 lance-corporals (*Gefreiten*).
28 privates.
1 artificer.
2 transport drivers.
10 horses (1 riding).
2–2-horsed supply wagons.
Total—1 officer and 44 other ranks.

The section was organized in three sub-sections, each with three light machine guns. Each sub-section was commanded by a corporal, the detachment for each light machine gun consisting of 1 lance-corporal and 3 men.

The transport consisted of two 2-horsed limbered wagons to carry the light machine guns, which were kept in boxes.

The men were armed with rifles, and each non-commissioned officer was, in addition, provided with field-glasses.

A series of 111 of these light machine gun sections was formed in 1916, viz. :—

| | |
|---|---|
| 1—87 .. .. .. .. .. .. .. | Prussian. |
| 88—99 .. .. .. .. .. .. .. | Bavarian. |
| 100—107 .. .. .. .. .. .. .. | Saxon. |
| 108—111 .. .. .. .. .. .. .. | Württemberg. |

These units were almost exclusively employed on the Eastern Front. They appear to have been disbanded, as a consequence of the issue of the '08/'15 pattern light machine gun to infantry units.

11. **The '08/'15 light machine gun.**—(*See* Plate 15.) The issue of the '08/'15 light machine gun began in March, 1917, on the scale of 3 to every infantry company. This allotment was eventually raised to 6 per infantry company, thus giving 2 guns to each platoon. The detachments for the light machine guns are found by the units themselves, a light machine gun group consisting of 1 *Unteroffizier* or lance-corporal and 8 men with one light machine gun. In each company the light machine guns are supervised by a senior N.C.O. and an armourer-assistant. Each battalion has been provided with a field wagon (1895 pattern) for transporting the light machine guns.

The '08/'15 light machine gun (*l.M.G. 08/15*), though water-cooled, can be carried and operated by one man. It has been evolved from the '08 pattern machine gun by making the following changes :—

(a.) The diameter of the barrel casing has been reduced from 5·3 inches to 3·5 inches, and its capacity from 7 to 5 pints.

(b.) The thickness of the breech casing has been reduced from ·16 inch to ·12 inch.

(c.) The ejector tube has been discarded. The empty cases are ejected through an aperture in the front of the breech casing.

(d.) The rear cross-piece has been replaced by a rifle butt and pistol grip.

(e.) The sledge mounting has been discarded for a bipod with adjustable pivot.

(f.) The gun is fitted with a rifle sling.

The ballistics are similar to those of the '08 pattern machine gun, but the light machine gun is not so accurate. Belts containing either 100 or 250 rounds are used.

| | |
|---|---|
| Total weight, with barrel casing filled .. .. .. | 43 lbs. (with bipod). |
| Weight of water filling .. .. .. .. .. | 6 lbs. (5 pints). |
| Length (overall) .. .. .. .. .. | 53 inches. |
| Length of butt .. .. .. .. .. .. | 1 foot. |
| Height of axis above the ground .. .. .. | 11 inches. |

The gun is fitted with a muzzle attachment and flash obscurer.

12. **Automatic carbine.**—German aeroplanes are sometimes equipped with an automatic carbine, called *Flieger-Selbstlader-Karabiner 15 für 7mm. Munition*, which closely resembles the Mexican Mondragon automatic carbine, but is apparently manufactured in Germany.

The chief characteristics of this weapon are :—

(a.) It is actuated by gas pressure and not by recoil.

(b.) It is provided with a magazine, containing 10 cartridges ; an auxiliary magazine (*Ansteckmagazin*), in the form of a drum, can also be employed. This latter magazine holds 30 cartridges which can only be fired as single rounds.

The issue of this weapon is possibly being extended to the other arms.

# CHAPTER VII.

## CAVALRY.

1. **General organization.**—The German cavalry is organized in—

      (*a.*) Independent cavalry divisions.
      (*b.*) Divisional cavalry.

In peace, the cavalry was not organized in divisions, except in the case of the Guard cavalry, but each Army Corps District provided two or three cavalry brigades. On mobilization, 11 cavalry divisions were formed, the regiments surplus to the requirements of the cavalry divisions furnishing the divisional cavalry of infantry divisions. A few cavalry brigades are employed independently.

In peace, the German cavalry consisted of 110 cavalry regiments, each of five squadrons. On mobilization, each regiment left one squadron behind at its home station to act as a depôt squadron.

Most cavalry regiments now have a fifth squadron in the field, and some a sixth, but these extra squadrons are detached as divisional cavalry. A regiment, forming part of a cavalry division, consists of four squadrons and a machine gun squadron.

The war establishment of a squadron is :—

      4 officers.
      163 other ranks (150 sabres).
      178 horses.
      3 vehicles.

2. **Organization of a cavalry division.**—11 cavalry divisions were formed on mobilization, and this number has not been increased, except for temporary formation now dissolved.

The normal composition of a cavalry division is as follows :—

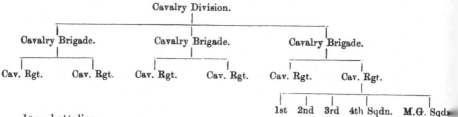

*Jäger* battalion.
1 or 2 cyclist companies.
Machine gun *Abteilung.*
Horse artillery *Abteilung* (3 batteries).
Cavalry pioneer detachment (1 officer and 33 other ranks).
Signal detachment (*Nachrichten-Abteilung*), comprising 1 heavy or 2 light wireless stations, and the telephone squads of the regiments.

The war establishment of a cavalry division is—

> 283 officers.
> 4,955 other ranks.
> 5,590 horses.
> 216 vehicles.

3. **Employment of cavalry divisions.**—Before the war, the German cavalry was taught to rely more on the fire action of artillery, machine guns and carbines than on the *arme blanche.* Mass and shock tactics were discouraged, special stress being laid on vigorous offensive action by small cavalry detachments.

The German cavalry divisions displayed little enterprise or initiative at the beginning of the campaign. Their tactics during the initial advance were marked by extreme caution, and seemed directed towards passive reconnaissance rather than to offensive action. During the retreat from the Marne to the Aisne, and again in October, 1914, the German cavalry rendered valuable assistance to its infantry. Reinforced by *Jäger* battalions and machine gun batteries, and sometimes even by heavy artillery, the cavalry divisions effectively extended the northern flank of the battle-line, and fought stubborn rearguard actions until relieved by the arrival of the infantry divisions.

From the autumn of 1914 to December, 1916, the cavalry divisions, with one exception, were employed on the Eastern Front, where the operations partook more of the nature of open warfare than in the West. One cavalry division was, however, retained in Belgium for the purpose of policing the country and guarding the Dutch frontier.

When the German retirement to the "Hindenburg Line" took place in March, 1917, an opportunity was created for open warfare, when cavalry could again perform its normal rôle. Three cavalry brigades, drawn from the 2nd and 7th Cavalry Divisions, were sent from Belgium to the Somme area to assist in covering the retirement. The withdrawal of the First Army, between Arras and Péronne, was covered by infantry rearguards and squadrons of divisional cavalry. The retirement of the Second Army, between Péronne and the Oise, which was a more extensive manœuvre, was covered by three cavalry brigades and five cyclist battalions. The cyclists were used to hold bridge-heads, villages and strong points, with the object of delaying the pursuit and covering the pioneer detachments which effected the demolitions. The mission of the cavalry was chiefly reconnaissance; patrols were left behind the rearguards to watch and report on the progress of the pursuit; these patrols fell back slowly, avoiding engagements, but keeping touch with the British and French advanced troops.

During the latter half of 1917, the 6th and 7th Cavalry Divisions were employed dismounted to hold quiet sectors of the line in the Vosges.

4. **Divisional cavalry.**—Originally, each infantry division had two or three squadrons of divisional cavalry, and in some cases a whole cavalry regiment. Only one squadron is now allotted to each infantry division.

During trench warfare, the squadrons of divisional cavalry assist the infantry by taking turns in the trenches. When not thus employed, these units do duty in patrolling the roads, as escorts, and in finding guards, posts, piquets and orderlies.

The divisional cavalry is often used in manning observation posts in trench warfare.

5. **Cavalry units formed during the war.**—Since the beginning of the war, 39 Reserve cavalry regiments have been formed—in addition to a certain number of Ersatz regiments, Landwehr and Landsturm squadrons and Reserve Cavalry *Abteilungen.*

These units are principally allotted as divisional cavalry to new formations; some of them, more especially the Landsturm squadrons, are employed in guarding neutral frontiers and in patrolling the occupied territories and the lines of communication.

During 1917 a great many of these units were broken up.

6. **Dismounted cavalry units.**—During 1916, a number of regiments employed as divisional cavalry were withdrawn from the front, dismounted, and converted into dismounted rifle regiments (*Schützen-Regimenter*). The units thus dismounted were chiefly Reserve and Ersatz formations.

Dismounted rifle regiments are equivalent to infantry battalions and are organized as follows :—

4 squadrons.

1 machine gun company.

Each squadron consists of three platoons and a trench mortar detachment, so that it resembles an infantry company. The men are armed with carbines and bayonets and are equipped as infantrymen.

In some cases the squadrons are called companies.

Dismounted rifle regiments are attached to infantry divisions. They take over sectors of the line, usually in quiet parts of the front, to relieve infantry units for operations elsewhere. About 50 cavalry regiments had been dismounted in this way by the end of 1917.

7. **Armament.**—The armament of the cavalry is the same for all mounted regiments. At the beginning of the war, officers and staff-serjeants were armed with sword and revolver; corporals with lance, sword and revolver; lance-corporals and privates with lance, sword and carbine. At the end of 1914, bayonets were issued to the cavalry,* and in July, 1915, their swords were withdrawn.

(*a.*) **Lance.**—The steel lance (*Stahlrohrlanze*) has a four-edged point of forged steel forming one piece with the shaft, which is of cast steel and hollow.

| | |
|---|---|
| Length .. .. .. .. .. | 10 feet 6 inches. |
| Weight .. .. .. .. .. | 3·94 lbs. |
| Point of balance .. .. .. .. | 5 feet 0½ inch from the point. |

(*b.*) **Automatic pistol.**—The revolver formerly in use has been replaced by the '08 automatic pistol, which takes eight cartridges.

| | |
|---|---|
| Calibre .. .. .. . .. | ·354 inch (9 mm.). |
| Weight .. .. .. .. .. | 1·8 lbs. (835 grammes). |
| Weight of bullet .. .. .. .. | 125 grains (8 grammes). |

(*c.*) **Carbine.**—The '98 pattern carbine (*Karabiner 98*) is similar in design to the '98 pattern rifle and takes the same ammunition.

| | |
|---|---|
| Calibre .. .. .. .. .. | ·311 inch (7·9 mm.). |
| Weight .. .. .. .. .. | 7·93 lbs. |
| Length .. .. .. .. .. | 43¼ inches (5½ inches shorter than rifle). |
| Length of barrel .. .. .. .. | 23½ inches. |
| Sighted up to .. .. .. .. | 2,200 yards. |

8. **Saddlery and personal equipment.**—The saddle is somewhat similar to that in use in the British Service, but is lighter and higher in the arch and the flaps are deeper and

---

* The more recently formed *Jäger zu Pferde* regiments had already been equipped with the bayonet prior to mobilization.

wider. The girth-buckle protector flaps are of numnah, and the panels are made of the same material. A thick woollen blanket (7 feet 7 inches by 6 feet 4 inches) is folded in four under the saddle. The stirrups are wide and heavy, and are made of nickelled metal. The girths are of the Cape pattern and a surcingle is carried. The wallets in which the kit is carried are large and roomy, more of the nature of saddlebags. In the near wallet is a pocket for cartridges, and the shoe case is attached to the outside of it. A spade or hatchet can also be attached.

The bits differ from those in use in the British Army, the bridoon being much thicker and the big bit has a considerably lower port and shorter cheek.

A short piece of rope, with a ring at one end, is carried over the carbine bucket. When a number of these ropes are joined together one long picketing rope is made, which passes over two long stakes carried in one of the baggage wagons and forms the picket line to which the head ropes are attached.

A corn sack, shaped like a sausage, is strapped in rear of the saddle over the rolled cloak.

The carbine is usually carried in a bucket, fitted with a flap to button over the butt, on the near side of the saddle in an almost vertical position, except in the Bavarian cavalry, where it is carried in a case fixed to the off wallet and rests on the man's thigh. On patrol work and when a fight is imminent, however, the carbine is carried slung over the shoulder.

A mess-tin made of aluminium, holding $4\frac{1}{4}$ pints, is carried in a leather case on the near side of the saddle. The tin cover can be used as a cup or frying pan, and a separate handle for this cover fits inside the mess-tin. The water-bottle is the same as that of the infantry, and is carried in the same manner.

When fully equipped in marching order the weight carried by the troop horse without the man is about 100 lbs.

An officer's saddlery and equipment consists of an officer's regulation saddle, blanket (Woilach), two wallets, one saddlebag, shoe case, greatcoat cover, corn sack, drinking bucket and leather head rope.

9. **Equipment.**—Cavalry regiments acting with cavalry divisions are provided with telephone and bridging equipment, together with tools and explosives for effecting demolitions.

(a.) **The telephone equipment** consists of two army telephones and 15,300 yards of "cavalry wire," the whole being carried on horseback. Each regiment has two telephone squads, each of two non-commissioned officers and two men.

(b.) **The bridging equipment** of a cavalry regiment consists of four half-boats of galvanized steel, together with the necessary transoms, chesses and other stores. The half-boats are 11 feet $3\frac{1}{2}$ inches long, 5 feet 2 inches broad, and weigh about $2\frac{1}{2}$ cwt. They are lashed together stern to stern, thus forming a complete boat, which can carry 8—10 men with their equipment. The bridging material is carried in two 6-horsed cavalry bridge wagons.

The material carried by a cavalry regiment is sufficient to construct about 21 yards of footbridge (Brückensteg), or 13 yards of light bridge (Laufbrücke), or about $8\frac{1}{4}$ yards of bridge to take field guns (verstärkte Laufbrücke). This material can also be formed into a raft capable of transporting 30 infantry men with their equipment, or four horses and horseholders, or one field gun and limber.

(c.) **The explosives** carried by a cavalry regiment consist of 40 explosive cartridges and fuzes.

10. **Designation of cavalry regiments.**—The Active cavalry regiments, although all similarly armed and equipped, are differently designated, as follows :—

1 Regiment of *Gardes du Corps.*
1 Guard Cuirassier Regiment.
8 Cuirassier Regiments.
  (No. 1 is known as the " Body Cuirassier Regiment.")
2 Guard Dragoon Regiments.
26 Dragoon Regiments.
  (No. 3 is known as the " Horse Grenadier Regiment.")
  (Nos. 20 is known as " Body Dragoon Regiment," and Nos. 23 and 24 as
    " Guard Dragoon Regiments.")
  (Nos. 25 and 26 are Württemberg.)
1 Body Guard Hussar Regiment.
20 Hussar Regiments.
  (Nos. 1 and 2 are known as " Body Hussar Regiments.")
  (Nos. 18, 19 and 20 are Saxon. )
3 Guard *Ulanen* Regiments.
21 *Ulanen* Regiments.
  (Nos. 17, 18 and 21 are Saxon.)
  (Nos. 19 and 20 are Württemberg.)
1 Saxon Guard Cavalry Regiment (*Garde-Reiter-Regiment*).
1 Saxon *Karabinier* Regiment.
13 *Jäger zu Pferde* Regiments.
2 Bavarian *Ulanen* Regiments.
2 Bavarian Heavy Cavalry Regiments (*Schwere-Reiter-Regimenter*).
8 Bavarian Light Horse Regiments (*Chevaulegers-Regimenter*).

There are 39 Reserve cavalry regiments, formed during the war, each of 4 squadrons. They are designated as follows :—

3 Heavy Reserve Cavalry Regiments.
1 Saxon Reserve *Reiter* Regiment.
1 Guard Reserve Dragoon Regiment.
11 Reserve Dragoon Regiments (numbered 1 to 8, 12, 13 and Württemberg).
10 Reserve Hussar Regiments (including 1 Saxon).
1 Guard Reserve *Ulanen* Regiment.
8 Reserve *Ulanen* Regiments (including 1 Saxon).
1 Reserve *Jäger zu Pferde* Regiment.
3 Bavarian Reserve Cavalry Regiments.

The uniform varies for the different types of regiment, as follows :—

Cuirassier and dragoon regiments wear a tunic and spiked helmet.
Hussar regiments wear a braided *Attila*, fur busby, and shoulder cords instead of
  shoulder straps.  (*See* Plate 3.)
*Ulanen* regiments wear a double-breasted tunic (*Ulanka*), lance-cap (*Tschapka*),
  and rounded shoulder-straps.  (*See* Plates 3 and 9.)
Saxon *Ulanen* regiments wear ordinary shoulder straps.
Bavarian *Chevaulegers* regiments wear a spiked helmet.
*Jäger zu Pferde* regiments wear a grey-green uniform similar to that of *Jäger*
  battalions.  They wear a black steel helmet.

# CHAPTER VIII.

## ARTILLERY.

### A.—Field Artillery.

1. **General organization.**—Prior to mobilization there were 642 batteries of horse and field artillery, or rather less than 1 battery per battalion of infantry. This proportion has been slightly increased during the war, and there is now rather more than 1 field battery per battalion. The total number of field batteries at the beginning of 1918 was about 2,900.

Field artillery includes horse artillery (*reitende Artillerie*). Horse artillery is allotted to cavalry divisions (*see* page 62). Field artillery proper is entirely allotted to infantry divisions. It consists of—

Field gun batteries, equipped with the 7·7-cm. field gun, and
Field howitzer batteries, equipped with the 10·5-cm. light field howitzer.

In peace, batteries consisted of 6 field guns or 4 light field howitzers, but during 1915 all field batteries were reduced to 4 guns, in order to provide material for new formations. In April, 1916, artillery establishments were still further reduced by withdrawing the lead horses from ammunition columns and transport wagons.

During 1916 a series of independent field artillery batteries, numbered from 801 to 915, was formed. These batteries have been used to reinforce the artillery of divisions on the Eastern Front.

2. **Divisional artillery organization.**—The artillery of an Active division was originally known as a field artillery brigade* (*Feldartillerie-Brigade*), usually commanded by a Major-General.

During the early stages of the war the divisional artillery organization varied somewhat in Active, Reserve and new-formation divisions.

In Active divisions, the field artillery brigade was organized as follows :—

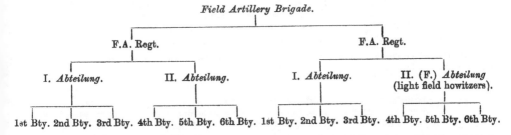

*Field Artillery Brigade.*

---

* Not to be confused with the British Field Artillery Brigade of 3 or 4 batteries, the German equivalent for which is "*Abteilung.*" The Major-General commanding a German Field Artillery Brigade corresponded to the C.R.A. of a British Division.

The *Abteilungen* were numbered I. and II., and the batteries from 1—6 in each regiment.

The artillery of the divisions formed since mobilization is organized in a slightly different manner, and the number of batteries has been reduced from 12 to 9. These 9 batteries form one field artillery regiment, divided into three *Abteilungen*, two of which are equipped with field guns and the third with light field howitzers. This organization has now become general.

The divisional artillery consists entirely of field batteries, and is now organized as follows :—

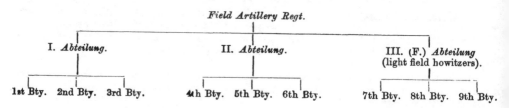

Field howitzer batteries now form $\frac{1}{3}$ of the total field artillery. In peace, field howitzer batteries formed $\frac{1}{8}$ of the total, as only one *Abteilung* in each Army Corps was equipped with light field howitzers.

3. **Divisional artillery headquarters.**—When the divisional artillery was reduced from 2 regiments, each of 6 batteries, to 1 regiment of 9 batteries, the field artillery brigade formation became eliminated. As, however, the divisional artillery commander is in command of *all* the artillery, heavy as well as field, allotted to the divisional sector, it was necessary to provide the division with a divisional artillery headquarters (*Artillerie-Kommando*), and one of these is now attached to each divisional headquarters.

4. **Independent field artillery regiments.**—During 1917, the reduction of the divisional artillery from 12 to 9 batteries was extended to all divisions, the surplus batteries thus set free being used as a nucleus for providing the new formations with artillery, as well as to form a number of independent field artillery regiments. These independent regiments, about 80 in number, form a General Headquarters reserve of field artillery, and are allotted to different sectors of the front as the situation requires.

By the beginning of 1918, including both independent and divisional artillery regiments, the German Army comprised 2,900 field batteries, compared with about 2,300 battalions of infantry.

5. **Organization of a field battery (gun or howitzer).**—A field battery is commanded by a captain (*Batterie-Führer*), and is organized in two sections (*Züge*), each commanded by a subaltern. There is a third subaltern to supervise ammunition supply, and a fourth to act as forward observing officer. Another officer is attached for transport duties.

The vehicles and transport of the battery are organized as follows :—

*Firing Battery (Gefechts-Batterie).*

    4 guns or howitzers (6-horsed).
    4 ammunition wagons (6-horsed).*
    1 observation wagon (6-horsed).

*1st Line Transport (Gefechts-Bagage).*

    4 led horses.
    1 limbered store wagon (4-horsed).
    1 travelling kitchen (2-horsed).

*Train (Grosse Bagage).*

    1 store wagon (4-horsed).
    1 forage wagon (4-horsed).
    1 supply wagon (4-horsed).

*Battery Commander's Staff (Batterie-Trupp).*

    2 *Unteroffiziere* with director.
    3 orderlies (1 with the stereo-telescope
       and 1 with signalling flags).
    2 mounted telephonists.
    All the above carry small spades and
wire cutters.

One bicycle was allowed for each battery in 1917 in order to save the wear and tear
of horses.

The establishment of a battery is :—

    6 officers.
    21 non-commissioned officers.
    64 gunners.
    45 drivers.
A total of 6 officers and 130 other ranks.

6. **Field artillery training.** — Field artillery training in the German Army is
supervised by an inspector of practice camps. (*Inspekteur der Artillerie-Schiessschulen,* or
*General von der Artillerie Nr. 1*). He ranks as an Army Artillery Commander.

The central School of Gunnery (*Artillerie-Schiessschule*) is at Jüterbog, south of Berlin,
where there is a depôt field artillery brigade (*Ersatz-Feldartillerie-Brigade Jüterbog*).

There are four regular practice camps in the occupied portion of France, and two on
the Eastern Front. Each of these camps has a divisional artillery headquarters permanently
allotted to it for the purpose of command and training. These headquarters are as
follows :—

| Camp. | Artillery Command. | | | Transferred from |
|---|---|---|---|---|
| Maubert-Fontaine (west of Charleville) .. .. | 5th .. .. | | , | 5th Division. |
| Thimougies (east of Tournai) .. .. .. | 7th Guard .. | | .. | 1st Guard Reserve Division. |
| Sebourg (east of Valenciennes) .. .. | 124th .. | .. | .. | 28th Reserve Division. |
| Signy-l'Abbaye (north of Rethel) .. .. | 134th .. | .. | .. | 4th Ersatz Division. |
| Grodno .. .. .. .. .. .. | 80th .. | .. | .. | 80th Reserve Division. |
| Orany .. . .. .. .. .. | 86th .. | .. | .. | 86th Division. |

Temporary camps are formed as required, *e.g.,* at Beverloo, Exaerde and Ciney.

At each practice camp there is a permanent depôt *Abteilung.* These are numbered in
a series commencing with 1001.

---

* The firing battery wagons are known as the *Staffel.*

**7. The field gun.**—There are two patterns, viz., the 1896 n/A. and the 1916 field guns.

**The 1896 n/A. field gun.**—The 1896 n/A. pattern field gun (*Feldkanone 96 n/A.*) is the old 15-pr. converted to a Q.F. gun. It is mounted on a shielded recoil carriage.

(*a.*) **The gun.**—The gun consists of an inner tube, rifled with 32 grooves, the rear half of the inner tube being covered by a jacket which is shrunk on and secured by a screw ring half-way between breech and muzzle. The breech end of the jacket is shaped to take the breech wedge, and has a lug for the attachment of the recoil buffer. Three recoil guides, shrunk on to the gun, enable it to recoil along the buffer slide.

The single-motion wedge breech action has an axial striker. The breech lever is placed above the breech and is actuated from the right side of the gun.

(*b.*) **The carriage.**—The upper carriage consists of the cradle, buffer-cylinder and traversing gear. The recoil buffer and running-out springs are contained in the cradle and are placed beneath the gun. The cradle pivots and traverses on a gimbal in the centre of the carriage axle itself.

The carriage is mounted on 4-ft. $5\frac{1}{8}$-in. wheels. The wheel-track is 5 ft. ; The axletree carries a shield, which is 5 ft. 6 in. high when fully extended, and two axletree seats.

The box trail is provided with a spade and traversing lever, and carries two seats, one for the layer and one for the loader. The tyre-brakes are combined with a rope-brake on the axletree arms.

The horse artillery gun is the same as that of the field artillery, but no men are carried on the axletree seats.

(*c.*) **The sights.**—The sighting gear consists of a toothed arc tangent sight fitted with a panoramic dial sight (*Rundblick-Fernrohr*) and a collimator sight for direct laying. The tangent sight works in a sight-bracket on the left side of the cradle and is fitted with a bubble level. The graduations, which are on the lower face, extend from 1 to 60 in hundreds of metres, and from zero to something over 15 in degrees of arc. The only graduations on the degree scale which are marked are 0, 5, 10 and 15 degrees.

As the line of sight is not independent of the gun elevation, a corrector slide, interposed between the tangent sight and the sight bracket, enables the trajectory to be modified, thus altering the height of burst. Each corrector graduation is equivalent to an alteration of $8\frac{1}{2}$ minutes in the angle of sight.

(*d.*) **Vehicles.**—The limber has a steel pole; the centre and lead horses are hooked to a master-bar on the point of the limber pole. Collars are used, but breast harness was introduced experimentally in July, 1917. Three men are carried on the limber The ammunition box is of steel plate and holds 36 rounds* in baskets containing three rounds each. The total weight behind the team is about 43 cwt., including two gunners on the axletree seats and three on the limber.

The wagon body is of similar construction, but carries 54 rounds.† In action, the wagon body is unlimbered on the right side of the gun, the perch being then supported by a prop. The shielded lid falls down to protect the gunners in action. Three men are carried on the wagon limber and one on the wagon body.

Two store wagons (*Vorratswagen*) accompany the battery. One is limbered and carries rations, medical and veterinary chests, tools and spare parts. The limber carries

---

* When long shell are carried, the box holds 24 long shell and 6 ordinary shell or shrapnel.
† Long shell are never carried in the wagon body.

ammunition. The other store wagon is 4-wheeled and carries the field forge, artificers' tools, spare clothing, equipment, and officers' baggage.

**The 1916 field gun** (*see* Plate 13).—Towards the close of 1916, some of the batteries then recently formed were equipped with a new field gun called *K.i.H.* (*Kanone · in Haubitzlafette* or gun on howitzer carriage). Subsequently, a modified form of this design was introduced, which is known as *F.K. 16* (*Feld-Kanone 16* or 1916 field gun), and it is with this piece that field gun batteries are being re-armed. It is not known (*April, 1918*) to what extent this re-armament has already been carried out, but it is being pushed with all speed.

(*a.*) **The gun.**—The gun is similar in construction to the 1916 n/A. gun, but is about 2 feet longer. There is no difference in the breech mechanism.

(*b.*) **The carriage.**—The buffer and carriage are those of the '98/'09 light field howitzer, *i.e.*, the cradle is mounted, like a cantilever on rear trunnions, on a small top carriage which is pivoted on the carriage proper. A double balance spring, seated on a transom on the carriage, thrusts against the cradle and supports the weight of the gun. The running-out springs have been strengthened, as have also the balance springs and the elevating gear; the recoil is on the constant long recoil system; a buffer stop has been provided to prevent damage to the breech mechanism at high angles of elevation.

A circular platform weighing 2·8 cwt. is placed underneath the wheels when in action. It is attached to the trail by two hinged rods. This platform ensures steadiness in firing and allows of a wide arc of traverse without disturbing the level of the wheels. The upper part of the shield is detachable and the lower part hinged.

(*c.*) **The sights.**—The sights are the same as those of the '98/'09 light field howitzer, except for the graduations.

(*d.*) **Vehicles.**—The vehicles are apparently the same as those hitherto in use. A spring coupling has been adopted for the gun limber. The circular platform is carried on the wagon of the limbered ammunition wagon. A gun limber takes 24 shell and 24 cartridges. An ammunition wagon takes 60 shell and 60 cartridges, 54 super-charges and 20 flash reducers.

## Details of the 1896 n/A., and 1916 field guns.—

| | 96 n/A. pattern. | 1916 pattern. |
|---|---|---|
| Calibre | 3·03 in. (7·7 cm.) | 3·03 in. (7·7 cm.). |
| Total length of gun | 27·3 calibres (6' 10$\frac{11}{16}$") | 35 calibres (8' 10$\frac{6}{16}$"). |
| Weight of gun in action | 19·3 cwt. | 27·5 cwt. |
| Weight of circular platform | None provided | 2·8 cwt. |
| Weight of gun limbered up, without gunners. | 35·6 cwt. | 45 cwt. |
| Limits of elevation | − 12°, + 16° | −10°, + 40°*. |
| Amount of traverse | 8° | 8°. |
| Weight of charges.. | ·7 lbs., 1·2 lbs. | ·8 lbs., 1·3 lbs., 1·5 lbs. |
| Rifling— | | |
|    Twist .. | Increasing. | Uniform (1 in 21). |
|    Pitch .. | 4°—7° 9' | 8° 25'. |
|    Number of grooves .. | 32 | 32. |

* The practical limits are − 9° 30' and + 38°.

*'96 n/A. pattern. 1916 pattern.*

Muzzle velocity—
   With reduced charge.
      With normal charge and 1915  1,526 f.s.   1571 f.s.
        pattern shell.
      With super-charge and 1915    —     1745 f.s.
        pattern shell.
      With super - charge and    —     1968 f.s.
        stream-line shell (*C-Ge-schoss*).

Maximum ranges—
   With reduced charge and 1914 pattern shell, 6,562 yards.
   With normal charge—
      1896 shrapnel (time)  ..  7,655 yards   8,421 yards.
      1915 pattern shell (percus-  9,186 yards*  9,405 yards.
        sion).

With super-charge.
   1915 pattern shell (percussion)  ..     —    10,389 yards.
   Stream-line shell (*C-Geschoss*)  ..    —    11,264 yards.

## 8. Field gun ammunition.—†

### (a.) Projectiles :—

(i.) *1896 n/A. gun.*—Fixed ammunition is used. Three rounds are packed in a basket, the total weight being 60 lbs. The following types of shell were in use during the campaign of 1917, but it is probable that by now the less effective types have become obsolete :—

1914 cast iron H.E. shell, with bursting charge of 0·4 lb. of amatol (issued with reduced propellant charge only).

1915 (short) H.E. shell with bursting charge of 0·84 lb. of amatol or picric acid, or with a reduced bursting charge of 0·5 lb.

Long H.E. shell with bursting charge of 2 lbs. of amatol.

Long gas shell (blue, yellow and green cross ; *see* page 89).

1896 pattern (converted) shrapnel, containing 300 lead bullets or 220 steel bullets.

Star shell *Leuchtgeschoss L/3.8* (*i.e.,* 3.8 cal. long). Maximum range, 4,812 yards.

The long shell weighs 16·2 lbs. with pointed fuze, and 15·8 lbs. with round-nosed fuze ; similarly, the 1915 pattern weighs either 15·5 lbs. or 15 lbs. Gas shell vary in weight from 15—15·5 lbs., according to the fuze and the filling.

(ii.) *1916 gun.*—Separate ammunition is used. Of the above-mentioned shell, the 1915 and long H.E., the long gas and the 1896 (converted) shrapnel are fired by the new gun. In addition, a stream-line H.E. shell, with instantaneous fuze and tapered base (*C-Geschoss*) has been introduced for use at long ranges ; it weighs 13 lbs. only, and has a comparatively small bursting charge (1·3 lb.). Its splinter effect is stated to be better than that of the long H.E. shell.

---

\* With trail sunk. 6,000 yards only, with the maximum elevation of 16° on the carriage.

† For further details regarding ammunition and range tables, *see* " Notes on German Shells " (S.S. 420) and " Notes on German Fuzes " (S.S. 306).

*Smoke producers.*—33 per cent. of all field gun H.E. shell, *i.e.*, one in each basket, contain a smoke producer. The other two shell in a basket, which do not contain a smoke producer, are marked with a vertical black stripe.

### (*b.*) **Fuzes (1896 n/A. and 1916 guns)** :—

*Features of interest.*—The non-delay type of fuze has been replaced by an instantaneous fuze and a delay action fuze. Fuzes are now made pointed, being struck with a radius of about 6 calibres. Zinc alloy and steel are employed to the exclusion of copper (brass). Safety powder pellets have been discarded for centrifugal bolts.

The following patterns are now in use :—

*Dopp. Z. 96 n/A.*—An old round-nosed T. & P. fuze, made of aluminium ; graduated in metres of range up to 7,000 m. (7,655 yards). Used with the 1896 pattern (converted) shrapnel.

*K.Z. 11 Gr.*—Ditto, graduated up to 7,200 m. (7,874 yards). Used with H.E. shell, particularly with the 1915 pattern, against aircraft (in which case it contains no percussion system).

*L.K.Z. 11 Gr.*—A pointed T. & P. fuze, made of zinc alloy ; graduated formerly up to 7,200 m. (7,874 yards) and more recently up to 5,000 m. (5,468 yards) only. Used with the 1915 and long H.E shell.

*L.K.Z. 16 m. V.*—A delay action fuze, enclosed in a cap of mild steel, designed for penetrating earth cover, &c. Used with the 1915 and long H.E. shell.

*E.K.Z. 16.*—A pointed fuze, made of zinc alloy ; the prototype of all German instantaneous fuzes. It is issued closed at the top by a lead seal, which is torn off just before loading and a short rod of steel or white metal inserted. On impact this rod drives the needle on to the percussion cap and so detonates the shell. Used with the long H.E. shell only.

*E.K.Z. 17.*—Identical in shape to the above, but the cap is made of steel. The simplicity of its mechanism, however, marks a revolution in German principles of fuze design. It is stated to be liable to cause prematures in the bore. Used with the 1915 H.E. shell and with gas shell.

*K.Z. 14.*—The original round-nosed non-delay action fuze is still sometimes used with gas shell. A later pattern, *K.Z. 14 n/A.*, is used with the 1914 cast-iron H.E. shell.

A picric acid exploder wrapped in paraffined paper, and contained in a steel gaine, is used with fuzes employed with H.E. shell. A powerful detonator is embedded in the picric acid. The gaine usually screws into the lower portion of the fuze.

(*c.*) **Charges.**—(i.) *1896 n/A. gun.*—The charge consists of a propellant similar to cordite made up in the form of tubes. The normal charge is generally used, but for economy in propellants, and in order to obtain a steep angle of descent, the 1914 H.E. cast iron shell is issued with a reduced charge.

(ii.) *1916 gun.*—Cartridges are issued separately packed in baskets containing three cartridges. The cartridge case as issued contains the normal charge (*Gebrauchsladung*), the upper portion of which is in a bag and can be removed when a reduced charge (*kleine Ladung* is required. The super-charge is issued separately. Flash reducers are used for night firing.

9. **The light field howitzer.—The '98/'09 light field howitzer.**—This light field howitzer (*leichte Feldhaubitze 98/09*) is the old 1898 pattern field howitzer entirely remodelled and mounted on a shielded recoil carriage.

(*a.*) **The howitzer.**—The howitzer has a single-motion wedge breech with axial striker, and the construction in general is similar to that of the field gun, but on some of the older howitzers the breech lever works from front to rear instead of from right to left. The bore is rifled with 32 grooves.

(*b.*) **The carriage.**—The carriage is a shielded recoil carriage. The buffer is on the constant long-recoil system with running out springs. The cradle is on rear trunnions with a balance spring in front. The wheels are 4 feet in diameter, and the wheel-track is 5 feet.

(*c.*) **The sights.**—The sighting gear is somewhat more complicated than that of the field gun, but carries a similar panoramic dial sight. The oscillating sight bracket has a range drum graduated in metres for each of the 8 charges, so that elevation is given in terms of the range. As in the case of the field gun, slight alterations to the elevation can be made by means of a corrector (*Regler*). Each corrector graduation is equivalent to an alteration of $13\frac{1}{2}$ minutes in the angle of sight.

(*d.*) **Vehicles.**—The wagon and limber are similar to those of the field gun, except that the shell-baskets are carried upright instead of on their side. Each basket carries two complete rounds, and weighs 79—84 lbs. The limber carries 24 rounds and the wagon (with limber) carries 58.

**The 1916 and Krupp light field howitzers.**—Two new howitzers are known to have been introduced; the 1916 pattern (*l. F.H. 16*) and the Krupp (*l. F.H. Kp.*). Both differ from the '98/'09 howitzer in the following particulars:—

A longer piece, a larger number of partial charges, a heavier full charge and considerably increased range. Captured howitzers which may possibly be of the 1916 pattern are 22 calibres in length. They are mounted on the '98/'09 carriage.

### Details of light field howitzers:—

| — | '98/'09 pattern. | 1916 pattern. | Krupp pattern. |
|---|---|---|---|
| Calibre .. | 10·5 cm. (4·13″) | 10·5 cm. (4·13″) | 10·5 cm. (4·13″). |
| Rifling (grooves) | 32 | 32 | .. |
| Length of howitzer .. | 11·9 calibres | 22 | .. |
| Weight of howitzer in action .. | 22¼ cwt. | .. | .. |
| Weight limbered up without gunners | 37 cwt. | .. | .. |
| Limits of elevation .. | −13°, +40° | .. | .. |
| Amount of traverse .. | 4° | .. | .. |
| Number of charges .. | 8 | 9† | 10 |
| Weight of full charge .. | 1·1 lb. | .. | .. |
| M.V. with full charge .. | 991 f.s.* | .. | .. |
| Maximum range—— | | | |
|   Shrapnel (time) .. | 7,655 yards | At least 7,655 yards | At least 7,655 yards. |
|   1915 and long H.E. shell (percussion). | 7,655 yards | 9,186 yards | 9,733 yards. |
|   Streamline H.E. shell (percussion) (*C-Geschoss*). | .. | 10,936 yards | 11,210 yards. |

\* With Charge No. 7.  † No. 9 is used at ranges between 6,999 and 10,936 yards.

10. **Light field howitzer ammunition.***—All light field howitzers fire separate ammunition.

(*a.*) **Projectiles.**

(i.) *'98/'09 howitzers.*—The following types are now in use :—

    1914 H.E. cast-iron shell, with bursting charge of 0·66 lb.

    1915 H.E. shell, with full bursting charge of 3·3 lbs. of amatol, or a reduced bursting charge of 0·77 lb.

    Long H.E. shell, with full bursting charge of 4·0 lbs. of amatol, or a reduced bursting charge of 3·3 lbs.

    Long gas shell (blue, green and yellow cross ; *see* page 89).

    1916 pattern shrapnel, containing 300 lead bullets, or 450 steel bullets.

The above shell weigh 34·5 lbs. each.

Star shell (*Leuchtgeschoss L/3·3* or star shell 3·3 calibres long) ; this shell bursts in the air like a shrapnel and releases a parachute from which a magnesium flare is suspended. Weight, 27·5 lbs. ; maximum range, 4,740 yards.

(ii.) *1916 and Krupp howitzers :—*

The 1916 and Krupp light field howitzers fire the same shell as the '98/'09 pattern howitzer, with the exception of the 1914 H.E. cast-iron shell. In addition, they fire a stream-line shell (*C-Geschoss*), similar in design to that fired by the 1916 field gun.

*Smoke producers.*—50 per cent. of the H.E. shell contain a smoke producer. The other 50 per cent. (*i.e.,* one in each basket) are marked with a vertical black stripe running the full length of the shell.

(*b.*) **Fuzes.**—All light field howitzer shell are issued fuzed.

*Features of interest.*—

(i.) A considerable proportion of H.E. shell is issued with T. and P. fuze.

(ii.) The introduction of a percussion fuze which can be set for either delay or non-delay action.

(iii.) The introduction of instantaneous fuzes.

(iv.) As regards materials, the employment of zinc alloy and iron to the exclusion of copper.

The following patterns are now in use :—

*H.Z. 05 Schr.* A T. and P. fuze graduated up to 7,000 m. (7,655 yards). Used with the 1916 pattern shrapnel.

*H.Z. 05 Gr.* Similar to the above, but made of brass and steel : can also be set for delay action. Used with the long and 1915 H.E. shell.

*H.Z. 16.* A percussion fuze, made of zinc alloy with a steel cap, and painted grey : can be set for either non-delay or delay action by means of a setting stud. Used with the 1915 and long H.E. shell.

*E.H.Z. 16, E.H.Z. 17* and *E.H.Z. 16 C.* Round-nosed instantaneous howitzer fuzes, similar as regards construction, to the instantaneous field gun fuzes *E.K.Z. 16, E.K.Z. 17* and *E.K.Z. 16 C,* described on page 73.

*H.Z. 14 Fb.* The original non-delay fuze, *H.Z. 14,* gained a reputation for causing prematures, which led to the addition of a centrifugal safety bolt, *Fliehbolzen* (abbreviated to *Fb.* or *Fliehb.*). The improved pattern is still used with the 1914 H.E. and the 1915 H.E. shell with reduced bursting charge. The original *H.Z. 14* fuze is still used with green cross gas shell.

---

  \* For further details regarding ammunition and range tables, *see* " Notes on German Shells " (S.S. **420**) and " Notes on German Fuzes (S.S. 306).

(*c.*) **Charges.**—The charges of flaked powder (*Würfelpulver*) are made up in bags. The cartridge case is either of brass or steel. Flash reducers are used.

11. **Observation wagon and stores.**—Every field battery is provided with a 6-horsed observation wagon. This wagon is unlimbered at the observing station and carries a tripod observation ladder with body-shield, admitting of observation from a height of 18 feet above the ground. The observation wagon carries also the "scissors" stereo-telescope (*Scherenfernrohr*), range-finder (*Entfernungsmesser*), director (*Richtkreis*) and telephone equipment.

Directors, dial sights, &c., of the field artillery are graduated round the circle from 0 to 6400, the main circle being divided into 64 parts, and the 100ths added by means of a micrometer screw. The smallest division (*Teilstrich*) is equivalent to the French *millième, i.e.,* the angle subtended by 1 metre at 1,000 metres (= 3·375 minutes).

In the foot artillery the unit of angular measurement was formerly one-sixteenth of a degree (=3·75 minutes), and dial sights, &c., were graduated from 0 to 5,760.

A War Ministry Order, dated 25th December, 1916, pointed out the inconvenience due to the existence of two systems of graduating sights, directors, &c., and laid down that, in future, the foot artillery would adopt the system of graduation hitherto used by the field artillery. The sights of all natures of gun and howitzer are now graduated in accordance with this system.

In each field artillery *Abteilung*, and in each battery, there is a telephone squad (*Fernsprech-Trupp*); in peace each telephone squad was equipped with two army telephones and 3,280 yards of army cable, but this allowance has probably been increased.

## B.—Foot Artillery.

1. **Peace organization.**—Prior to mobilization, the German Army comprised 24 foot artillery regiments (*i.e.,* one per Army Corps District). The regiments were designed for employment as Corps artillery, and were organized as follows :—

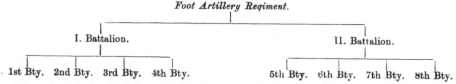

*Foot Artillery Regiment.*

I. Battalion.  II. Battalion.

1st Bty. 2nd Bty. 3rd Bty. 4th Bty.  5th Bty. 6th Bty. 7th Bty. 8th Bty.

The armament consisted of 15-cm. heavy field howitzers and 21-cm. mortars. Battalions equipped with 21-cm. mortars had only two batteries.

The peace strength of the German heavy artillery amounted to about 400 batteries.

Most of the foot artillery regiments had, in peace, one or two *Bespannungs-Abteilungen* (draught-horse detachments), which were attached in turn to each battery in order to train the personnel for mobile operations.

2. **Expansion during the war.**—The expansion of the foot artillery has continued steadily during the war. In January, 1918, there were nearly 5½ times as many heavy batteries as existed in peace.

On mobilization, each Active foot artillery regiment formed a Reserve regiment which was soon ready to take the field.

As the production of guns increased, each foot artillery regiment also formed a Landwehr regiment, and some of the batteries of the Ersatz (depôt) battalions and Landsturm battalions of regiments have also appeared in the field.

The number of battalions in a regiment has also been raised, some regiments having three, four or even five battalions.

In addition to the batteries belonging to Active, Reserve, Landwehr, Ersatz and Landsturm foot artillery battalions, a number of independently numbered foot artillery batteries were formed in 1915 and 1916, numbered from 101 to 150, and from 200 to 800. A great many of these batteries were equipped with the armament of captured fortresses, or from the fortresses in Germany, and were not horsed. A number were also equipped with the old 9-cm. field gun. Independent battalions, numbered from 21 upwards, were also formed.

During 1916, the series of high-numbered batteries greatly increased, and a new series of foot artillery battalions, numbered from 40 upwards, was formed. These battalions consisted of three or four batteries. Some of their batteries were merely formed by re-numbering existing batteries of the independent series and providing them with horses.

A considerable number of naval long-range batteries were added to the Field Army during 1916 and 1917.

By the beginning of 1918, the total number of foot artillery batteries in the field had risen to about 2,250.

### 3. Distribution and allotment of foot artillery units.—The numbering and original formation of foot artillery units afford no clue to their distribution in the field.

Foot artillery regiments no longer exist as tactical units, and only remain as part of the designation of batteries. The battalions, also, have been largely broken up, and batteries do not necessarily work together under their original battalion staff.

During the latter part of 1916, there was a tendency to revert to a more permanent organization, and a great many independent batteries were grouped together in battalions of three or four batteries.

These anomalies in organization and command have made it difficult to follow the distribution and allotment of foot artillery units in the field.

The following points are, however, established :—

(a.) Batteries are not permanently allotted to Corps or divisions, but are allotted to certain sectors of the front in accordance with the tactical objectives or the situation at the moment. The normal allotment is 8 or 9 heavy batteries to a quiet divisional sector, and 16 on an active battle front. These batteries sometimes form mixed groups with the field batteries.

(b.) The heavier calibres and long-range guns on railway mountings, are grouped together for counter-battery work or for special tasks under higher commanders.

(c.) Batteries other than those included under (b) are all under the orders of the divisional artillery commander in whose sector they are placed. When the division moves, the batteries remain in position.

In battle sectors, a Corps headquarters is frequently given a special artillery staff (*Artilleriestab zur besonderen ucerwendung*), which keeps in touch with the various divisional artillery staffs in the Corps, and directly controls the Corps long-range heavy artillery group.

At the headquarters of every Army there is an artillery adviser (*General von der Artillerie*).

### 4. Organization of foot artillery batteries.—The organization of foot artillery batteries varies very considerably according to the calibre. The following table shows the

normal number of pieces in German foot artillery batteries according to their calibre, as established by recent documents :—

| Nature of battery. | Number of guns or howitzers. |
|---|---|
| 10 cm. gun   ..      ..      ..      ..      .. | 4 |
| 13 cm. gun   ..      ..      ..      ..      .. | 2 |
| 15 cm. gun   ..      ..      ..      ..      .. | 2 |
| 15 cm. howitzer      ..      ..      ..      .. | 4 |
| 21 cm. howitzer (mortar)   ..      ..      .. | 3 |

9-cm. gun batteries have 6, 8 and sometimes 12 guns, but these are obsolescent.

The establishment of a 21 cm. mortar battery would appear to include 3 mortars, 6 officers, 200 men, 100 heavy and 25 light draught horses. The normal strength of a 15 cm. howitzer battery is 4 officers and 120 other ranks. Batteries do not appear to be horsed in all cases, and, in general, the number of horses has been considerably reduced from the establishment laid down prior to mobilization. In other respects, the normal organization and equipment of heavy batteries does not differ greatly from that of field batteries.

5. **Armament of foot artillery batteries.**—The proportion of guns to howitzers in the German foot artillery is approximately—

Guns   ..      ..      ..      ..      ..      ..      25 per cent.
Howitzers..      ..      ..      ..      ..      ..      75 per cent.

The heavy guns in commonest use are—

10-cm. (4·1-inch) gun.
13-cm. (5·3-inch) gun.
15-cm. (5·9-inch) gun (of various types).
24-cm. (9·4-inch) naval gun.

The three first-mentioned calibres are represented in approximately equal proportions, but there is a tendency to increase the number of 15-cm. high-velocity naval guns.

A number of foot artillery batteries are armed with the old 9-cm. (3·5-inch) field gun, and in many sectors, batteries are identified which are armed with the old German 12-cm. heavy gun, the French 120-mm. long gun, or the Belgian 12-cm. gun. There are a few batteries of 21-cm., 28-cm., 30·5·cm., 35·6-cm. and 38-cm. guns of naval origin.

The calibres of the heavy howitzer batteries have been standardized to a much greater degree than in the case of the heavy gun batteries. The two standard calibres are—

15-cm. (5·9-inch) howitzer, forming 50 per cent. of the total armament of the foot artillery.

21-cm. (8·3-inch) mortar, forming 25 per cent. of the total armament of the foot artillery.

A few heavy howitzer batteries of 28-cm. (11-inch), 30·5-cm. (12-inch), and 42-cm. (16·5-inch) calibre exist, but they are comparatively rare.

The Germans, in most cases, use the term " mortar " (*Mörser*) for howitzers of 21-cm. calibre and upwards.

6. **The 15-cm. heavy field howitzer.**—As stated above, 50 per cent. of the German foot artillery is equipped with 15-cm. heavy field howitzer batteries. There are four patterns of 15-cm. heavy field howitzer (*schwere Feld-Haubitze*).

*Particulars of 15-cm. heavy field howitzers.*

| —— | Original pattern. (s.F.H.) | 1902 pattern. (s.F.H. 02) | 1913 pattern. (s.F.H. 13) | Long 1913 pattern. (lg.s.F. H. 13) |
|---|---|---|---|---|
| Calibre | 14·97 cm. (5·89″). | 14·97 cm. (5·89″). | 14·97 cm. (5·89″). | 14·97 cm. (5·89″). |
| Rifling, grooves | 36 | 36 | 36 | 32 |
| Length of howitzer | 10·8 calibres. | 12 calibres. | 14 calibres. | 17 calibres. |
| Weight of howitzer with breech block. | 21⅓ cwt. | 15¾ cwt. | 15½ cwt. | 16¼ cwt. |
| Weight of carriage | 19 cwt. | 23½ cwt. | ? | 26¾ cwt. |
| Weight limbered up, without gunners. | 53½ cwt. | 53½ cwt. | ? | ? |
| Limit of elevation | 65° | 42° | 45° | 45° |
| Amount of traverse | ? | 3° 36′ | about 4° | about 4° |
| Number of charges | 7 | 6 | 7 | 8 |
| Weight of full charge | 1·9 lbs. | 2·6 lbs. | 3·0 lbs. | ? |
| M.V. with full charge | 905 f.s. | 1,066 f.s. | 1,196 f.s. | ? |
| Maximum range with full charge. | 6,616 yards.* | 8,147 yards.* | 9,296 yards.* | 9,296 yards.* |

* With shell with false cap, probably 1,000–2,000 yards more.

(*a.*) **The original howitzer.**—The howitzer is mounted on an old type of heavy limbered carriage. The recoil is checked by means of tyre brakes, actuated by wire ropes which wind round the inner flanges of the wheels. The howitzer need not be fired from a platform, but in soft ground mats are placed under the wheels and trail.

(*b.*) **The 1902 howitzer.**—The howitzer is mounted on a recoil carriage with spade, buffer and running-out springs. The recoil is on the constant recoil system. The cradle rotates on trunnions placed in front of the carriage axle. The carriage is not shielded.

The howitzer has a single-motion wedge breech action with an axial striker. It is fitted with a dial sight but not with an independent line of sight. The range drum is graduated in degrees from 9° to 42°, and also in metres of range for each of the six charges.

Six gunners are carried on the limber, but no ammunition.

(*c.*) **The 1913 howitzer.**—This is an improved type with increased range and steadiness when firing. Howitzers of recent manufacture are fitted with an air recuperator (*Luftvorholer*). The recoil is on the constant recoil system. The cradle is mounted on rear trunnions, the weight of the forepart of the howitzer and cradle being taken up by two balance springs placed one on either side of the top carriage. The carriage is provided with a shield, and the wheels with girdles.

(*d.*) **The long 1913 howitzer** (*see* Plate 14) embodies the following noteworthy features in its design :—

A very long piece, rear trunnions, air recuperator, variable recoil, 8 charges, a hinged spade.

The *howitzer* consists of a single tube, 17 calibres long, over which are shrunk a muzzle ring, two guide rings, and a breech jacket. The breech is of the usual German sliding wedge type, with axial percussion striker.

The *cradle* is mounted on a top carriage on rear trunnions, placed only 20 inches from the face of the breech. The trunnions are vertically above the carriage axle. Two balance springs, one on either side of the cradle, take the weight of the piece. The maximum length of recoil is about 59 inches.

The *top carriage* is pivoted in front of the carriage axle on the carriage proper.

The *carriage proper* is remarkable for the length of the trail. It is fitted with a hinged shield, in which the usual central shutter has been replaced by a hood. The spade is hinged on an eccentric, and can be clamped both when folded up and when let down. The carriage is mounted on wooden wheels, 49 inches in diameter, fitted with 4½-inch tyres.

The *sights* are mounted on an oscillating bracket and are canted to allow for drift. The range drum is graduated in hundreds of metres for 8 charges and also in degrees.

### 7. **Ammunition of the 15-cm. heavy field howitzer.**[*]—

(*a*.) **Projectiles.**—The projectiles in common use are—

> 1912 and 1912 n/A. (long) H.E. shell with bursting charge of 13·4 lbs. of trinitro-anisol and dinitrobenzene.
>
> 1914 (short) H.E. shell with bursting charge of 5·5 lbs. of amatol. This shell is the most employed. With a view to economising copper it has been issued (experimentally) with a zinc driving band.
>
> 1914 (short) H.E. cast iron shell with bursting charge of 3·1 lbs. of amatol and T.N.T.
>
> Gas shell (green, yellow and blue cross, *see* page 89). The 1912 n/A. (long) shell case is used for gas shell.

In order to obtain increased range with undiminished accuracy, the 1914 (short) H.E. shell, which has a 1 calibre head, is now fitted with a hollow pointed false cap made of thin mild steel. This cap must be struck with a radius of about 6 calibres. The length of the shell has been increased from 3 to 4½ calibres. The consequent increase in range is not known, but is probably from 1,000—2,000 yards, so that the maximum range of the howitzers now mostly in use would be about 11,000 yards.

All three patterns of H.E. shell weigh about 92 lbs.; the gas shell weighs about 95·5 lbs. Each shell is packed in a separate basket, the total weight being about 100 lbs.

A proportion of H.E. shell contain smoke producers and are marked on the shoulder with a black "R" (*Rauchentwickler*).

(*b*.) **Fuzes.**—The ammunition is mostly issued fuzed; *Gr. Z. 04* fuzes are, however, issued separately, packed in soldered tin boxes. Gas shell of recent patterns are also issued unfuzed.

The following fuzes are now employed with all four patterns of 15-cm. howitzers :—

*Dopp. Z. 15.*—Time and percussion fuze, which can be set for either delay or non-delay action; made of brass and steel; graduated up to 41 seconds. Used with the 1912 and 1912 n/A. H.E. shell.

---

[*] For further details regarding ammunition and range tables, *see* "Notes on German Shells" (S.S. 420) and "Notes on German Fuzes" (S.S. 306.)

[†] This shell has recently been found filled with a mixed charge of trinitroanisol and dinitrobenzene.

*Gr. Z. 04.*—A percussion fuze, made of brass or of white metal and steel ; can be set for either non-delay or delay action.  Used principally with the 1912 pattern (long) H.E. shell.

*Gr. Z. 14.*—Made of brass and steel ; a simplified variation of the above ; non-delay action only.  Used principally with the 1914 and 1914 A patterns (short) H.E. shell.

*Gr. Z. 14 n/A.*—The improved pattern of *Gr. Z. 14*, from which it can be distinguished by the thin plate riveted over the top of the body ; a centrifugal safety bolt is provided in addition to the safety powder pellet.  Used principally with the 1914 H.E. shell and with gas shell.

*Gr. Z. 17.*—A new instantaneous fuze, made of steel and white metal.  It apparently has a projecting rod like the *E.K.Z. 17* (*see* page 73).  Used with the 1912 n/A. and 1914 H.E. shell.

(*c.*) **Charges.**—The charges of flaked powder (*Würfelpulver*) are made up in bags. The cartridge cases are of either brass or steel and are packed in flat baskets containing 5 apiece.  Flash reducers are used for night firing.

8. **The 21-cm. mortar.**—Apart from various patterns of obsolete bronze mortars, the three following patterns of German 21-cm. mortar are now in use :—

(*a.*) " 21-cm. mortar " (*21 cm. Mörser* or *21 cm. Mrs.*).—Dating from 1902 ; an obsolete piece, still however in use.

(*b.*) " Mortar " (*Mörser* or *Mrs.*).—Introduced in 1910 and still being issued in 1917 ; the piece with which most 21-cm. mortar batteries are equipped.

(*c.*) " Long mortar " (*langer Mörser* or *lg. Mrs.*).—The latest pattern.

*Particulars of 21-cm. Mortars.*

| — | 21 cm. Mortar. (*21-cm. Mrs.*) | Mortar. (*Mrs.*) | Long Mortar. (*lg. Mrs.*) |
|---|---|---|---|
| Calibre .. .. .. .. .. | 21·1-cm. (8·3″) | 21·1-cm. (8·3″) | 21·1-cm. (8·3″) |
| Rifling, grooves .. .. .. | 64 | 64 | |
| Total length of mortar .. .. | 10 calibres | 12 calibres. | |
| Weight of mortar with breech block . | 59 cwt. | 51¾ | |
| Weight of carriage .. .. .. | 36 cwt. | ? | |
| Limits of elevation .. .. .. | − 6°, + 70° | 0, + 70° | |
| Amount of traverse .. .. .. | ? | 4° | |
| Number of charges .. .. .. | 17 (11)* | 9 | |
| Weight of full charge .. .. | 6·8 lbs. | 12·3 lbs. | |
| M.V. with full charge .. .. | 1,010 (1,158)† f.s. | 1,203 (1,332)† f.s. | |
| Maximum range .. .. .. | 8,421 (8,968) † yards | 10,280 (9,952)† yards. | 11,155 (10,280)† yards |

(*a.*) **The 21-cm. mortar (original pattern).**—The carriage is provided with travelling wheels, but in action these are replaced by small firing wheels or trucks, which only project as far as the prolongation of the lower surface of the trail.  In action, the carriage rests on a platform constructed of two layers of baulks of timber.  The recoil is

* 17 charges are used with the 1896 pattern shell, and 11 with the 1914 and 1914 A patterns.
† The figures in brackets refer to the 1914 and 1914 A (short) shell, the other figures refer to the 96 and 1896 n/A. (long) shell.

checked by two movable inclined planes, which are placed on either side of the carriage so that the firing trucks have to run up them when the carriage recoils.

For purposes of transport, the mortar is dismounted from its firing carriage and placed on a special wagon. The firing carriage, when fitted with its transport wheels, is attached to a special limber.

(*b.*) **The "Mortar."**—The *Mortar* (*see* Plate 16) consists of a single tube, over which are shrunk a guide ring, a plain ring and the breech jacket. The breech is a sliding wedge breech, with axial percussion striker. The axis of the bore when horizontal is about 5 feet 3 inches above the ground level. A tray, handled by 4 men, is used for loading The shell is rammed by hand, the men standing on the trail. On the march, the mortar is carried on a special wagon.

*The cradle* encircles the piece. The buffer is placed above the mortar. The cradle rotates on rear trunnions on a top carriage. This admits of a constant long recoil. The weight of the piece is taken by a helical balance spring, mounted on a gimbal placed some 14 inches in front of the carriage axle.

The *top-carriage* is pivoted on the carriage proper immediately in rear of the carriage axle.

The *carriage* has a trail 14 feet 9 inches in length, measuring from the carriage axle It is mounted on steel wheels 4 feet 7 inches in diameter, with $4\frac{3}{4}$-inch tyres. The brake shoes act on both faces of inner flanges on the wheels. Girdles are used on soft ground and for firing. Wicker mats are also issued to place beneath the wheels. The shield is detachable.

The *sights* are mounted on an oscillating bracket and canted so as to allow for drift The range drum is graduated in degrees and in hundreds of metres for 9 charges, for both low and high angle fire.

(*c.*) **The "Long mortar."**—Nothing is known about the long mortar except the particulars given in the table, but it is frequently referred to in documents and is probably the type now being manufactured.

9 **Ammunition of the 21-cm. mortar.**\*—(*a*) **Projectiles.**—The shell used with these mortars are supplied fuzed. Gas shell of recent pattern are, however, issued unfuzed. Each shell is packed in a separate basket.

The following patterns of shell are in common use:—

1896 *n/A.* (long) H.E. shell with bursting charge of 40·4 lbs. of T.N.T.
1914 (short) H.E. shell with bursting charge of 17·0 lbs. of amatol.
1914 *A* (short) H.E. shell with bursting charge of 13·9 lbs. of amatol.
1896 *n/A.* (long) type gas shell (mostly yellow cross, *see* page 89).

The 1896 *n/A.* shell weighs about 262 lbs., and the 1914 and 1914 *A* shell about 184 lbs.

(*b.*) **Fuzes.**—Only percussion fuzes are used.

*kz. Bd. Z. 1C.*—Base fuze made of brass and screwed into a steel gaine; can be set for either non-delay (*0 V.*), short delay (*1 V.*), or long delay (*2 V.*). Used with the 1896 n/A. H.E. shell.

*Gr. Z. 04* and *Gr. Z. 04/14.*—Made of brass and steel; nose fuzes. They can be set for either delay or non-delay action. Used with the 1914 and 1914 A (short) H.E. shell

---

\* For further details regarding ammunition and range tables, *see* "Notes on German Shells" (S.S. 4 and "Notes on German Fuzes" (S.S. 306).

*Gr. Z. 92.*—An old-fashioned nose fuze made of brass. Used with the 1896 n/A. gas shell. This is a base-fuzed shell which has been plugged and the point of the shell cut off and tapped to receive a nose fuze.

(*c.*) **Charges.**—The charge is of powder in flat rings, made up in bags. Cartridge cases are of brass and are packed in flat baskets containing 2 apiece.

### 10. Howitzers and mortars of 28-cm. and larger calibres.—These include the following : —

28-cm. (11-inch) howitzer on travelling carriage.
28-cm. (11-inch) coast defence howitzer.
30·5-cm. (12-inch) heavy coast defence howitzers '98 and '09.
30·5-cm. (12-inch) Austrian howitzer.
30·5-cm. (12-inch) Krupp howitzer.
42-cm. (16·5-inch) mortar.

Information concerning the projectiles, maximum ranges, &c., of these weapons, is contained in " Notes on German Shells" (S.S. 420).

### 30·5-cm. Austrian mortar.—The following is a rough description of the 1911 pattern. There is also apparently a later pattern which is 14 calibres long and has a maximum range of 13,124 yards.

The *mortar* recoils within a circular cradle of cast steel. Above the cradle are the two buffer cylinders below it are the three cylinders of the hydro-pneumatic recuperator. The central cylinder contains glycerine, the other two glycerine and compressed air.

The *cradle* is mounted on trunnions on a carriage formed by two upright members braced in front and mounted on a circular steel base. The latter is pivoted on a circular mounting bolted to a rectangular steel platform.

The *platform* is built up in the form of 3 flat boxes laid side by side and connected by hinges. On the march the central box is laid flat on the truck, the two others hanging vertically on either side.

The mortar with its platform is transported on 3 vehicles hauled by one 100 h.p. Daimler tractor. The mortar is also known to be transported on a motor truck.

The following particulars refer to the 1911 pattern :—

| | |
|---|---|
| Calibre | 12 inches (30·5 cm.). |
| Rifling | 68 grooves. |
| Length of mortar | 10 calibres. |
| Weight of mortar | about 7 tons. |
| Weight of carriage | „ 10 „ |
| Weight of platform | „ 7 „ |
| Limits of elevation | + 45° + 75°. |
| Amount of traverse | 120° on platform, 60° without platform. |
| Maximum range | 10,499 yards. |
| Weight of shell | 838 lbs. |
| Weight of bursting charge | 77 lbs. |
| Weight of propellant (full charge) | 26·4 lbs. |
| Rate of fire | 1 round every 6 minutes. |

### 30·5-cm. German mortar.—Krupp manufactures a mortar similar to the Austrian mortar described above. About 10 of these batteries are reported to have been identified in the Western Front. A battery consists of two mortars.

11. **10-cm. guns.**—There are four patterns of German 10-cm. gun, known respectively as *10-cm. gun, 10-cm. gun '04*; *10-cm. gun '97, 10-cm. gun '14,* which in German documents are grouped in pairs as above for purposes of reference regarding range (*see* diagram to face page 88). These are all long-range high-velocity guns and fire the same ammunition.

**The 1904 gun.**—The principal details of the '04 pattern gun are as follows:—

| | |
|---|---|
| Calibre | 4·13 inches (10·5 cm.). |
| Length of gun | 30 calibres. |
| Weight of gun | 26½ cwt. |
| Weight of carriage | 27¾ cwt. |
| Weight limbered up without gunners | 69 cwt. |
| Limits of elevation | − 5°, + 30°. |
| Amount of traverse | 3° 56'. |
| Weight of charge | 5 lbs. |
| Muzzle velocity | 1,830 f.s. |
| Maximum percussion range | 11,264 yards. |

The breech is of the single-motion vertical wedge pattern. The firing device consists of a striker actuated by a lever and counter spring. The gun is mounted on a recoil carriage fitted with a hydraulic buffer, running-out springs, and trail with spade. The buffer is below the gun and is pivoted on a cradle; the trunnions of the latter being in front of the axle of the carriage. There is no shield. The sighting arrangements are similar to those of the 7·7-cm. field gun (*see* page 70).

**The 1914 gun.**—The 1914 gun made its appearance on the Western Front during 1915, and by the end of 1917 was probably in general use. It differs principally from the '04 pattern by the length of the piece, which is at least 35 calibres and its maximum range (T. and P.) of 12,085 yards. It fires the same shell as the other patterns, but has separate ammunition. A reduced propelling charge is also used, with which the maximum range is 8,968 yards.

There are three further patterns of 10-cm. gun, known, according to their mounting, as *10-cm. gun with overhead shield, 10-cm. gun in turret,* and *10-cm. reinforced gun in turret* which fire the same ammunition as the above, with the exception of the most modern shell, the 1915 H.E.

*The 10-cm. coast defence gun on wheeled carriage* is also employed against land targets firing a shell known as the "1916 pattern H.E.," with a bursting charge of 4 lbs. and a maximum range of 16,295 yards. This is separate ammunition. The propellant charge weighs 15·4 lbs. With the reduced charge of 9·9 lbs., the maximum range is 12,249 yards.

12. **Ammunition of 10-cm. guns.\***—(*a.*) **Projectiles.**—The weight of a complete round is approximately 53 lbs. The projectiles in use are as follows:—

"10-cm. H.E. shell" with bursting charge of 1·48 lbs. of picric acid.
1914 H.E. shell with bursting charge of 1·98 lbs. of amatol.
1914 A H.E. shell with bursting charge of 1·54 lbs. of amatol.
1915 H.E. shell with bursting charge of 4 lbs. of picric acid.
1896 shrapnel, containing 680 lead bullets.

Each of the above projectiles weighs 39·5 lbs.

---

\* For further details regarding ammunition and range tables, *see* "Notes on German Shell" (S.S. 420), and "Notes on German Fuzes" (S.S. 306).

(*b.*) **Fuzes.**—The following fuzes are used:—

*Dopp. Z. 92 f. 10 cm. K.*, also marked *Dopp. Z. 92 K. 15.* An old-fashioned T. and P. fuze made of brass, graduated up to 26 seconds. Used with shrapnel. Maximum range, 9,296 yards.

*Dopp. Z. 92 lg. Brlg.*—An improved variation of the above, graduated up to 41 seconds. Used with shrapnel. Maximum range, 12,085 yards.

*H. Z. 14 Vorst* and *K.Z. 16 f. 10 cm. K.* Percussion fuzes. Used with the 1914 and 1914A H.E. shell.

*Gr. Z. 04.*—Percussion fuze (delay and non-delay action). Used with the 1915 H.E. shell.

(*c.*) **Charges.**—The charge consists of a propellant similar to cordite, made up in the form of tubes. The reduced charge is used whenever possible. The cartridge cases are of brass.

13. **The 13-cm. gun.**—(*a.*) **The gun.**—The 13-cm. gun is a long-range, high-velocity Q.F. gun which was introduced before the present war to replace the 15-cm. long gun. The principal details are given below :—

| | |
|---|---|
| Calibre | 5·31 inches (13·5 cm.) |
| Total length of gun | 15' 6½" = 35 calibres. |
| Weight of gun in action | 114 cwt. |
| Weight of carriage | 55 cwt. |
| Limit of elevation | +26° |
| Amount of traverse | 4° |
| Weight of charge | 22·5 lbs. |
| Weight of reduced charge | 17·2 lbs. |
| Muzzle velocity with full charge | 2,280 f.s. |
| Maximum range— | |
| Percussion (H.E. shell) | 15,748 yards. |
| Time (shrapnel) | 15,311 yards. |

The *gun* recoils on a cradle, which is pivoted on a *top-carriage.* The latter is mounted on the *carriage proper* on forward trunnions.

The *gun* consists of an "A" tube, a "B" tube, and a jacket, over which are shrunk three rings. The recoil guides are secured to the gun by screws. The breech is of the usual Krupp single-motion sliding-wedge type. The gun is fired by a self-cocking axial percussion striker.

(*b.*) **The cradle and carriage.**—The *cradle*, containing the hydraulic buffer and running-out springs, is placed below the gun, and is pivoted in a small top-carriage. The recoil is constant, and has a normal length of about 52 inches.

The *top-carriage* is a U-shaped steel casting, mounted on forward trunnions on the carriage proper.

The *carriage* proper consists of a trail formed with flanged steel sides connected by ransoms. In addition to a small fixed spade, there is a large hinged spade (shown folded). The wheels are either of wood or steel. The shield is hinged and folds back flat on the gun. The carriage brakes consist of shoes working on both faces of inner flanges on the wheels, and are operated by the hand-wheel in front of the carriage. The hand-wheels operating the elevating and traversing gears are mounted on the left of the gun.

(*c.*) **The sights.**—The sighting arrangements are similar to those of the 1896 n/A. field gun (*see* page 70).

14. **Ammunition of the 13-cm. gun.**\*—(*a.*) **Projectiles.**—Shell and cartridge are separate. The projectiles in common use are as follows:—

13-cm. H.E. shell, with bursting charge of 7·7 lbs. of T.N.T.
1914 pattern H.E. shell, with bursting charge of 5·5 lbs. of T.N.T.
13-cm. shrapnel, containing 1,170 lead bullets.

The above projectiles weigh about 89 lbs. each.

(*b.*) **Fuzes.**—*lg. Bd. Z. 10.* Percussion base fuze, made of brass; can be set for non-delay (*0.V.*), short delay (*1 V.*), and long delay (*2 V.*) Used with the 13-cm. H.E shell.

*Gr. Z. 14.* Percussion nose fuze, non-delay action only, made of brass and steel; used with the 1914 H.E. shell.

*Dopp. Z. 92 f. 10 cm. K.*; also marked *Dopp. Z. 92 K. 15.* An old-fashioned T. and P. fuze, made of brass; graduated up to 26 seconds. Used with shrapnel; maximum range (time), 10,936 yards.

*Dopp. Z. 92 lg. Brlg.* An improved variation of the above; graduated up to 41 seconds. Used with shrapnel; maximum range, 15,311 yards.

(*c.*) **Cartridge cases.**—These are of brass.

15. **Older patterns of guns employed by the foot artillery.**—A certain number of foot artillery batteries are armed with guns of older patterns. Particulars of those which are most commonly in use are given in the table below; all four types are mounted on old-fashioned non-recoil carriages.

### Particulars of guns of older patterns.

| — | 9-cm. field gun '73/'88. (*9 cm. K.*) | 12-cm. heavy gun. (*s. 12 cm. K.*) | 15-cm. gun with chase rings (*Ringkanone*). | 15-cm. long gun. (*lg. 15 cm. K.*) |
|---|---|---|---|---|
| Calibre | 8 ·8 cm. | 12 ·03 cm. | 14 ·97 cm. | 14 ·97 cm. |
| Total length of gun | 23 ·9 calibres | 23 ·4 calibres | 23 calibres | 30 calibres |
| Weight of gun | 8¼ cwt. | 25½ cwt. | 61¼ cwt. | 66¼ cwt. |
| Weight of carriage | 15 cwt. | 22½ cwt. | 37¼ cwt. | 52 cwt. |
| Weight limbered up without gunners. | .. | 66½ cwt. | .. | 76 cwt. |
| Limits of elevation.. | −10° +41° | −5° +40° | − 5° +35° and +37° | − 4° +40° |
| Weight of charge (single charge of flaked powder, similar to cordite, contained in bag). | 1 ·5 lbs. | 2 ·9 lbs. | 6 lbs. | 8 ·8 lbs. |
| Muzzle velocity | 1,450 f.s. | 1,280 f.s. | 1,499 f.s. | 1,640 f.s. |
| Maximum range— | | | | |
|     Time .. | 7,109 yards | 7,218 yards | 7,546 yards | 8,968 yards |
|     Percussion | 7,109 yards | 7,984 yards | 8,640 yards | 10,936 yards |

\* For further details regarding ammunition and range tables, *see* "Notes on German Shells" (S.S. 42) and "Notes on German Fuzes" (S.S. 306).

Certain 9-cm. batteries are known to have been re-armed with captured French and Belgian 12-cm. guns, and others with 15-cm. howitzers but the guns are probably still allotted to sectors as anti-tank and infantry guns.

There is also a " Long 15-cm. gun with chase rings" (*lg. 15 cm. R.K.*) which fires the same ammunition as the *Ringkanone*, but its maximum time and percussion ranges are 7,655 and 8,749 yards, respectively.

### 16. The 15-cm. experimental gun on wheeled carriage (*15 cm. Vers. K.i.R.L.* or *15 cm. Versuchs-Kanone in Rad-Lafette*).

—A long-range gun which made its appearance in 1916. The gun is rifled with 48 grooves. The pitch of the rifling is 7°. (For ranges, *see* diagram to face page 88). It fires the following ammunition :- –

1903 H.E. shell, with bursting charge of 7·2 lbs. of T.N.T. and *Gr. Z. 04* fuze (*see* page 81).

Ditto, with false cap (7·5 c.r.h.) and bursting charge of 8·1 lbs.

1903 shrapnel (grey) and 1903 shrapnel (grey) with false cap.

The T. and P. fuzes *Dopp. Z. 92 f. 10 cm. K.*, *Dopp. Z. 92 K. 15* and *Dopp. Z. 92 lg. Brlg.* (*see* page 85) formerly used with this shrapnel have been superseded by the clockwork fuze *Dopp. Z. 16*. This fuze is remarkable for its cheapness, simplicity and accuracy. Its introduction has rendered practicable the engagement of kite balloons by heavy guns firing at very long ranges (20,000 yards and upwards).

### 17. The 15-cm. gun, 16.

—Probably an improved pattern of the above firing the same ammunition. (For ranges *see* diagram to face page 88).

### 18. Naval guns.

—A large number of German naval guns are employed on the Western Front. These are either spares, or old guns from dismantled warships, or guns that were on order for foreign navies at the outbreak of war. They are mounted in three different ways, viz :—

On wheeled road-carriage (*in Rad-Lafette*).
On railway mounting (*Eisenbahn-Geschütz*).
On platform mounting (*Bettungs-Geschütz*).

These are all Q.F. guns.

The guns most frequently identified are the 15-cm. Q.F. gun L/40, and the 24-cm. Q.F. gun L/40.

### Particulars of naval guns.

| Pattern of gun. | 10·5-cm. Q.F. gun. | 15-cm. Q.F. gun. | 17-cm. Q.F. gun. | 21-cm. Q.F. gun. | 24-cm. Q.F. gun. |
|---|---|---|---|---|---|
| German abbreviation. | *10·5 cm., s.K.L/35 or s./10 cm. K.* | *15 cm., S.K.L/40 or s./15 cm. K.* | *17 cm., S.K.L/40.* | *21 cm. S.K.L/45.* | *24 cm. S.K.L/40.* |
| Mountings .. | .. | On wheeled carriage. | On wheeled carriage. *17 cm. K.i.R.L.* On platform mounting. *17 cm. K. Bett-Gesch.* On railway mounting. *17 cm. K. Eis.* | On railway mounting. *21 cm. S.K.L/45 Eis.* | On platform mounting. *24 cm. S.K.Bett.-Gesch.* On railway mounting. *24 cm. S.K.L/40 Eis.* |

| Pattern of gun. | 10·5-cm. Q.F. gun. | 15-cm. Q.F. gun. | 17-cm. Q.F. gun. | 21-cm. Q.F. gun. | 24-cm. Q.F. gun. |
|---|---|---|---|---|---|
| Rifling, grooves .. | 32 | 44 | 52 | 64 | 72 |
| Type of projectile | H.E., 2 c.r.h., nose fuze. | H.E., false cap, ? c.r.h., nose fuze. | H.E., pointed, 8 c.r.h., false cap, tapered base, nose fuze. | H.E., pointed, 10 c.r.h., base fuze. | H.E., pointed, 10 c.r.h., base fuze. Shrapnel, pointed, 10 c.r.h., false cap, clockwork nose fuze. |
| *Weights*— | | | | | |
| Shell    ..    .. | 38·69 lbs. | 94·5 lbs. | 141 lbs. | 253·53 lbs. | 332·90 lbs. |
| H.E.    bursting charge. | 1·65 ,, | 9·85 ,, | 14·17 ,, | 17·95 ,, | 33·06 ,, |
| Full propellant charge. | 6·39 ,, | 20·28 ,, | 38·1 ,, | 65·04 ,, | 94·80 ,, |
| Reduced propellant charge. | None in use. | 11·02 ,, | 24·9 ,, | None in use. | 78·2 ,, |
| *Maximum ranges*— | | | | | |
| Full charge (time) | (H.E.), 10,389 yards. | (H.E.), 14,983 yards. | .. | .. | (Shr.), at least 22,000 yards. |
| Full charge (percussion). | 10,389 yards | 20,451 yards | 25,700 yards. | 29,200 yards. | 29,090 ,, |
| Reduced charge (percussion). | .. | 11,400 ,, | .. | .. | .. |

**35·6-cm. gun.**—There are known to exist a certain number of *35·6-cm. coast defence guns* manufactured by Krupp.  One of these 35·6-cm. guns was mounted on a rectangular concrete platform, the excavation for which measured 45 feet × 55 feet and was 10 feet deep.

The following particulars refer to a gun located south-west of Lille :—

| | |
|---|---|
| Calibre    ..    .    ..    .. | 35·56 cm. (14 ins.) |
| Rifling    ..    ..    ..    .. | 72 grooves. |
| Type of shell    ..    ..    .. | H.E. with pointed false cap. |
| Fuze    ..    ..    ..    .. | Base fuze *Spgr. m. K.* |
| Colour of shell    ..    ..    .. | Yellow. |
| Weight of shell    ..    ..    .. | 12¼ cwt. approx. |
| Maximum range reported..    .. | 50,300 yards, corresponding to an estimated time of flight of 105 seconds. |
| Rate of fire..    ..    ..    .. | 1 round every 7 minutes. |
| Size of craters    ..    ..    .. | 8–14 feet deep; 20–27 feet in diameter. |

**38-cm. gun.**—A naval gun, probably 45 or 50 calibres in length, mounted, on land, on a pivot mounting in a circular concrete pit.  It would appear, from the examination of an abandoned pit, that the gun recoils in a cradle, mounted on trunnions on the main girders

# MAXIMUM RANGES OF GERMAN GUNS, HOWITZERS AND MORTARS.

## FIELD ARTILLERY

### (a) FIELD GUNS

* Range with maximum elevation of 16° on carriage.

### (b) LIGHT FIELD HOWITZERS

## FOOT ARTILLERY

### (a) MEDIUM RANGE GUNS

### (b) HIGH VELOCITY & LONG RANGE GUNS

FEATURES OF SPECIAL INTEREST.

1. The introduction of new patterns of guns, howitzers and shell, by which the range of the field artillery has been considerably increased.

2. The increased range of some of the high-velocity guns, due to the adoption of stream-line shell (with and without false caps).

3. The introduction of howitzer shell (15-cm. and 42-cm.) with false caps.

* With reduced charge.
† With super-charge.

*Maximum ranges in yards :—*T = with time fuze.    P = with percussion fuze.

## Maximum Ranges of German Guns, Howitzers and Mortars—*continued.*

### (c) HEAVY FIELD HOWITZERS & MORTARS

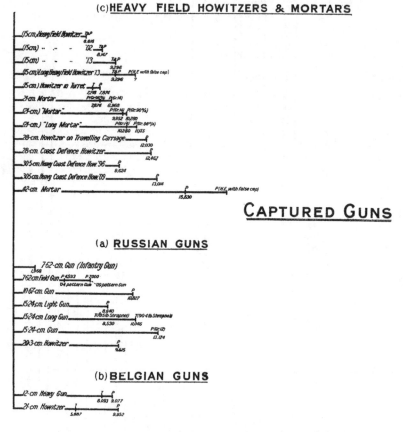

## CAPTURED GUNS

### (a) RUSSIAN GUNS

### (b) BELGIAN GUNS

*Maximum ranges in yards.*

T = with time fuze.     P = with percussion fuze.

of a steel bridge which spans half the pit. This bridge resembles in construction that of the half of a turntable. One end is pivoted in the centre of the pit, the other runs on a circular track laid round its edge. Where an all round traverse is not required, the pit has the shape of a sector of a circle.

*Particulars.—*

| | | | |
|---|---|---|---|
| Calibre | .. | .. | 38·1 cm. (15-inch.). |
| Types of shell | .. | .. | Pointed H.E. and H.E. with pointed false cap. |
| Weight of shell | .. | .. | 14¾ cwt. |
| Fuze | .. | .. | Base fuze, *Spgr.m.K.* |
| Maximum range reported | | | 46,000 yards. |

## 19. Ammunition of naval guns—

(*a.*) **Projectiles.**—All naval H.E. shell are painted yellow, usually with a black nose. Both shells and fuzes are stamped with a crown surmounted by a capital M. The bursting charge of compressed T.N.T. or picric acid is in a millboard container.

In order to obtain increased range with these naval guns, few of which were new, the old naval shell were fitted with a pointed false cap. The results were so satisfactory that new types of shell were adopted which had a pointed head struck with a radius of 10 calibres (10 c.r.h.). The latest type of long-range shell, evolved by the Germans, is the 17 cm. H.E. shell with pointed false cap (8 c.r.h.) and tapered base (1 in 7), with which a range of 25,700 yards is obtained. The shell complete with cap is 4·7 calibres long.

(*b.*) **Fuzes.**—*Dopp.Z.S./43.*—An old-fashioned T. & P. fuze, made of brass, graduated up to 43 seconds. Used with 10·5-cm. and 15-cm. H.E. shell.

*Dopp. Z. 16.*—Clockwork time fuze used with 24-cm. shrapnel (*see* page 87). There are no graduations on the fuze. A graduated fuze setter is used.

*Percussion nose fuzes* of various patterns are used with 10·5-cm., 15-cm. and 17-cm. H.E. shell. These fuzes bear no marking. They are graze fuzes with centrifugal safety devices.

*Spgr. m. K. = Sprenggranatenzünder mit Klappensicherung, i.e.,* fuze for H.E. shell, with centrifugal safety device; a percussion base fuze. The body is of lacquered steel and the cap and moving parts of brass. Used with 21, 24, 35·6 and 38-cm. H.E. shell.

20. **Artillery gas shell.**—During the autumn of 1917 the following types were in use :—

| Type. | Filling. | Nature. |
|---|---|---|
| Green cross .. | Diphosgene .. .. .. . .. | Lethal. |
| Green cross 1 .. | Diphosgene with 30—66 per cent. chloropicrin | Lethal. |
| Green cross 2 .. | 60 per cent. phosgene, 25–30 per cent. diphosgene, 10-15 per cent. diphenylchlorarsine. | Causes sneezing in addition to lethal effect. |
| Blue cross .. .. | Diphenylchlorarsine + H.E. .. .. .. | Causes sneezing in addition to H.E. effect. |
| Yellow cross .. | Dichlorethyl sulphide .. .. .. .. | Lethal, and attacks the eyes and skin. |
| Yellow cross 1 .. | An unknown variation of the above. | |

* For further details regarding ammunition, *see* "Notes on German shells" (S S. 420) and "Notes on German Fuzes" (S. S. 306).

All these types of gas shell were fired by each of the following guns, the only exception being green cross 2, which was not fired by 7·7-cm. field guns :—

(7·7-cm.) field guns 96 n/A. and '16.
(10·5-cm.) light field howitzers '98/'09, '16 and Krupp.
10-cm. guns '04 and '14.
15-cm. heavy field howitzers '02, '13, and long pattern '13.
15-cm. long gun.
21-cm. mortar, " mortar," and 21 cm. long mortar.

## C.—Mountain Artillery.

No mountain artillery units existed in peace, although the requisite material was available to form several batteries. About 25 mountain batteries have been created during the war. They are grouped in *Abteilungen* of 3 batteries each, and are allotted to divisions operating in the Balkans, Carpathians, Alps and Vosges. The personnel of mountain batteries is drawn mainly from the mountainous districts of Bavaria, Württemberg and Baden.

A mountain gun battery (*Gebirgskanonen-Batterie*) consists of four 7·5-cm. Q.F. mountain guns. The gun has a single-motion wedge breech action and fires both shrapnel and H.E. shell. The recoil buffer is placed beneath the gun.

Mountain batteries are organized for pack transport. The gun and breech-block form one load. A complete gun forms seven loads.

A few mountain batteries are armed with mountain howitzers. Mountain batteries are normally employed in independent sections.

*Establishment of a section of a mountain gun battery (December, 1916).*

2 lieutenants.
1 *Vizewachtmeister*.
6 *Unteroffiziere*.
1 mounted orderly (bombardier).
26 gunners.
31 drivers.
2 train drivers.
2 mountain guns.
31 mules, 10 riding horses.

The loads are distributed as follows :—

| | |
|---|---|
| Mountain guns (7 mules each) .. .. .. | 14 mules. |
| Entrenching tools .. .. .. .. .. | 2 ,, |
| Forge and farriers' tools .. .. .. .. | 2 ,, |
| Observation stores .. .. .. .. .. | 2 ,, |
| Medical equipment .. .. .. .. .. | 1 ,, |
| Cooking equipment .. .. .. .. .. | 2 ,, |
| Ammunition .. .. .. .. .. .. | 6 ,, |
| Spare.. .. .. .. .. .. .. | 2 ,, |
| Total .. .. | 31 ,, |

## D.—Miscellaneous.

1. **Close-range batteries.**—A certain number of light field or fortress guns are employed by the Germans for defensive purposes in trench warfare. This form of defence was developed considerably during 1916 and 1917 in order to combat our tanks, but the experience of 1917 showed that these units were of no special value.

At first these units were equipped with 3·7-cm., 5-cm., 5·7-cm. (Belgian) and 6-cm. guns, and were known as *Revolverkanonen-Abteilungen* or *Schützengrabenkanonen-Abteilungen.* The personnel consisted partly of infantrymen and partly of artillerymen, the guns being semi-permanently allotted to infantry regimental sectors.

During 1917 a series of 50 "infantry-gun" batteries (*Infanterie-Geschütz-Batterien*) was formed, armed with captured 7·62-cm. field guns.

**The 7·62-cm. infantry gun** (*Infanterie-Geschütz* or *Inf.-Gesch.*) is the Russian field gun (rifling, 24 grooves), which has been cut down from 30 to 16·4 calibres in length and fitted with new sights graduated up to 1,800 m. (1,968 yards) only. The gun is mounted on a recoil carriage on low wheels, 43⅝ inches in diameter. It fires a 13-pdr. H.E. shell, of German manufacture, fitted with a non-delay action fuze (*K.Z. 14*).

"Infantry-gun" batteries are permanently allotted to each Army assault battalion. Otherwise, these batteries are generally employed either as anti-tank guns or as forward guns for close defence. Batteries allotted to assault units are used in support of raids and other enterprises.

At the same time, another series of 50 "close-range" batteries (*Nahkampf-Batterien*) was formed, armed with the German 7·7-cm. field gun, mounted on low wheels, about 3 feet in diameter. The gun is on trunnions forward of the carriage axle, instead of being mounted directly on the carriage axle like the ordinary field gun.

Long shell with pointed fuze were employed against tanks, and also a special anti-tank shell with hardened steel point and internal delay action percussion fuze.

Infantry-gun and close-range batteries consisted of—

> 2 officers,
> 60–70 other ranks,
> 6 guns.

They had neither transport nor horses. Normally one battery was allotted to each divisional sector on active fronts.

Captured orders issued in May, 1917, show that the German General Staff had found the 7·7-cm. close-range batteries unsuitable, and they were probably all withdrawn by the end of 1917.

There appears to be a tendency now to employ the small calibre guns, such as 3·7-cm. and 5-cm., for the close defence of artillery positions and for dealing with tanks which succeed in getting through the barrage.

2. **Dummy batteries.**—Maroons are employed for imitating both the flash and report of a German gun and the bursts of our shell. The German maroon has the appearance of a large ball of tarred string. It consists of a number of charges of powder (either smokeless or black) made up in boxes of thick cardbord, the whole being bound with several layers of tarred twine. The charges can be fired either simultaneously or at intervals, by means of safety fuse.

3. **Smoke generators.**—The Germans employ smoke generators based on the reaction of chlorsulphonic acid on lime, which produces a cloud of heavy white smoke.

Three patterns of this type of smoke generator are in use :—

| Designation. | Approximate dimensions. | | Total weight. | Weight of lime. | Quantity of chlorsulphonic acid. |
| --- | --- | --- | --- | --- | --- |
| | Height. | Diameter. | | | |
| | ft. in. | ft. in. | lb. | lb. | pints. |
| Nebel-Trommel N.T. (smoke drum) .. | 2  4 | 1  7 | 209 | 63 | 37½ |
| Nebel-Topf N.L. (smoke pot)..    .. | 3  0 | 1  3 | 152 | 39 | 21½ |
| Nebel-Kasten N.K. (smoke box)    .. | 1  4 | 1  2 | 75 | 24 | 15½ |

Each generator consists of an iron container (drum or sphere) filled with chlorsulphonic acid, which is suspended on trunnions in or above an iron drum containing lumps of quicklime.

The action of the acid on the lime produces an opaque cloud of white smoke, which is non-poisonous but causes a slight irritation of the throat.

These generators are used for forming smoke screens.

## E.—Ammunition Supply.

1. **First line.**—(a.) Each infantry battalion is accompanied by four company small-arm ammunition carts (*Kompagnie-Patronen-Wagen*), each carrying 14,400 rounds.

(b.) Each field artillery *Abteilung* was formerly accompanied by a light ammunition column (*leichte Munitionskolonne* or *leichte Feldhaubitz-Munitionskolonne*), consisting of—

> 24 ammunition wagons (4-horsed) carrying 2,160 rounds (1,152 of long shell).
> 1 store wagon (4-horsed).
> 1 travelling kitchen (2-horsed).

A light ammunition column is divided into three sections. These columns no longer form part of field artillery *Abteilungen*, but in 1917 were grouped in the train echelons allotted to divisional and Corps sectors (*see* page 134).

(c.) Each horse artillery *Abteilung* (with a cavalry division) is accompanied by a light ammunition column consisting of—

> 14 ammunition wagons (4-horsed)
> 7 small-arm ammunition wagons.
> 1 supply wagon.
> 1 store wagon.
> 2 forage wagons.
> 1 travelling kitchen.

(*d.*) Each horse-drawn foot artillery battery is accompanied by a foot artillery battery ammunition column (12 ammunition wagons), which replenishes its supply from the ammunition refilling points. A horsed foot artillery ammunition column normally consists of—

> 12 ammunition wagons (4 horsed).
> 1 store wagon.
> 1 forage wagon.
> 1 forge wagon.

Some of these units are also Army troops. The heavier natures of artillery are provided with mechanical transport.

In places where the ground is impassable for limbers, field artillery ammunition is packed on the battery horses. Each horse carries 240 lbs. of ammunition, *i.e.*, either 12 field gun shell in 4 baskets, or 6 light field howitzer shell in three baskets. In the latter case, the third basket is lashed on top of the saddle. Except for rope lashings, no special equipment is required (*e.g.*, canvas ammunition carriers).

## 2. Divisional ammunition columns.—Each division was originally provided with—

(*a.*) 2 infantry ammunition columns, and

(*b.*) 3 or 4 artillery ammunition columns (one of which was a field howitzer ammunition column). There was one artillery ammunition column for each field artillery *Abteilung* in the division.

(*a.*) Formerly, one infantry ammunition column was 6-horsed and the other was 4-horsed, but in April, 1916, they were all reduced to the 4-horse establishment. The infantry ammunition columns were composed as follows :—

| 1st Infantry Ammunition Column. | 2nd Infantry Ammunition Column. | Vehicles. |
|---|---|---|
| 23 | 34 | Small-arm ammunition wagons. |
| 2 | 2 | Store wagons. |
| 1 | 1 | Field forge. |
| 1 | 1 | Travelling kitchen. |

(*b.*) The artillery ammunition columns are composed as follows :—

> 21 ammunition wagons (4-horsed).
> 2 store wagons (4-horsed).
> 1 travelling kitchen (2-horsed).

At the beginning of 1917, the infantry and artillery ammunition columns were all broken up and converted into "new pattern ammunition columns" (*Munitions-Kolonnen n/A.*). These, like the light ammunition columns, are now sector troops, and are grouped in the train echelons, described on page 134.

Foot artillery *park companies* are allotted to Armies and Corps for work in connection with unloading ammunition and mounting heavy guns.

Ordnance repair workshops (*Instandsetzungswerkstätten*) exist at Thorn, Posen, Mainz, Metz and Cologne. They are under the control of the Munitions Supply Department of the War Ministry.

**3. Chain of ammunition supply.**—The following table shows the chain of ammunition supply for a field battery (gun and howitzer) before the reorganization of the ammunition columns :—

| Where carried. | | Number of rounds per gun. | Number of rounds per howitzer. |
|---|---|---|---|
| Firing battery and first line transport. { 4 gun-limbers, each 36 rounds (*howr. 24*) | | 36 ⎫ | 24 ⎫ |
| 4 wagon bodies, each 54 rounds (*howr. 32*) .. | | 54 ⎬ 135 | 32 ⎬ 88 |
| 4 wagon limbers, each 36 rounds (*howr. 26*) .. | | 36 | 26 |
| limber of store wagon, 36 rounds (*howr. 26*) .. | | 9 ⎭ | 6 ⎭ |
| Light ammunition column (24 wagons) .. .. .. .. | | 179 | 116 |
| Artillery ammunition column (21 wagons) .. .. .. .. | | 158 | 101 |
| Total carried in division .. .. .. .. | | 472 | 305 |

**4. Expenditure of ammunition.**—A large number of German documents, captured in 1917, lay stress on the necessity for economy in ammunition expenditure, often with reference to the abnormal expenditure on days of battle.

The following reasons are usually put forward in support of the necessity for economy :—

(*a.*) Difficulties of production.

(*b.*) Difficulties of ammunition supply.

(*c.*) Strain on artillery material.

(*d.*) Bad laying and impossibility of observation with abnormal expenditure of ammunition.

Nevertheless, the ammunition expenditure appears to have kept up to the Somme standard, and even to have increased, during the spring battles in 1917, as is shown by the following table :—

*Specially high expenditure of ammunition by individual batteries on individual battle days.*

| Type of battery. | Somme battle, 1916. | Spring battles in 1917. |
|---|---|---|
| Field gun (4—7·7-cm. guns) .. .. .. | Over 4,500 | Up to 3,450. |
| Light field howitzer (4—10·5-cm. howitzers) .. .. | Over 3,000 | Up to 3,100. |
| Heavy field howitzer (4—15-cm. howitzers) .. .. | Over 1,200 | Up to 1,600. |
| 21-cm. howitzer (3—21-cm. howitzers) .. .. .. | Over 750 | Up to 1,200. |
| 10-cm. gun (4—10-cm. guns) .. .. .. .. | .. | Up to 1.175. |

From this it is seen that the maximum expenditure of the heavier natures increased considerably in the 1917 spring battles, while the only decrease recorded was in 7·7-cm. field gun ammunition.

**5. Ammunition reserves.**—(*a*) *Strategical allotment of ammunition and supervision of ammunition supply.* (i.) The strategical allotment is controlled by a special section of the General Staff at General Headquarters: " *Abteilung Op. Mun.*" On the Russian Front the control is delegated to a director of ammunition supply (*Chef des Feldmunitionswesens beim Oberbefehlshaber Ost*). On each of the remaining fronts there is an ammunition distributing centre (*Munitions-Vermittlungsstelle*); these are situated at Mézières, Bucharest and Uskub. At the headquarters of each Group of Armies on the Western Front there is an ammunition information officer (*Munitions-Nachrichten-Offizier*).

(ii.) At Group (Corps) Headquarters, a General Staff Officer, or other senior officer permanently allotted to the Group Staff, is responsible, under the Chief of the General Staff of the Group, for ammunition supply.

(iii.) At divisional headquarters an officer attached to the staff performs similar duties.

Permanent officers, assisted by technical personnel, are detailed to control the depôts in rear. On battle fronts, special staffs are formed (*Park-Kommandos*) to supervise work in the ammunition depots, railheads and distributing centres.

The work of ammunition columns in the Groups is supervised by permanent sector echelon staffs (*Staffelstäbe*).

(*b.*) *Stocks in battery positions.*—(i.) German orders are continually laying stress on the necessity for having an adequate supply of ammunition, dumped in the zone of the batteries, during a defensive battle. This supply is not, however, all dumped in the battery position, but is widely distributed in small pits and dug-outs, in the vicinity of the battery positions and in that of the reserve and alternative positions. In practice, about one day's allotment is dumped in the battery position, and the remainder in the vicinity.

(ii.) Crown Prince Rupprecht's Group of Armies, in May, 1917, laid down the following as the maximum totals for these small dumps :—

| | | |
|---|---|---|
| Light calibre, up to | .. .. .. .. | 120 rounds. |
| Medium, up to | .. .. .. .. .. | 60 ,, |
| Heavy, up to | .. .. .. .. .. | 30 ,, |

Shell and cartridges are kept separate as far as possible.

It is hoped by only having these small dumps to avoid heavy losses in ammunition from hostile fire, also that, when forced to change its position during battle, a battery will always find some ammunition in the vicinity of its new position.

(iii.) The following were laid down at varying dates as the amounts of ammunition considered essential to be kept in and near battery positions during a defensive battle :—

## Ammunition stocks in battery positions.

| Type of battery. | Report of "B" Group, First German Army, July, 1916. | Report of "A" Group, First German Army, Sept., 1916. | Memorandum issued by German G.H.Q. in May, 1917. |
|---|---|---|---|
| Field gun batteries (4—7·7-cm. guns) .. .. | 2,200 | 3,000 to 3,500 | 3,000 |
| Light field howitzer batteries (4—10·5-cm. howitzers) | 2,200 | 3,000 | 3,000 |
| Heavy field howitzer batteries (4—15-cm. howitzers) | 1,400 | 1,800* | 1,500 |
| 21-cm. howitzer batteries (3—21-cm. howitzers) .. | 450 | 750 | 900 |
| 10-cm. gun batteries (4—10-cm. guns) .. .. | 1,600 | .. | 1,800 |
| Heavy flat-trajectory batteries.. .. .. .. | .. | .. | 200 per gun |

* Includes 300 gas shell.

The following points are of interest in this connection :—

The amounts laid down in May, 1917 (*see* table above), were considered as sufficient for three days' normal battle expenditure. (It is interesting to compare this with the actual maximum expenditure *on one day* during the spring battles in 1917, as shown in paragraph 4 above.)

A document issued by the Wytschaete Group in April, 1917, shows that in normal sectors these amounts were reduced by one third.

Gas shell are generally brought up immediately before a gas-shell bombardment, and are therefore not dumped for any length of time in battery positions.

During the Flanders battle, prisoners' statements show that the orders about dumping ammunition were disregarded owing to the difficulty of ammunition supply, and that as much as 5,000 to 6,000 rounds were sometimes dumped in or near the battery positions.

(*c.*) *Ammunition reserves in rear.*—In September, 1916, it was considered by " A " Group, First German Army, that the whole of the divisional ammunition columns should be kept filled in battle.

The following extracts are taken from a memorandum on ammunition supply, issued by German General Headquarters in May, 1917 :—

(i.) It is only in exceptional cases that Groups keep ammunition reserves on rail.

(ii.) Groups receive their ammunition through Army Headquarters from the trains allotted to Armies by Groups of Armies ; Groups of Armies make the necessary demands on General Headquarters.

(iii.) Armies and Groups of Armies must have mobile ammunition reserves (if necessary trains made up of various types of ammunition) at their disposal ; this is necessary in order that ammunition can be sent up in good time, in the case of increased expenditure in any sectors. The remainder of the ammunition is stored in the lines of communication ammunition depôts.

(iv.) To meet cases in which supply by rail is not sufficient, Army Headquarters have ammunition mechanical transport columns at their disposal.

# CHAPTER IX.

## ENGINEERS AND PIONEERS.

**General.**—Duties corresponding to those of the Royal Engineers in the British Army are divided in the German Army between—

    A.—(1.) The Corps of Engineers (*Ingenieur-Korps*).
        (2.) Fortress Construction Officers (*Festungsbau-Offiziere*).
    B.—The Corps of Pioneers (*Pionier-Korps*).

A (1), A (2) and B are distinct corps, but all three are under the Inspector-General of the Engineer and Pioneer Corps (*General-Inspektion des Ingenieur- und Pionier-Korps und der Festungen*).

There is a General of the Engineer and Pioneer Corps at General Headquarters on the Western Front.

### A.—The Corps of Engineers (and Fortress Construction Officers).

The Corps of Engineers consists only of officers, who are engaged solely in the design, construction, maintenance and organization of fortresses. Engineer and pioneer officers receive the same training and are interchangeable from one service to the other.

Fortress construction officers are promoted from among qualified pioneer non-commissioned officers who undergo a special course of training.

### B.—The Corps of Pioneers.

**1. General.**—The Corps of Pioneers carries out all the work connected with field engineering, and comprises the following units :—

        Field companies.
        Mining companies.
        Bridging trains.
        Searchlight sections.
        Park companies.

The Corps of Pioneers also furnishes the personnel for trench mortar units * (*see* page 102) and for the manipulation of flame projectors, cloud gas and gas projectors.

A certain number of electro-technical units are also formed by pioneers for the purpose of constructing and running electric light and power stations close to the firing line. These units are generally formed locally as Corps or divisional troops and are variously known as—

        *Starkstrom-Abteilungen.*
        *Hochspannungs-Abteilungen.*
        *Elektrotechnische Abteilungen.*
        *Elektriker-Trupps.*

**2. Pioneer battalions.**—The establishment of pioneers in peace, apart from bridging and searchlight units, was one battalion of four companies in each Army Corps, and eight battalions of fortress engineers. Attached to the Guard Pioneer Battalion was an experimental company (*Pionier Versuchs-Kompagnie*).

---

\* With the exception of the infantry regimental *Minenwerfer* detachments (*see* page 45).

On mobilization, each of the Corps battalions was expanded by means of two Reserve companies into two battalions; the first battalion was allotted to the Active Corps, and consisted of the 1st, 2nd and 3rd Active field companies, while the second battalion was allotted to the Reserve Corps, and consisted of the 4th Active field company and the 1st and 2nd Reserve companies. The normal allotment of pioneers to a Corps was, therefore, at the beginning of the war, three companies.

Four Reserve pioneer battalions have been formed during the war, each consisting of three companies. Two new pioneer battalions, the 37th and 38th, were formed in 1917.

The original pioneer battalions no longer exist as units in the field, though the name is retained in the designation of the field companies.

In 1917, the pioneer units in each division were reorganized and grouped in a divisional pioneer battalion. The staffs of the original pioneer battalions were utilized to complete these units, and a number of new pioneer battalion staffs were formed.

A divisional pioneer battalion consists of :—

> 2 field companies.
> 1 *Minenwerfer* company.
> 1 searchlight section.

There is a Pioneer Staff Officer (*Stopi*) attached to each Group Headquarters. At each Army Headquarters there is a Pioneer General, with 1 adjutant, 1 officer for pioneer services, 1 officer for *Minenwerfer* services, and 1 senior officer with 3 subalterns to supervise the supply of material.

### 3. Pioneer regiments.—The eight fortress battalions (Königsberg, Posen, Cologne, Ehrenbreitstein, Strassburg, Metz, Mainz and Graudenz), which existed in peace, were expanded on mobilization into 10 pioneer regiments, numbered 18, 19, 20, 23, 24, 25, 29, 30, 31, and Bavarian. Each pioneer regiment consists of four to six field companies and a park company, in addition to several Reserve and Ersatz companies.

The pioneer regiments have been split up during the war and their companies allotted to different sectors as Army troops. The companies of pioneer regiments were at first employed on special technical tasks, such as mining or electrical work, while the companies of pioneer battalions were used exclusively on field works.

In 1917, the original pioneer regiments were converted into pioneer battalions, and although the companies were in some instances allotted as field companies to divisions, the majority of the companies were retained as Army troops.

Each pioneer regiment comprises a siege train (*Belagerungstrain*) and a park company.

During the war, three new pioneer regiments have been formed, namely the Guard Reserve Pioneer Regiment and the 35th and 36th Pioneer Regiments. These units are employed in manipulating flame-projectors and cloud gas.

The Guard Reserve Pioneer Regiment consists of 3 battalions, each of 4 companies. It is specially trained for offensive operations in conjunction with the use of *Flammenwerfer*. The battalion is under the orders of G.H.Q., and the companies are allotted as required to Army assault battalions. The men wear Guard collar patches, and in addition, a skull and cross-bones on the left sleeve.

The 35th and 36th Pioneer Regiments are specially trained in the offensive use of cloud gas and gas projectors. Each regiment consists of 2 battalions; each battalion is organized in 3 companies and a park company. A battalion normally handles 5,000 or 6,000 gas cylinders or as many as 1,000 gas projectors.

There is an Inspector of Gas Regiments (*Inspekteur der Gasregimenter*) at General Headquarters, and an Anti-Gas Inspector in Germany (*Inspekteur des Gasschutzdienstes*).

Gas questions are dealt with by the Chemical Section of the War Ministry (*see* page 37 ) and there is a Central Gas School (*Heeresgasschule*) in Berlin.

4. **Pioneer field companies.**—The Reserve and reconstituted divisions, formed in 1914 and 1915, were each provided with either one or two divisional pioneer companies, and this number was, in many cases, increased by the addition of Ersatz, Landwehr and Landsturm units. The new-formation divisions have all been provided with independent pioneer companies.* By the end of 1917, the number of field companies in the German Army had risen to nearly 700, so that over two companies were available for each division, instead of the three per Corps which were available on mobilization. In 1917, the number of field companies allotted to each division was finally fixed at two, the surplus field companies being allotted to Armies and Groups as required for the construction of back lines.

The establishment of a pioneer field company is—

> 4 officers.
> 1 medical officer and 1 paymaster.
> 262 other ranks.
> 20 horses.
> 7 vehicles.

A field company is organized in three sections (*Züge*), which can act independently No bridging material is carried.

The horses and transport drivers are provided by the Train. The transport is a follows :—

> 1 pioneer store wagon (*Gerätewagen*) (4-horsed).
> 3 pioneer store wagons ⎫
> 1 baggage wagon ⎪
> 1 supply wagon ⎬(2-horsed).
> 1 travelling kitchen ⎪
> 1 pack horse ⎭

The armament and equipment of field pioneers is the same as that of the infantry (*see* pages 47-52), except that long-handled spades are carried instead of the small entrench ing tool, and the bayonet is of a special pattern with a saw-back. The ammunition pouches are also different. (*See* Plate 9.)

5. **Mining companies.**—In peace, mining was only practised by the fortress pioneer battalions, and when trench warfare commenced at the end of 1914, mining operations were usually undertaken by the Army troops companies of pioneer regiments (*see* paragraph 3). These companies were gradually supplemented by trained miners with-drawn from the infantry, and tunnelling companies (*Berg-* or *Stollenbau-Kompagnien*) were improvised under divisional or regimental arrangements.

It was not until 1916 that a regular series of pioneer mining companies was created. The Prussian, Saxon and Württemberg companies (*Pionier-Mineur-Kompagnien*) were

---

* About 20 of these independent companies are known as Garrison pioneer companies, and are employed in Germany or on the L. of C.

numbered above 200, and the Bavarian companies (*Mineur-Kompagnien*) from 1 to 13. By the beginning of 1918, over 50 independent mining companies had been identified. These units are more or less permanently allotted to sectors of the front, so that continuity in mining policy is obtained. Mining operations are controlled by the divisional commander of the sector in which they take place, but the engineer officer on the spot is authorized to blow mines on his own initiative when the situation requires such action. Ammonium nitrate explosives such as *Perdit, Donarit, Westphalit,* &c., are employed. For reasons mainly of economy, attempts are being made to generalize the employment of liquid air as an explosive, and instruction is given in its use.

In parts of the front where active mining operations are in progress, a mining group of two or three mining companies is usually allotted to a divisional sector, and placed under the orders of the pioneer battalion commander of the division holding that sector.

The establishment of a mining company is 4 officers and about 250 other ranks.

6. **Bridging trains.**—Bridging trains were formerly attached to divisions, Corps and Armies, but, at the end of 1916, they were withdrawn from lower formations and re-organized as G.H.Q. troops, being allotted to Armies as required. As the details of the new organization are not available, the old composition of bridging trains is described below.

(*a.*) **A divisional bridging train** (*Divisions-Brücken-Train*) used to form part of every division. The bridging train was attached to the divisional pioneers, but the personnel and horses were all drawn from the Train.

The bridging train is organized in two sections and a reserve section.

The establishment of a divisional bridging train is—

> 2 officers.
> 59 other ranks.
> 98 horses.
> 21 vehicles.

The bridging material is carried on—

> 12 pontoon wagons (each carrying a half-pontoon).
> 2 trestle wagons.
> 1 shore transom wagon.

These wagons are 4-horsed.

The six pontoons of a divisional bridging train are of galvanized steel and are bipartite. The bow pieces have a raised bow to give extra safety in rough water. Both bow and stern pieces are 14 feet 9 inches long, 4 feet 7 inches wide, and 2 feet 9½ inches deep internally. The bow piece weighs 661 lbs. and the stern piece 683 lbs. The freeboard (amidships) of the bipartite pontoon varies from 31 inches (unloaded) to 3½ inches (with a load of 7¾ tons).

(*b.*) **A Corps bridging train** (*Korps-Brücken-Train*) was formerly attached to the headquarters of every Corps. It is organized in two half-columns and a reserve section and has a pioneer detachment of 2 officers and 64 other ranks.

The establishment of a Corps bridging train is·—

> 2 officers  
> 54 other ranks } pioneers.  
> 4 officers  
> 138 other ranks } train.  
> 1 medical officer, 1 veterinary officer, 1 paymaster.  
> 239 horses.  
> 39 vehicles.

The bridging material is carried on—

> 26 pontoon wagons (each carrying 1 whole pontoon).  
> 2 trestle wagons.

These wagons are 6-horsed, but the establishment of horses is believed to have been reduced recently.

The 26 pontoons carried by a Corps bridging train are galvanized steel whole pontoons, $26\frac{1}{4}$ feet long, 4 feet 11 inches wide, and 2 feet $9\frac{1}{2}$ inches deep internally, weighing about 1,102 lbs. The bow and stern are similar to those of the bipartite pontoon, and their buoyancy is practically the same.

(c.) **Bridging capacity.**—Normal bridge is designed to take all weights up to $3\cdot14$ tons. For 21-cm. mortars, long 15-cm. guns and all vehicles weighing between $3\cdot14$ and $4\cdot92$ tons, normal bridge is strengthened by doubling the baulks under the wheel tracks. For the army mechanical transport trains (greatest weight on each back wheel of tractor, $3\frac{1}{4}$ tons) the bridge must be constructed with twice the number of pontoons required for normal bridge, the number of baulks is increased from five to nine and the chesses are doubled.

This type of heavy bridge may be used by fully loaded mechanical transport trains across rivers with a velocity not exceeding $5\cdot1$ miles an hour.

The bridging capacity of the divisional and Corps bridging trains is as follows:—

| Nature of bridging train. | Bridge. | | | Time of construction. | Number of pioneer companies required. |
|---|---|---|---|---|---|
| | Light. | Normal. | Heavy. | | |
| | yards. | yards. | yards. | hours. | |
| 1 divisional bridging train .. .. .. | 65·6 | 38·3 | 21·9 | $\frac{1}{2}$–1 | $\frac{1}{3}$–1 |
| 2 divisional bridging trains.. .. .. | 131·2 | 76·6 | 43·7 | 2 | $\frac{2}{3}$–1 |
| 1 Corps bridging train .. .. .. | 185·9 | 142·2 | 82 | 3 | 1–2 |
| 1 Corps and 2 divisional bridging trains .. | 328 | 218·7 | 131·2 | 5 | 2 |
| 1 Corps and 3 divisional bridging trains .. | 393·7 | 251·5 | 153·1 | 5 | 2 |
| 1 Corps and 4 divisional bridging trains .. | 459·3 | 295·3 | 175 | 6 | 2–3 |

The pontoon equipments can be used as rafts and flying bridges, capable of ferrying heavy guns and army mechanical transport

**7. Searchlight sections.**—On mobilization, the searchlight units consisted of one field searchlight section (*Scheinwerferzug*) attached to each of the 26 pioneer battalions of the Active Corps, and one fortress searchlight section with each of the 10 fortress pioneer regiments.

A number of the Reserve Corps formed during 1914 and 1915 were provided with Reserve searchlight sections, and the majority of the original fortress sections have appeared in the field, and have been replaced by newly formed heavy and light fortress searchlight sections.

The Corps searchlight sections have now mostly been allotted to divisions.

In addition to the sections originally attached to Corps, a new series of divisional searchlight sections have been formed during the war, mainly numbered between 200 and 400.

The normal establishment of a searchlight section is—

> 2 officers.
> 38 other ranks.
> 25 horses.
> 7 vehicles.

The technical equipment comprises—

(*a.*) *Heavy* 90-cm. electric-light projector, with motor, dynamo and scaffolding, the whole being transported on three vehicles.

(*b.*) *Light* 60-cm. electric-light projector, carried in trunnions on a telescopic mast mounted on a limbered wagon. The dynamo, which is carried on the limber, is driven by a 6-h.p. motor. The total weight behind the team is about 35 cwt.

(*c.*) *Portable* searchlights, of which there are two patterns. One has an electric-light projector of 25 to 35-cm. diameter. The other, which is the more common type, has an oxy-acetylene (*A.S.*) projector of 25 or 30-cm. diameter. Both of these patterns can be carried on a man's back.

A divisional searchlight section is usually equipped with two light and four portable searchlights, or one searchlight of each of the above types.

There is a Searchlight Depôt (*Scheinwerfer-Ersatz-Bataillon*) at Spandau, and an Anti-aircraft Searchlight School (*Flak-Scheinwerfer-Schule*) at Hannover.

Anti-aircraft searchlight sections (*Flak - Scheinwerferzüge*) are attached to the anti-aircraft artillery guarding fortresses and munition factories. Each anti-aircraft searchlight section consists of 3 non-commissioned officers and 10 men, with one 90-cm. naval projector, which is said to have a range of 1,500 metres.

**8. Park companies.**—Pioneer park companies are composed of men of the Armed Landsturm (*see* page 143). They are attached to Armies as required, and are employed in handling pioneer stores at the railheads and at the large pioneer depôts on the lines of communication. In all, 55 pioneer park companies have been identified.

**9. Trench mortar units.**—German trench mortar units are pioneer formations. In principle, trench mortars are served by pioneers, and trench guns by artillerymen, but in practice the personnel is largely drawn from the infantry.

Every infantry battalion is now provided with a *Minenwerfer* section, equipped with 4 light *Minenwerfer*, grouped in a regimental *Minenwerfer* detachment (*Abteilung*), which normally comprises 12 light *Minenwerfer* and 24 *Granatwerfer*.

There is a *Minenwerfer* officer attached to the headquarters of every infantry regiment.

(*a.*) **Minenwerfer companies.**—Every division has a *Minenwerfer* company per-manently allotted to it and forming part of the divisional pioneer battalion. These companies are in general numbered on a regular system :—

Each Active division has a *Minenwerfer* company bearing the same number (*e.g.*, the 7th Division has the 7th *Minenwerfer* Company).

Each Reserve division has a *Minenwerfer* company bearing the same number + 200 (*e.g.*, the 7th Reserve Division has the 207th *Minenwerfer* Company).

Each Landwehr division has a *Minenwerfer* company bearing the same number + 300 (*e.g.*, the 7th Landwehr Division has the 307th *Minenwerfer* Company).

Each new formation division has a *Minenwerfer* company having the same number + 210 (*e.g.*, the 221st Division has the 431st *Minenwerfer* Company).

A *Minenwerfer* company is organized in three sections, one heavy and two medium, the former armed with four heavy and the latter with eight medium *Minenwerfer*. Each section (*Zug*) is divided into sub-sections (*Trupps*), two for each *Minenwerfer*. A sub-section consists of two non-commissioned officers and four to five men. A company consists of 8 officers, 41 non-commissioned officers and 201 men.

Before the light *Minenwerfer* were issued to infantry battalions, *Minenwerfer* companies were equipped with 3 heavy, 6 medium and 12 light *Minenwerfer*.

There are also a few mountain *Minenwerfer* companies, numbered from 170 to 175, mainly employed on the Eastern Front, and provided with pack animals and vehicles suitable for mountain transport. A mountain *Minenwerfer* company is equipped with four medium and eight light *Minenwerfer*.

(*b.*) **Minenwerfer battalions.**—In addition to the divisional and mountain *Minen-werfer* companies, there exist 13 *Minenwerfer* battalions, which form a reserve at the disposal of General Headquarters, and are used to reinforce particular sectors.

A *Minenwerfer* battalion consists of—

4 companies, each equipped with six heavy and four light *Minenwerfer*.
Draught-horse detachment (*Bespannungsabteilung*).
Mechanical transport échelon (*Kraftwagenstaffel*).

Each company has a strength of about 5 officers, 180 other ranks and 50 horses.

The central *Minenwerfer* school is at Markendorf (near Jüterbog), and each *Minenwerfer* battalion has a depôt in Germany for training of personnel.

## 10. Particulars* of trench mortars ("**Minenwerfer**") :—

| Description of *Minenwerfer*. | Description of shell. | Weight of shell. | Weight of charge. | Most favourable range. | Distinctive marking on shell. | Fuze. |
|---|---|---|---|---|---|---|
| | | lbs. | lbs. | yards. | | |
| *Heavy "Minenwerfer."* Calibre—25 cm. (9·84 in.). Weight in action—11¼ cwt. †Personnel required—21 men. Rate of fire—20 rounds per hour. | Heavy H.E. | 207·2 | 103·6 | 219–601 | .. | *Z.s.u.m.W.M.* (T. and P.) |

* From "Die Minenwerfer," translated and issued as S.S. 624. For later information, *see* "Notes on German Shells (S.S. 420).

† Personnel required to carry the *Minenwerfer* into action.

| Description of *Minenwerfer*. | Description of shell. | Weight of shell. | Weight of charge. | Most favourable range. | Distinctive marking on shell. | Fuze. |
|---|---|---|---|---|---|---|
| | | lbs. | lbs. | yards. | | |
| *1916 Heavy " Minenwerfer."*<br>Calibre—*25 cm.* (9·84 in.).<br>Weight in action—15 cwt.<br>†Personnel required—28 men.<br>Rate of fire—20 rounds per hour. | 1916 heavy H.E. | 207 ·2 | 103 ·6 | 547–1094 | .. | With or without delay action. (P.) |
| *Heavy " Minenwerfer."**<br>(" Flügelminenwerfer.")<br>Calibre—*24 cm.* (9·45 in.).<br>Weight in action—25 cwt.<br>†Personnel required—42 men.<br>Rate of fire—20 rounds per hour. | Heavy H.E., fitted with vanes. | 220 ·5 | 92 ·6 | 492–1312 | .. | Each shell is issued with 2 fuzes — one practically instantaneous, the other delay action. (P.) |
| *Medium " Minenwerfer."*<br>Calibre—*17 cm.* (6·69 in.).<br>Weight in action—9½ cwt.<br>†Personnel required—17 men.<br>Rate of fire—30–35 rounds per hour (H.E.).<br>Rate of fire—40–45 rounds per hour (gas). | Medium H.E.<br><br>Medium gas. | 109 ·1<br><br>92 ·6 | 26 ·4<br><br>22–24 ·2 (liquid). | 164–984<br><br>328–1094 | ..<br><br>White bands. | Z.s u.m. W.M. (T. and P.)<br>Z.s.u.m. W.M. (T. and P.) |
| *1916 Medium " Minenwerfer."*<br>Calibre—*17 cm.* (6·69 in.).<br>Weight in action—11 cwt.<br>†Personnel required—21 men.<br>Rate of fire—30–35 rounds per hour (H.E.).<br>Rate of fire—40–45 rounds per hour (gas). | 1916 medium H.E.<br><br>Medium gas. | 109 ·1<br><br>92 ·6 | 26 ·4<br><br>22–24 ·2 (liquid). | 328–1258<br><br>437–1750 | Three black bands.<br><br>White bands. | With and without delay action. (P.)<br>Z.s.u.m. W.M. (T. and P.) |
| *Old Light " Minenwerfer."*<br>Calibre—*7·6 cm.* (2·99 in.).<br>Weight in action—2 cwt.<br>†Personnel required—6 men.<br>Rate of fire—up to 20 rounds a minute for short periods.<br>Old pattern light *Minenwerfer* may only be fired with Charges II. to IV. | Light H.E.<br><br>Light gas. | 9 ·9<br><br>9 ·9 | 1 ·23<br><br>About 1 ·76 (liquid). | 328–1094 | ..<br><br>White bands. | l.W.M.Zdr. (T. and P.)<br>l.W.M.Zdr. (T. and P.) |

* *See* Ia/43035 A., dated 16th January, 1918.
† Personnel required to carry the *Minenwerfer* into action.

| Description of *Minenwerfer*. | Description of shell. | Weight of shell. | Weight of charge. | Most favourable range. | Distinctive marking on shell. | Fuze. |
|---|---|---|---|---|---|---|
| | | lbs. | lbs. | yards. | | |
| *New Light " Minenwerfer."* | | | | | | |
| Calibre—7·6 cm. (2·99 in.). | 1916 light H.E. | 9·9 | 1·23 | 328–1422 | Three black bands. | *l.W.M.Zdr.* 2. (T. & P.) *Az. 16 f.l.W.M.* (P.) |
| Weight in action—nearly 3 cwt. | | | | | | |
| *Personnel required—6 men. | | | About | | | |
| Rate of fire—up to 20 rounds a minute for short periods.† | Light gas. | 9·9 | 1·76 (liquid). | 328–1422 | Three white bands. | *l.W.M.Zdr.* 2. (T. and P.) |
| (*See* Plate 17 ) | Light message shell. | 9.9 | ·· | 328–1422 | *l.N.M.* Three black bands. | *l.W.M.Zdr.* 2. (T. and P.) |
| | | | oz. | | | |
| *" Granat-Schnellwerfer."* | H.E. | 1·7 (approx). | 1·5 | 150–700 (at least). | ·· | Time fuze (train of powder.) |
| 3·9 cm. rapid fire trench mortar. | | | | | | |
| Calibre—3·9 cm. approximate (1·5-in.). | | | | | | |
| Method of fire—searching fire in bursts of 3–6 rounds. | | | | | | |
| *" Granatwerfer "* (" stick " bomb-thrower). | | | | | | |
| Weight in action—88 lbs. | "Stick" bomb (pine-apple). | 4 | 0·5 | 66–208 | ·· | Percussion fuze. |
| Weight of thrower—53 lbs. | | | | | | |
| Weight of bed-plate—35 lbs. | Signal and message rockets. | ·· | ·· | ·· | ·· | |
| Personnel required—2 men. | | | | | | |

A 17-cm. ' Medium *Flügelminenwerfer* " has also been reported. It is said to fire an H.E. shell 123 lbs. in weight, fitted with vanes, at a range of at least 1,500 yards.

The old patterns of *Minenwerfer* have a very short gun and a rectangular bed-plate. The modern patterns have a much longer gun and are mounted on a circular bed-plate with all-round traverse.

* Personnel required to carry the *Minenwerfer* into action.
† It is stated that a rate of 44 rounds per minute has been attained.

## 11. Minenwerfer gas shell.

| German name for liquid filling. | Chemical implied. | Nature. | Distinctive marking.* | Calibre. |
|---|---|---|---|---|
| B-Stoff .. .. | Xylyl bromide .. .. | Lachrymatory | B .. .. .. .. | 7·6 cm. |
| | | | and one white ring .. | 17 cm. |
| C-Stoff .. .. | Mono or tri-chlormethyl chloroformate. | Lethal .. | C (in red or white) | 7·6 cm. |
| | | | and two white rings .. | 17 cm. |
| D-Stoff .. .. | Phosgene .. .. .. | Lethal .. | D .. | 7·6 cm. |
| | | | | 17 cm. |
| | | | and three white rings | 17·5 cm.† |
| | | | | 25 cm. |
| | | | or six white rings .. | 7·6 cm. |
| | | | or four white rings .. | |

**12. Gas projectors.**—In reply to our gas projector bombardments, the 18-cm. (7·1-inch) smooth-bore *Minenwerfer* has been employed as a gas projector. This *Minenwerfer* is an obsolete bronze muzzle-loading trench mortar. It is mounted on a non-recoil steel carriage, which is pivoted on a rectangular steel platform. Weight in action, 9 cwt.

The normal *charge* consists of perforated discs of smokeless powder, but a large charge of black powder is probably used with gas bombs.

According to prisoners' statements, the Germans have recently introduced a gas projector (*Gaswerfer*) similar to the Livens projector, described as a steel tube about 40 inches in length. The projectors are set up side by side on wooden frames, placed so that the projectors are " laid " as required. A base plate is apparently not used, as the shock of discharge is said to drive the projector into the ground.

The projectors are discharged simultaneously by electricity, as many as 1,000 being employed in a single operation.

The *bomb* employed with both these weapons is a thick-walled iron "rum jar" or " canister," 17·5 cm. in diameter. It weighs 66 lbs. and contains about 9 pints of liquid (phosgene) or a mixture of phosgene and chloro-picrin. With it is used the T. and P. *Minenwerfer* fuze *Z. s. u. m. W. M.*

A similar " blue cross " bomb is also used, in conjunction with the above, which contains a solid filling, a mixture of H.E. and a substance which causes irritation and pain in the nose and throat and often sneezing (contents by weight, 51 per cent. huxanitrodiphenylamnie + 49 per cent. diphenylchlorarsine).

When these projectors are discharged, a sheet of flame is seen to run along the German trenches accompanied by a loud explosion. The bombs are clearly visible in flight and make a loud whizzing noise. They burst with a loud detonation producing a thick white smoke.

---

\* The letters B, C and D are frequently missing.                    † Gas projector bomb.

# CHAPTER X.

## AIR SERVICE.

1. **General organization.**—In peace, the German aircraft troops formed part of the Communication Troops, but an Army Order of the 25th November, 1916, definitely established the Air Forces (*Luftstreitkräfte*) as a separate branch, taking precedence between the Pioneers and the Communication Troops. At the same time the Air Forces, including all aviation, balloon and anti-aircraft units, were placed under the orders of a General Officer Commanding the Air Forces (*Kommandierender General der Luftstreitkräfte* or *Kogenluft*), and the post of the Chief of the Field Aviation Service (*Chef des Feldflugwesens*) was abolished.

The General Officer Commanding the Air Forces is assisted by a Chief Staff Officer (*Chef des Generalstabes der Luftstreitkräfte*).

The administration of the Air Forces is carried out an Inspector-General (*Inspekteur der Flieger* or *Ideflieg*). The *Inspekteur der Flieger* is also in charge of training units (*Kommandeur der Fea* or *Kodofea.*)

2. **Training establishments.**—In Germany there are now 17 training squadrons (*Flieger-Ersatz-Abteilungen* or *Fea*), where pilots, observers and mechanics are trained, in addition to seven Bavarian flying schools.

These training squadrons are situated as follows:—

|       |    |    |                           |
|-------|----|----|---------------------------|
| 1st   | .. | .. | Altenburg.                |
| 2nd   | .. |    | Schneidemühl.             |
| 3rd   | .. | .. | Gotha.                    |
| 4th   | .. | .. | Posen.                    |
| 5th   | .. | .. | Hannover.                 |
| 6th   | .. | .. | Grossenhain (Saxony).     |
| 7th   | .. | .. | Braunschweig.             |
| 8th   | .. | .. | Graudenz.                 |
| 9th   | .. | .  | Darmstadt.                |
| 10th  | .. | .. | Böblingen (Württemberg).  |
| 11th  | .. | .  | Breslau.                  |
| 12th  | .. | .. | Cottbus.                  |
| 13th  | .. | .. | Bromberg.                 |
| 14th  | .. | .. | Halle a.S.                |
| 15th  | .. | .. | Königsberg.               |
| 1st Bavarian | .. | | Schleissheim (near Munich). |
| 2nd Bavarian | .. | | Fürth.                    |

The seven Bavarian flying schools are situated at Schleissheim, Neustadt, Fürth, Lager Lechfeld, Gersthofen, Bamberg and Germersheim.

The 12th, 13th, 14th and 15th, as well as the 2nd Bavarian Training Squadron were formed during 1917, while the Bavarian flying schools were expanded during the same period.

A training squadron is organized in four companies; the first (*Fliegerkompagnie*) consisting of pilots, the second (*Werftkompagnie*) of mechanics, and the third (*Ersatz-kompagnie*) comprising the personnel permanently employed at the training squadron. The fourth company (*Rekrutenkompagnie*) contains those men who have recently joined and are being instructed in discipline and drill.

The training squadrons for the personnel of giant machines (*Riesen-Ersatz-Abteilungen* or *Rea*) are at Döberitz and Cologne.

Flying schools, at which pilots undergo a course of preliminary training are attached to the greater number of training squadrons; these schools are generally civilian establishments, the property of various aircraft manufacturing firms. In every case the more advanced stages of instruction are undergone at the training squadrons themselves, after pilots have passed through the preliminary school.

While at certain training squadrons the training of observers is undertaken, the more important schools for observers are independent, *e.g.*, the observers' schools at Köln, Königsberg, Thorn, Jüterbog, Stolp and at Diest in Belgium.

**3. Organization in the field.**—At the Headquarters of each Army in the field there is an Aviation Commander (*Kommandeur der Flieger* or *Kofl*) and a Balloon Commander (*Kommandeur der Luftschiffer* or *Koluft*).

At the Headquarters of each Corps there is a Group Aviation Commander (*Gruppenführer der Flieger* or *Grufl*).

Aeroplane and observation balloon units are allotted to armies in accordance with the requirements of the situation.

Each Army in the field is provided with an Army Aircraft Park (*Armee-Flugpark*), which receives new machines from Germany and issues them to units in the field; a store of spare parts is kept and a small amount of repairing work is also carried out. These parks also maintain "pools" of pilots, observers and machine gunners, who are posted to units in replacement of casualties.

**4. Aircraft units.**—The standard aviation unit is the flight of 6 machines. The establishment of the flight is 115–120 all ranks. The establishment in machines of a bombing flight is 12 and that of a pursuit flight is 18 machines. The actual strength of the former seldom exceeds 10, and of the latter 14.

Observers in reconnaissance units are almost invariably officers, while the pilots in these units are generally non-commissioned officers.

Aerial gunners in protective flights, as well as their pilots, are always non-commissioned officers or privates.

Pilots in pursuit flights are either officers or non-commissioned officers.

In the case of bombing flights, observers are always officers, while the pilots may be either officers or non-commissioned officers; aerial gunners are not of commissioned rank.

Flights are designated according to the tasks which they perform, as follows :—

(*a.*) **Bombing flights** (*Bombenstaffeln*).—When first organized, at the beginning of 1916, these flights, then called *Kampfstaffeln*, were intended to act as fighting units (equipped with two-seater machines) and were grouped in six battle squadrons (*Kampfgeschwader O.H.L.* or *Kagohl*), each of six flights, allotted as required to armies by General Headquarters. During the Somme battle, the squadron organization was broken up and flights were transferred independently from one army to another; during the winter of 1916-1917 the *Kampfgeschwader* were partly reformed as bombing squadrons, the flights being employed almost entirely on long distance bombing expeditions and equipped mainly with large twin-engine machines. A number of these *Kampfstaffeln* were transformed into protective flights (*Schutzstaffeln*).

At the beginning of 1918, 24 bombing flights (the name *Kampfstaffel* was changed to *Bombenstaffel* in December, 1917) had been identified. These were grouped in bombing squadrons (*Bombengeschwader* or *Bogohl*).

Recent information indicates that one uniform establishment of three flights per squadron, with 12 machines per flight, is now being introduced.

(*b.*) **Pursuit flights** (*Jagdstaffeln* or *Jasta*).—These first appeared during the Somme battle, and are equipped throughout with single-seater fighter machines. Before the formation of pursuit flights, two or three single-seater fighter machines were attached to some reconnaissance units. Pursuit flights are allotted to active sectors of the front as required; the principle is to keep the main groups of pursuit flights near the boundaries of armies or between two active sectors.

Pursuit squadrons are attached to the Headquarters of each Army on an active front and work directly under the Army Aviation Commander. During the battles of 1917, pursuit flights were formed into groups (*Jagdstaffelgruppen*), each consisting of about 4 flights ; this organization was, however, purely temporary, and was replaced in 1918 by the organization of pursuit flights into squadrons (*Jagdgeschwader*), each of 4 pursuit flights. Several cases have been found where two or three pursuit flights working independently have been allotted to a Corps working directly under the Group Aviation Commander; this, however, has only been the case in sectors of intense activity.

Early in 1918, 56 pursuit flights and two naval pursuit flights had been identified. There are two pursuit flight schools at Valenciennes.

(*c.*) **Fighting single-seater flights** (*Kampfeinsitzerstaffeln* or *Kest.*)—These are allotted to important centres, munition factories, railway junctions and depôts, for the purpose of home defence. Ten of these units have been identified. They are stationed at Mannheim, Saarbrücken, Mainz, Stuttgart, &c.

(*d.*) **Reconnaissance flights** (*Fliegerabteilungen* and *Fliegerabteilungen* "*A*").—The reconnaissance units in the German Air Service were formerly divided into two series : *Fliegerabteilungen*, of which at the beginning of 1918, 63 had been identified ; and *Flieger-abteilungen* "*A*" (numbered between 200–299), all of which, at the beginning of 1918, had been identified. The duties and composition of these two types of units do not differ in any way and are now all known as *Fliegerabteilungen*. They are allotted to :—

- (*a.*) *Divisions* for trench reconnaissance, photography, contact patrol work and artillery observation ; one flight is usually allotted to each division in active sectors.
- (*b.*) *Corps* for trench reconnaissance, photography and artillery observation throughout the Corps counter-battery area ; three to four flights are usually allotted to each Corps on active fronts.
- (*c.*) *Armies* for long-distance reconnaissance and photography ; one or two flights are allotted to Army Headquarters.

A few naval reconnaissance flights (*Marine-Landfliegerabteilungen*) have been identified working with the Naval Corps in Flanders, also in the Gulf of Riga and the Ægean Sea.

Flights allotted to divisions and Corps are under the Group Aviation Commander ; flights working for Armies (called *AOK Abteilungen*) are under the Army Aviation Commander. Each of these is provided with a mosaic section (*Reihenbildzug*).

(*e.*) **Protective flights** (*Schutzstaffeln* or *Schusta*).—On principle, one of these is allotted to each reconnaissance flight working with a division or Corps on active fronts, but in practice it is more often found that one protective flight works for two or even three reconnaissance flights. At the beginning of 1918, 32 of these units had been identified. Cases have occurred where several of these flights have been formed into a group for offensive action against ground targets.

(*f.*) **Giant aeroplane flights** (*Riesen-Flugzengabteilungen*).—These are employed on long-distance bombing. Only three of these units had been identified at the beginning of 1918 ;

they are numbered 500 and over. Flights consisted originally of two machines, but appear now to comprise six machines.

5. **Types of aeroplanes.**—The main types of aeroplanes in use at the beginning of 1918 were as follows :—

### (a.) Single-seater fighters.

*Albatros D. 5.*—Tractor biplane ; 160 h.p. *Mercedes* engine ; " V " type interplane struts, one pair on each wing. Two '08 pattern machine guns. firing through the airscrew, actuated by a direct flexible drive interrupter gear.

*Albatros D. 5 A.*—The same as D. 5, only of heavier construction.

*Pfalz D. III.*—Tractor biplane ; 160 h.p. *Mercedes* engine. " V " type interplane struts, one pair on each wing. Two '08 pattern machine guns, firing through the airscrew, actuated by a direct flexible drive interrupter gear.

*Fokker Triplane.*—Tractor triplane ; the engine is an imitation by the Oberursel Company of the 110 h.p. *Le Rhone.* One wide interplane strut between each plane on each wing. Two '08 pattern machine guns, firing through the airscrew, actuated by a direct flexible drive interrupter gear.

*Note.*—This machine is frequently equipped with captured British and French rotary engines.

### (b.) Two-seater fighters.

*Hannoversche Waggon-Fabrik.*—Tractor biplane ; 200 h.p. *Opel-Argus* engine one pair of " V " type interplane struts on each wing ; double tail-plane ; two elevators, one above and one below the fuselage. One '08 pattern machine gun, firing through the airscrew, and one Parabellum on a turret mounting in the observer's cockpit.

*Halberstadt.*—Tractor biplane ; 160 h.p. *Mercedes* engine. Top plane level with top longerons ; pilot's and observer's seats close together, giving good visibility for both. Light construction.

### (c.) Two-seater reconnaissance machines.

*L.V.G.*—Tractor biplane ; 200 h.p. *Benz* engine ; two pairs of vertical type interplane struts on each wing. One '08 pattern machine gun, firing through the airscrew, actuated by an interrupter gear ; Parabellum gun on a turret mounting in the observer's cockpit.

*D.F.W.*—Tractor biplane ; 200 h.p. *Benz* engine, two pairs of vertical type interplane struts on each wing. One '08 pattern machine gun, firing through the airscrew, actuated by an interrupter gear. One Parabellum gun on a turret mounting in the observer's cockpit.

*Rumpler.*—Tractor biplane ; generally fitted with 260 h.p. *Mercedes* engine, but some-times with a 260 h.p *Maybach* engine. Two pairs of vertical type interplane struts on each wing. One '08 pattern machine gun, firing through the airscrew, actuated by an interrupter gear. A Parabellum gun on a turret mounting in the observer's cockpit.

*Albatros.*—Tractor biplane ; 260 h.p. *Mercedes* engine ; two pairs of vertical type interplane struts on each wing. One '08 pattern machine gun, firing through the airscrew, actuated by an interrupter gear. A Parabellum gun on a turret mounting in the observer's cockpit.

### (d.) Contact patrol two-seaters.

\* *A.E.G.*—Tractor biplane ; 200 h.p. *Benz* engine. This machine is designed for low flying and is protected beneath by quarter-inch sheet steel armour-plating.

\* *Junker.*—200 h.p. *Benz* engine. This machine is designed for low flying and is constructed entirely of metal, large extensions on top planes, no interplane cross-bracing wires.

---

\* Specimens of these machines have not yet been captured.

\* *Albatros.*—New armoured type: 260 h.p. *Mercedes* engine; two pairs of vertical type interplane struts on each wing. This machine is designed for low flying and is armoured.

### (e.) Bombing machines.

*Gotha.*—Three-seater twin-engine pusher biplane; two 260 h.p. *Mercedes* engines; three pairs of vertical type interplane struts on each wing; three Parabellum guns, one in the forward nacelle, the other two in the gunners' cockpit aft; a tunnel built obliquely through the fuselage allows one of these guns to fire downwards and to the rear; approximately 900 lbs. weight of bombs carried.

*Friedrichshafen.*—Four-seater twin-engine pusher biplane; two 260 h.p. *Mercedes* engines; two Parabellum guns: approximately 750 lbs. weight of bombs carried.

*A.E.G.*—Four-seater twin-engine tractor biplane: two 260 h.p. *Mercedes* engines; three Parabellum guns, one in the observer's nacelle forward, and two in the gunner's cockpit aft, one of which fires through a trap door in the bottom of the fuselage. 418 lbs. weight of bombs carried.

\* *Rumpler.*—Three-seater twin-engine pusher biplane, fitted either with two 260 h.p. *Mercedes* or two 260 h.p. *Maybach* engines.

\* *Giant Aeroplane* (*Riesenflugzeug*).—Biplane, *Lizenz* type, with four 300 h.p. *Maybach* engines; two pusher and two tractor airscrews. The span is about 140 feet, and the bomb carrying capacity about 5,000 lbs. There are three nacelles, the centre one, with three cockpits, carrying the commander, two pilots and gunners, while each of the side nacelles carries two engines. The crew consists of nine. Four machine guns are carried, one in front and three in rear, one of which fires downwards. Fuel is carried for a flight of 9 hours.

6. **Observation balloons.**—The balloon service in the field is directly controlled by the General Commanding the Air Forces. The supply of personnel and material is assured by the Inspectorate of Balloon Troops (*Inspektion der Luftschiffertruppen* or *Iluft*) in Berlin. In Germany, there are six depôt units (*Luftschiffer-Ersatz-Abteilungen* or *Lea*) at Reinickendorf, Darmstadt, Düren, Mannheim, Königsberg and Munich.

At the Headquarters of each Army in the field is a Balloon Commander (*Kommandeur der Luftschiffer* or *Koluft*), and a balloon report centre (*Ballon-Zentrale*).

A balloon detachment (*Feld-Luftschiffer-Abteilung*) is allotted to each Corps headquarters. The balloon detachment, which is merely a staff, consists of 3 officers and about 30 other ranks, mostly employed in connection with photography, maps and signals.

Each balloon detachment controls 2 or 3 balloon sections (*Ballonzüge*). A balloon section has 2 balloons, one of which is normally kept filled, the other being in reserve. The section is composed of 3 officers and about 110 other ranks. One of the balloon sections on a Corps front is specially told off for tactical observation, and provides the "infantry balloon," which communicates direct with the headquarters of divisions. Otherwise, balloons are almost entirely used in connection with artillery observation, and are linked up direct with the artillery group commanders. The balloon observers are mostly artillery officers. 125 balloon sections have been identified.

The balloons in use are of three sizes, containing 600, 800 and 1,000 cubic metres of gas, respectively. The winding gear consists of a winch and a petrol engine, mounted on separate vehicles, which are coupled together when the balloon is working.

---

\* Specimens of these machines have not yet been captured.

**7. Airships.**—Only the naval airship service now exists. The military airship service was broken up during 1917, the useful airships being transferred to the Navy, together with the majority of the military airship sheds. The personnel was distributed partly to the Navy and partly to the military balloon service.

Zeppelin airships are constructed at Friedrichshafen (3 slips) and Spandau (2 slips). The framework is of aluminium. The period of construction extends over 8 to 9 weeks.

Schütte-Lanz airships are now built at Mannheim and Königswusterhausen, near Berlin (one slip each). The period of construction is longer, the framework being of 3-ply wood and very highly finished.

Non-rigid Parseval ships have been practically abandoned.

Airships were formerly allotted indiscriminately to the military and naval services according to current requirements.

During the war the size, the bomb carrying capacity and climbing power of airships have all increased considerably.

The "Super-Zeppelin" airships of 2,000,000 cubic feet capacity first appeared in the summer of 1916. These ships had six engines.

A modified type was introduced at the beginning of 1917. The ships are of the same capacity, but all unnecessary weight has been discarded.

There are only five engines actuating four propellers. Each propeller has a direct drive and is placed at the stern of each of the four cars. The after propeller is driven by a pair of engines set tandemwise.

The number of the crew is 2 officers and 16 or 17 other ranks as against a total of 22 in 1916.

These ships can climb to 20,000 feet carrying a load of at least 3,500 lbs. of bombs.

At the end of 1917 about 19 ships of 2,000,000 cubic feet capacity were in commission.

The most important airship station is Ahlhorn, which will have accommodation for 12 airships. Nordholz will have accommodation for 8 modern airships and two small training ships. Other North Sea stations are Wittmund (4 ships) and Tondern (2 modern ships). Numerous smaller stations (formerly tenanted by military airships) exist.

The principal Baltic stations include Seerappen, Seddin, Wainoden.

The station of the naval experimental ship is at Jüterbog, near Berlin, formerly the headquarters of the Army Airship Training School.

The bomb load when raiding is as high as 4,000 lbs. The H.E. bombs are pear shaped bombs of 100, 220 or 660 lbs. weight. Incendiary bombs weighing 20 to 25 lbs. are also carried.

## B.—Anti-aircraft organization.

**1. General organization.**—Anti-aircraft artillery is under the control of the Commander of the Air Forces, but the personnel is drawn from the artillery.

German anti-aircraft units consist of:—

Anti-aircraft batteries.
Anti-aircraft sections.
Mobile anti-aircraft guns.
Anti-aircraft machine guns.

German anti-aircraft guns are known as *Flaks* (*Flug-Abwehr-Kanonen*).

**2. Organization in Germany.**—(*a.*) *Command.*—Anti-aircraft defence in German is controlled by the Commander of the Home Aerial Defences (*Kommandeur des Heima Luftschutzes*, abbreviated to *Kmdr. Heim. Luft.*), whose headquarters are at Frankfurt a. M This officer is in turn subordinate to the General Officer Commanding the Air Forc (*Kommandierender General der Luftstreitkräfte*). The local command of groups of an aircraft units at important places, such as Duisburg, Essen, Friedrichshafen, Mannheim and Rottweil, is centred in *Flak-Gruppen* or *Flak-Kommandos*. The Home Aerial Defence Troops (*Heimat-Luftschutz-Truppen*) wear red shoulder straps bearing a shell with wings.

(*b.*) *Aeroplane reporting service.*—The Commander of the Home Aerial Defences has under his orders an Aeroplane Reporting Service (*Flugmeldedienst*) controlled by three *Stabsoffiziere des Flugmeldedienstes* (*Stabsoffz. Melde Heim.*), the principal being the *Stabsoffizier des Flugmeldedienstes Süd* at Karlsruhe. These officers control a number of Aeroplane Observation Posts (*Fliegerwachen, Fliegerwarten*).

(*c.*) *Fixed anti-aircraft sections* (*Ortsfeste Flakzüge*) form two separate series of units, numbered from 1 to 150, and from 601 upwards, with the letter "O" affixed to each number. They are all located in the interior of Germany or in rear of the Zone of the Armies. To each section is attached an anti-aircraft searchlight section (*Flakscheinwerferzug*), consisting of 3 non-commissioned officers, 10 men, and one 90-cm. naval projector.

(*d.*) *Anti-aircraft batteries.*—In addition to the anti-aircraft batteries (*Flak-Batterien*) allotted to Armies in the field, there is a series numbered between 1 and 100, employed in defending towns, railway junctions and munition factories.

(*e.*) *Schools and depôts.*—In Germany there are a number of anti-aircraft depôts (*Flak-Ersatz-Abteilungen*) under the Commander of the Anti-Aircraft Depôts (*K. der Flakean*) at Frankfurt a/M. The Anti-Aircraft School of Instruction is at Ostend, and the Anti-Aircraft Searchlight School (*Flak-Scheinwerfer-Schule*) is at Hannover.

### 3. Organization in the field.—(*a.*) *Command.*—In each Army the anti-aircraft units (including anti-aircraft searchlights) and the aircraft reporting service are placed under the control of an officer at Army Headquarters, known as the Commander of the Anti-Aircraft Guns (*Kommandeur der Flugabwehrkanonen*, abbreviated to *Koflak*).

In each Corps the anti-aircraft defences are organized in a group (*Flakgruppe*), under an officer known as the Commander of the Anti-Aircraft Group (*Flakgruko*).

(*b.*) *Aircraft reporting service.*—The anti-aircraft defences in an Army are organized in several lines of observation, connected to the corresponding lines of the Armies on the flanks. These lines consist of aircraft reporting and look-out stations (*Fliegerwachen, Flugwachen,* or *Fliegerwarten*) and aircraft report centres (*Flugmeldestationen*), which are in telephonic communication.

The Commander of the Anti-Aircraft Guns (*Koflak*) is responsible for the supervision of the entire system.

(*c*) *Anti-aircraft sections* (*Flakzüge*) are armed with guns of 7·7-cm., 9-cm. or 10-cm. calibre. There are two series, one numbered from 1 to 200, and the other from 401 to 500. These units were formerly attached to divisions but are now sector troops. They are horse-drawn.

(*d.*) *Sections of automatic anti-aircraft guns* are armed with automatic or Q.F. guns of 2-cm. and 3·7-cm. calibre. They are distinguished by the letter "M" (*Maschinen-Flakzüge*), and form a separate series numbered between 1 and 200.

(*e.*) *Anti-aircraft guns on motor lorries* are usually 7·7-cm. guns employed singly, and are designated *Kraftwagen-Geschütze* or *Kraftwagen-Flugabwehrkanonen* (*K-Flaks*). They form a special series numbered between 1 and 100, the number being followed by the letter "K."

(*f.*) *Anti-aircraft batteries* (*Flak-Batterien*) in the field consist of three series, one numbered from 301 to 400, another from 501 to 600, and the third from 701 upwards. These batteries, like the *Flakzüge*, are armed with 7·7-cm., 9-cm. or 10-cm. guns. There is also a further series (numbered between 101 and 200) mounted on motor lorries (*K Flak-Batterien*). An anti-aircraft battery consists of 4 guns (3 if on motor lorries).

4. **Anti-aircraft guns.**—(*a.*) *2-cm. gun.*—The German designation is *2 cm. Flak-Grabenkanone* or *2 cm. Flugzeugkanone.* This gun fires tracer shot; maximum range, 3,500 yards, or a maximum height of 2,734 yards; rate of fire, 120 rounds per minute.

(*b.*) *3·7-cm. guns.*—The German designations are *3·7 cm. Flak.* and *3·7 cm. Masch.-Flak.* (or *M.-Flak.*). The latter is of the 1-pr. pom-pom type, and probably fires both H.E. shell and tracer shot; maximum range, at least 3,280 yards.

(*c.*) *7·7-cm. guns.*—Various types of these are known :—

    (*a.*) The 96 n/A pattern field gun on an improvised mounting.

    (*b.*) A 7·7-cm. gun on a pedestal mounting (*7·7 cm. Sockel-Flak*).

    (*c.*) 7·7-cm. L/35 gun. This is probably the new 1916 pattern field gun or howitzer mounting (*K.i.H.=Kanone in Haubitz-Lafette.*)\* (*F.K. 16.*)\*

    (*d.*) 7·7-cm. guns mounted on motor lorries (*Kraftwagengeschütze*).

(*b.*) and (*c.*) are described in an official German publication as *pferdebespannte*=horse drawn.

7·7-cm. anti-aircraft guns fire a 15 lb. shell, the 1915 pattern H.E. shell with the *K.Z.11 Gr.* fuze. When used with anti-aircraft ammunition these fuzes contain no percussion system. As a distinguishing mark the cap of the fuze is painted yellow. The maximum range is 7,874 yards, and the rate of fire is about 20 rounds per minute.

(*d.*) *9-cm. gun.*—Some of the old-fashioned '73 and '73/'88 pattern 9-cm. field guns have been adapted for anti-aircraft work. They are known as *9 cm. K. 73 auf Sockel* and *9 cm Ballon-Abwehr-Kanonen (9 cm. B.A.K.).* They fire a 17½ lb. shell, the 1914 pattern H.E shell and the 1915 pattern shrapnel, both fitted with a time fuze marked *Dopp.Z.92.lg Brlg.o.Az.* (*o.Az.=ohne Aufschlagzündung*=without percussion fuze). The maximum range is 7,109 yards.

(*e.*) *10-cm. guns.*—The 10-cm. gun, 10-cm. gun '04, 10-cm. gun '97, and 10-cm. gun '1 are all used for anti-aircraft work on a pivot mounting (*Sockel*).

The following details are known :—

| Gun. | Shell. | Fuze. | Maximum range. | |
|---|---|---|---|---|
| | | | Time. | Perc'n. |
| { 10-cm. gun.. <br> { 10-cm. gun '04 <br> { 10-cm. gun '97 <br> { 10-cm. gun '14 | 10 cm. Gr. .. | Dopp. Z. 92 f. 10 cm. K. .. | yards. <br> 8,968 | yards. <br> — |
| { 10-cm. gun.. <br> { 10-cm. gun '04 <br> { 10-cm. gun '97 <br> { 10-cm. gun '14 | 10 cm. Schr. 96 | Dopp. Z. 92 lg. Brlg. .. | 11,264 <br><br> 12,085 | 11,264 <br><br> 12,085 |

---

\* A German official document, dated 18.9.16, states as follows with regard to the *K.i.H.* field gun, of which the 1916 pattern field gun is a modification :—

    "The *K.i.H.* field gun can be used for anti-aircraft fire, but is not designed for it. Anti aircraft fire entails elevations up to 70°, and to obtain these with a *K.i.H.* gun necessitate mounting it on a fixed mounting. This is not so easily done with a *K.i.H.* field gun as with 96 n/A field gun. The 96 n/A field gun on a fixed mounting is a more handy weapon for anti aircraft fire than the *K.i.H.* field gun ; besides, the latter should be diverted as seldom a possible from its legitimate employment, which is long range fire."

*( f.)  Heavy guns employed against captive balloons:—*

| Gun. | Shell. | Fuze. | Maximum range. | |
|---|---|---|---|---|
| | | | Time. | Perc'n. |
| | | | yards. | yards. |
| 12-cm. heavy gun (*s. 12 cm. K.*) | *12 cm. Schr. 15.* .. .. | *Dopp. Z. 92* .. .. | 7,218 | 7,983 |
| 13-cm. gun (*13 cm. K.*) .. | *13 cm. Schr.* .. .. .. | *Dopp. Z. 92 lg. Brlg* .. | 15,311 | 15,311 |
| 15-cm. experimental gun, on wheeled carriage (*15 cm. Vers. K.i.R.L.*). | *15 cm. Schr. 03 (gr.)* .. <br> *15 cm. Schr. 03 (gr.) (Haube)* | *Dopp. Z. 16* (clock-work fuze) .. | about 18,600 21,107 | about 18,600 21,107 |
| 15-cm. gun, with overhead shield (*15 cm K.i.S.L.*). | *15 cm. Schr. 03* .. .. <br> *15 cm. Schr. 03 (gr.)* .. <br> *15 cm. Schr. 30 (gr.) (Haube)* | *Dopp. Z. 92 lg. Brlg* .. <br> *Dopp. Z. 16* (clockwork fuze). | 16,186 over 17,500 | 17,060 over 17,500 |
| 15-cm. long gun (*lg. 15 cm. K.*) | *15 cm. Schr. 15* .. .. | *Dopp. Z. 92* .. .. | 8,968 | 10,936 |
| 15-cm. gun, with chase rings (*15 cm. R.K.*). | *15 cm. Schr. 15 m.v.F.* (*m.v.F.* = with forward driving band). | *Dopp. Z. 92* .. .. | 7,546 | 7,546 |
| 15-cm. long gun, with chase rings (*lg. 15 cm. R.K.*). | *15 cm. Schr. 15 m.v.F.* .. | *Dopp. Z. 92* .. .. | 7,929 | 7,929 |
| 24-cm. Q.F. gun L/40 .. .. | Shrapnel with false cap .. | *Dopp. Z. 16* (clockwork fuze). | at least 22,000 | at least 22,000 |

*(g.) Miscellaneous.*—Captured French (75-mm.) and Russian (7·62-cm. L/30) field guns have also been adapted for anti-aircraft work. The Russian guns are referred to in a document as *pferdebespannte 7·62 cm. russ. 00 u.02*, *i.e.*, 1900 and 1902 patterns 7·62-cm. Russian field guns, horse drawn. The most favourable range of the latter is from 5,500-7,500 yards.

Several of these converted Russian field guns, on wheeled carriage, have been captured. They fire a 15-lb. H.E. shell of German manufacture, fitted with *K. Z. 11 Gr.* time fuze, specially graduated in seconds up to 30 seconds.

In addition to the army guns enumerated above, there are various patterns of naval anti-aircraft guns, including an 8·8-cm. gun which is in general use on the Belgian coast. There are also 8·8-cm. naval guns on pivot mountings on railway trucks (*Eisenbahn-Sockel-Batterie.*)

5. **Anti-aircraft machine gun detachments.**—During 1917, two series of anti-aircraft machine gun detachments (*Flugabwehr-Maschinengewehr-Abteilungen* or *Flamga*) were formed; the first was numbered from 801 upwards, the second from 901 upwards. Of the former, only the first three have been identified; of the latter, the highest number

identified is 925. It is reported that each detachment consists of three companies of about 80 men under a lieutenant, the whole commanded by a captain. Each company is armed with 12 machine guns, '08 pattern, and each gun is served by one non-commissioned officer and 5 gun numbers. The full complement of ammunition for each gun consists of 18 cases with 2 belts of 250 rounds each, no tracer bullets.

6. **Balloon barrage detachments.**—Since the beginning of 1917 the Germans have endeavoured to protect important industrial centres by the employment of balloon barrage detachments (*Luftsperrabteilungen*). Each barrage comprises a number of captive balloons, which are let up to a maximum height of about 7,000 feet whenever an air raid is expected. The balloons are about 500 feet apart.

At the beginning of 1918, seven barrages had been identified, mainly stationed near Metz, Diedenhofen, Saarbrücken, Köln, and important iron-ore works in Lorraine.

There appears to be a continuous balloon barrage along the valley of the Saar from Dillingen to Saargemünd.

# CHAPTER XI.

## SIGNAL SERVICE.

1. **Peace organization.**—In peace the personnel of the Signal Service was found by the Telegraph Troops (*Telegraphentruppen*), consisting of :—

6 Prussian telegraph battalions and 7 fortress telephone companies.

1 Saxon telegraph battalion and 1 fortress telephone company.

1 Württemberg telegraph company and 1 fortress telephone detachment.

2 Bavarian telegraph battalions.

The officers were drawn mostly from the engineers and pioneers, some from the infantry and railway troops. The uniform of the Telegraph Troops was similar to that worn by the pioneers, but a shako was worn, and the shoulder straps bore a "T."

In January, 1917, the Telegraph Troops were separated from the Communication Troops, to which they formerly belonged, and were organized as a separate corps under the Director of Signals (*Chef der Feldtelegraphie*), who also controlled the telegraph and telephone systems in Germany.

2. **Present organization and command.**—In July, 1917, the Signal Service (*Nachrichtenwesen*) was completely reorganized and extended to embrace all means of communication, including telegraphs, telephones. power buzzers, listening sets, wireless telegraphy, visual and sound signalling, message-carrying projectiles, carrier pigeons and messenger dogs. The name *Telegraphentruppen* was changed to *Nachrichtentruppen*, and the Director of Signals (*Chef des Nachrichtenwesens*) was made directly subordinate to the Chief of the General Staff of the Field Army, being his adviser in all matters dealing with signals, as well as being the executive head of the Signal Service.

In each of the main theatres of war there is a Signal Brigade Commander (*Nachrichten-Brigadekommandeur*), and there is a Signal Commander (*Nachrichten-Kommandeur*) at the headquarters of each Army, Corps and division, and also with each fortress in Germany. A Prussian War Ministry order, issued in October, 1917, ordered the amalgamation of the staff of the Army Telephone and Army Wireless Commanders (*Akofern* and *Akofunk*) into one staff, viz., that of the Army Signal Commander (*Akonach*). Similar staffs at Group Headquarters are combined under the Group Signal Commander (*Grukonach*). In a division, all means of communication are under the direction of the Divisional Signal Commander (*Divkonach*). A Signal Service Adviser (*Nachrichtenreferent*) is attached to the headquarters of a Group of Armies. In trench warfare, Permanent Signal Officers are allotted to divisional sectors.

Each cavalry division is provided with a cavalry signal detachment.

Each Army Corps District in Germany has a Signal Depôt (*Nachrichten-Ersatz-Abteilung*), which is responsible for the supply and training of all personnel for the Signal Service. Each Army in the field has also a Signal School (*Nachrichtenschule*), usually with a Wireless School attached, where the training is completed, and an Army Signal Park for the supply of material.

3. **Regimental signalling detachments.**—Every infantry and artillery unit has its own regimental signalling detachment (*Truppen-Nachrichtenabteilung*). These are all subordinate to the Divisional Signal Commander (*Divkonach*) in technical matters. A regimental signalling detachment normally comprises 1 officer and 130–150 men, organized in telephone

and lamp signalling sections (*Fernsprechtrupps* and *Blinkertrupps*), and also provides the requisite personnel for carrier pigeons, messenger dogs, message projectors, &c.

**4. Telegraphy.**—Telegraph units are not allotted to formations in advance of Army Headquarters.

A Lines of Communication Telegraph Directorate (*Etappen-Telegraphen-Direktion*) connects the headquarters of each Army with neighbouring Armies, Corps, Groups of Armies and General Headquarters. The instruments used are the Siemens high-speed telegraph (*Schnelltelegraph*), with a speed of 24,000 to 30,000 words an hour, the Hughes' telewriter (*Fernschreiber*), and the ordinary sounder (*Klopfer*). The first two systems deliver the messages ready printed.

**5. Telephone units.**—At each Army Headquarters there are two Army Telephone Detachments (*Armee-Fernsprechabteilungen*), numbered in two series, *e.g.*, the Fourth Army has the 4th and 104th Army Telephone Detachments. Each of these units comprises a headquarters section (*Stationszug*) and 5 to 7 motor airline sections (*Kraftwagen-Fernsprech-Bauzüge*). The strength of a section (*Bauzug*) is :—

> 1 officer.
> 7 non-commissioned officers.
> 35 other ranks.
> 4 motor lorries.

These sections are numbered in a series commencing with 900.

Each Army in the field has an Army Telephone Park for the supply of material. The officer commanding the telephone units at Army Headquarters is known as the *Armee-Fernsprechkommandeur* (*Akofern*). He works directly under the *Nachrichtenkommandeur* at Army Headquarters.

A telephone detachment is allotted to each Group (Corps) and Divisional Headquarters. These detachments are numbered in series according to the formation to which they are attached, as follows :—

| | |
|---|---|
| Active and high-numbered divisions | Divisional number (*e.g.*, 11th with 11th Division). |
| Reserve divisions | 400 + divisional number (*e.g.*, 424th with 24th Reserve Division). |
| Landwehr divisions | 500 + divisional number (*e.g.*, 513th with 13th Landwehr Division). |
| Ersatz divisions | 550 + divisional number (*e.g.*, 554th with 4th Ersatz Division). |
| Active Corps | 600 + Corps number (*e.g.*, 607th with VI Corps). |
| Reserve Corps | 700 + Corps number (*e.g.*, 712th with XI Reserve Corps). |

The telephone commander at Corps Headquarters is known as *Kofern* or *Kofe*.

Special telephone detachments are attached to cavalry divisions, fortresses, and units engaged in mountain warfare.

During trench warfare, the Group (Corps) telephone detachment lays the requisite number of lines to divisional headquarters (including counter-attack divisions). The divisional telephone detachment connects divisional headquarters with brigades and regiments.

A telephone detachment consists of several sections, each carrying 25 miles of cable, which can be laid at the rate of about 1,000 yards in half-an-hour. In addition to air-line, two kinds of cable are employed : *Armeekabel*, which has a covering of woven yarn only, and *Feldkabel*, which is insulated with rubber.

**6. Earth current telegraphy.**—German listening sets are named after the engineer, Arendt, who designed them. An *Arendt* Detachment (*Ara*) is attached to the Headquarters of each Army, and comprises about 15 officers and 300 other ranks. The *Arendt* Detachment consists of a number of *Arendt* Groups (*Agru*), one for each Group (Corps) in the Army. An *Arendt* Group comprises several listening sets (*Abhörstationen* or *Astos*), one for each divisional sector. The personnel of each listening set consists of 10 to 20 non-commissioned officers and men. Each divisional sector is also provided with a mobile policing set to check German telephone conversations. These listening sets are attached to the divisional telephone detachment.

Power buzzer stations (*Erdtelegraphenstationen*), each consisting of a sending and receiving apparatus, are alloted to divisions in active sectors at the rate of 2 per infantry regiment. The personnel required for each station is 1 non-commissioned officer and 4 men, these being provided by the regimental signalling detachments (*see* paragraph 3 above). The average range of a power buzzer with amplifier is about 2,200 yards.

**7. Wireless telegraphy.**—Wireless stations are allotted to all formations down to divisions, and are fixed or mobile as required, or adapted for use with aircraft or in mountain warfare. Intercepting and compass stations are also allotted for detecting the enemy's wireless traffic. At each Army Headquarters there is an Army Wireless Detachment (*Armee-Funkerabteilung*) with 2 heavy wireless stations (range nearly 200 miles), 2 compass stations and 1 intercepting station. An Army Wireless Park is allotted to each Army for the supply of material. The wireless troops at Army Headquarters are under the orders of the *Armee-Funkerkommandeur* (*Akofunk*), who works directly under the *Nachrichtenkommandeur*.

Each Group (Corps) Headquarters has a Group Wireless Station (*Gruppen-Funkenstation* or *Grufusta*), with a range of about 60 miles, and 1 compass station. The Group Wireless Commander is known as *Gekofunk*.

A Prussian War Ministry order of the 30th May, 1917, shows that the aeroplane jamming stations (*Fliegerstörer*), which were formerly attached to Corps Headquarters, have become Group Wireless Stations (*Gruppen-Funkenstationen*). These are numbered in a series from 500 upwards. The same order shows that the heavy field wireless stations, intercepting stations and compass sections (*Richt-Empfang-Trupps*), which were formerly attached to Army Headquarters, but were numbered independently, have now been absorbed into the Army Wireless Detachment (*Armee-Funkerabteilung*). This means that the wireless organization has been simplified by amalgamating the previously existing independent wireless formations into centralized units at Army and Corps Headquarters.

On active sectors of the front, each divisional sector is provided with a divisional wireless detachment (*Divisions-Funkerabteilung* or *Difua*)* consisting of :—

1 divisional wireless station
1 infantry wireless station (2 large, 5 medium and 6 small sets).
1 artillery wireless section (2 large, 6 medium and 4 small sets).
} All portable sets.

---

* Formerly known as *Funker-Kleinabteilung* (*Fukla*).

The ranges of these sets are as follows :—

| | | | | | | |
|---|---|---|---|---|---|---|
| Divisional station | .. | .. | .. | .. | .. | 62 miles. |
| Large trench set | .. | .. | .. | .. | .. | 4,400 — 6,600 yards. |
| Medium trench set .. | .. | .. | .. | .. | .. | 2,200 — 3,300  ,, |
| Small trench set | .. | .. | .. | .. | .. | 600 — 1,100  ,, |

In addition to the above, every Army area contains a number of aviation fighting stations and aerodrome stations, according to the number of aviation units in the area. In active sectors, special wireless stations are allotted to heavy guns on railway mountings, working directly under Army and Corps Headquarters. Communication with aeroplanes is maintained by the wireless stations allotted to Armies, Corps, divisions and artillery groups.

Each cavalry division has a cavalry wireless detachment, with 1 heavy and 2 light stations. The respective ranges are 190 and 62 miles.

8. **Lamp signalling.**—Extensive use of lamp signalling (*Blinken*) is made by the Germans in the forward areas during trench warfare. The personnel required for a lamp signalling station is 1 non-commissioned officer and 4–6 signallers. These men are found by the regimental signalling detachments (*see* para. 3 above). The 1916 pattern apparatus (*Blinkgerät 16*) is actuated by dry batteries. It is easily portable and can be carried on horseback or on a bicycle. It is issued in three sizes :—

| | | | | | |
|---|---|---|---|---|---|
| Large signalling lamp .. | .. | .. | .. | range about 6,600 yards. |
| Medium  ,,  ,, .. | .. | .. | .. | ,,  3,300  ,, |
| Small  ,,  ,, .. | .. | .. | .. | ,,  900  ,, |

The 1917 pattern lamp is used for communicating with aircraft and observation balloons.

The following table shows the allotment of 1916 pattern signalling lamps to the various units in a division .—

| | *Large.* | *Medium.* | *Small.* |
|---|---|---|---|
| Divisional Headquarters  ..  ..  ..  ..  .. | 4 | 4 | .. |
| Infantry Brigade Headquarters  ..  ..  ..  .. | .. | 2 | .. |
| Infantry Regimental Headquarters..  ..  ..  .. | .. | 4 | .. |
| Infantry Battalion  ..  ..  ..  ..  .. | .. | 6 | 2 |
| Machine Gun Company  ..  ..  ..  ..  .. | .. | 4 | .. |
| Regimental *Minenwerfer* Detachment  ..  ..  .. | .. | 2 | 2 |
| Divisional Artillery Staff  ..  ..  ..  ..  .. | .. | 2 | .. |
| Field Artillery Regimental Headquarters ..  ..  .. | .. | 6 | .. |
| Field Artillery *Abteilung*  ..  ..  ..  ..  .. | .. | 10 | .. |
| Pioneer Company  ..  ..  ..  ..  ..  .. | .. | 2 | .. |
| *Minenwerfer* Company  ..  ..  ..  ..  .. | .. | 4 | .. |

Medium signalling lamps are also provided for heavy artillery on the following scale :—

| | | | | | |
|---|---|---|---|---|---|
| Foot artillery regimental headquarters | .. | .. | .. | .. | 4 |
| Foot artillery battalion | .. | .. | .. | .. | .. | 12 |
| Independent foot artillery battery | .. | .. | .. | .. | .. | 4 |

9. **Message-carrying projectiles.**—The Germans have recently introduced message-carrying projectiles to transmit written messages from front to rear.

A message rocket (*Meldewurfgranate*) is used from the front line to battalion head-quarters, and from forward observing officers to artillery command posts. It is projected either by means of the 1916 pattern "stick" bomb-thrower, or by a special "signal-thrower" to a range of 550 or 650 yards.

The signal-thrower (*Signalwerfer*) consists essentially of a rifle mechanism contained in a hollow steel rod, shod with a spike for planting in the ground. The rocket is made with a hollow shaft to slip over the rod of the signal-thrower, which contains the striker. The propellant charge and percussion cap are contained in the body of the rocket.

The signal-thrower is primarily intended for projecting light-signals, but can also be used for projecting message rockets. It is issued to all regimental staffs and units down to companies and batteries.

The light message shell (*leichte Nachrichtenmine*) is used between battalion, regimental and brigade headquarters, and as a means of communication between infantry and artillery. It is fired from the light *Minenwerfer*, the range being 1,422 yards.

A smoke-indicator cartridge (*Rauchmeldepatrone*), fired from a signalling pistol, is used by airmen for dropping written messages.

10. **Carrier pigeons.**—In each Army, the carrier pigeon service is controlled by the Army Signal Commander. Normally each Corps has a training loft (*Korpsschlag*); homing lofts (*Heimatschläge*), which are frequently mobile, are stationed near divisional headquarters.

The lofts are usually numbered consecutively throughout each Army. In some cases, the pigeons used by an Army are dyed a distinctive colour, as in the case of the Sixth Army, where the birds are generally dyed red.

Pigeon stations (*Abflugstellen*) are maintained at infantry and artillery command posts, and also with forward observing officers and infantry company commanders.

11. **Messenger dogs.**—A messenger dog section (*Meldehund-Trupp*) is attached to each Army Headquarters. This unit acts as a training school where dogs and attendants are trained, and issued to Corps and divisions as required. The Army messenger dog sections train dogs received from Germany, instruct the attendants and complete the training of dogs sent back from the front for further training.

Messenger dogs are allotted to the infantry signalling detachments (*see* page 117); a maximum of 12 dogs may be allotted to a regiment and 6 to a battalion. Each dog requires an attendant and an assistant attendant. These men are detailed by regiments or battalions and sent to the Army messenger dog section for a four weeks' course of training, after which they return to their units with trained dogs.

The dogs principally employed are of the German sheep-dog or wolf-hound breed. Messages are carried in a cylindrical tin case, about 6 inches long and $1\frac{1}{2}$ inch in diameter, attached to the collar. The average time to carry a message between battalion and company headquarters (about a mile) is from 6 to 8 minutes.

# CHAPTER XII.

## SURVEY.

**1. Survey department.**—In peace, the Prussian Survey (*Landesaufnahme*) was placed directly under the control of the Great General Staff. The survey was divided into three sections—trigonometrical, topographical and cartographical.

In war, the *Landesaufnahme* is under the Acting General Staff in Berlin, and is organized as follows:—

> Cartographical section.
> Trigonometrical section.
> Topographical section.
> Photogrammetric section.
> Geological section.
> Scientific computation office.
> Map room.
> Central directorate of surveys.

The subordinate personnel of the survey was in peace mainly civilian. The officers and non-commissioned officers employed on survey work are especially drawn from the artillery.

**2.—Organization in the field.**—In war, the whole of the survey is placed under the Director of Military Survey (*Chef des Kriegsvermessungswesens*) at General Headquarters.

At the Headquarters of each Army in the field there is a Survey Staff Officer (*Stabsoffizier des Vermessungswesens* or *Stoverm*), and one or two Survey Detachments *Vermessungs-Abteilungen*), which correspond to our Field Survey Companies. Each survey detachment has a map-printing section (*Karten-Felddruckerei*) attached, and is responsible for trigonometrical and topographical work, the preparation of artillery maps and boards, and the supply and issue of maps. Some Armies, *e.g.*, Second, Fifth and Sixth, have two survey detachments, but the majority have only one; 27 of these units have been identified. On the Lines of Communication of each Army in the field there is a map depôt (*Kartenlager*).

Each Corps and divisional headquarters comprises a topographical section (*Kartenstelle*), where trench maps can be overprinted and sketch-maps and plans can be drawn and reproduced. The personnel consists of an officer or survey official and a staff of qualified draughtsmen. These divisional and Corps topographical sections are actually branches of the Army Survey Detachment.

There is a General Staff Officer for Maps at the headquarters of each Corps.

Corps topographical sections are provided, wherever possible, with a lithographic power press.

**3. Duties of survey detachments.**—The survey detachment at the Headquarters of an Army in the field is responsible for all trigonometrical and cartographical work required by the Army as well as for the exploitation of aeroplane photographs. The following account of the duties of these units is compiled from the instructions on the subject issued by the Sixth German Army.

The following data must be sent direct by units to the survey detachment or Corps topographical section :—

  (a.) All reconnaissance reports, photographs, sketches, &c., concerning changes in the position of hostile batteries, defences, trenches, &c.

  (b.) Flash intersections obtained by the observation groups.

  (c.) Two copies of every aeroplane photograph, numbered and annotated.

The following work also devolves on the survey detachment :—

  (a.) Checking the triangulation network in the Army area, triangulating new trigonometrical points, erection of bench-marks.

  (b ) Topographical reconnaissance in order to correct existing maps ; partial re-surveys where necessary.

  (c.) Preparation of barrage maps and battery boards for field and heavy artillery, observation groups, &c. Trigonometrically fixing battery aiming points, observation posts and battery positions.

  (d.) Location of important points in the foreground by triangulation, plane-table and photogrammetric methods.

  (e.) Re-section of sound-ranging posts and observation group posts.

  (f.) Stereo-photogrammetric panoramas.

  (g.) Geological research. Assistance to the mining units and advice on questions affected by the condition of the ground.

  (h.) Reproduction of maps, enlargements and reductions, &c. When this work becomes too large to be dealt with in sufficient time, it is passed to the Cartographical Section of the General Staff in Berlin, or the Topographical Bureau in Munich.

  (i.) Inspection of captured maps, cadastral and mining plans, and utilization of the information obtained from these.

  (j.) Printing of maps, plans, sketches, orders and forms. Mounting maps and binding pamphlets.

  (k.) Photography and photogrammetry for technical and historical purposes.

  (l.) Preparation of relief maps in plaster or cardboard layers.

4. **Survey units working with artillery.**—The location of active hostile batteries is largely carried out by an elaborate chain of artillery survey units, viz. :—

**Observation groups** (*Artillerie-Messtrupps* or *Licht-Messtrupps*), and

**Sound-ranging sections** (*Schall-Messtrupps*).

These units count as artillery formations and wear artillery uniform; at least one officer in each must be an artillery officer. They are placed at the disposal of Armies, which allot them as required to Corps and divisions. The observation groups and sound-ranging sections are sector units and remain in their sectors when the formation to which they are allotted is relieved; they are, however, placed directly under the orders of the artillery commander of the division holding their sector. One observation group and one sound-ranging section are normally allotted to each divisional sector. The front covered by the posts of one of these units varies between 3 and 10 miles.

At the beginning of 1918, 175 observation groups, and 125 sound-ranging sections had been identified.

There is a school of instruction (*Artillerie-Messschule*) for the personnel of observation groups at Wahn (Germany).

There exists also a series of giant periscope (*Mastfernrohr*) detachments, which are attached to artillery groups. The detachment consists of one non-commissioned officer, and four men.

5. **Organization and functions of artillery survey units.**—Each observation group has four or five flash-spotting posts (*Licht-Messstellen*), and each sound-ranging section has four or five sound-ranging posts (*Schall-Messstellen*). If required, each unit can man six posts. Each of these units has a separate telephone system linking it up to a headquarters office (*Auswertungs-Stelle*) where the results are computed. These headquarters are situated together if possible, and conveniently near the divisional artillery headquarters. Transport and telephonic communication are provided by the divisional artillery headquarters. The strength of an observation group is about six officers and 100 men.

The information obtained by the above units is communicated direct to the artillery, and is then sent for accurate compilation to the Army Survey Detachments, which are responsible for the compilation and publication of maps.

The observation groups and sound-ranging sections not only locate hostile gun positions, but also range their own batteries. They work in close co-operation with the artillery intelligence officer, and with the divisional topographical section (*Kartenstelle*).

The following are the duties of artillery survey units according to the training manual issued in May, 1917 :—

(*a.*) Location of hostile batteries and other targets
(*b.*) Information from aeroplane photographs.
(*c.*) Observation of fire for their own artillery.
(*d.*) Observation of the enemy's movements.
(*e.*) Preparation and use of stereo-photographs.
(*f.*) Preparation of charts and tables showing the positions, number and activity of hostile batteries.
(*g.*) Preparation of battery boards and artillery maps.
(*h.*) Collection and collation of all reconnaissance reports concerning the sector.

6. **Maps.**—In peace the normal scales used were 1/100,000 for ordinary manœuvres, and 1/25,000 for detailed operations.

The small scale maps used by the Germans in the field are mainly 1/200,000 and 1/300,000 scales. An edition of the 1/200,000 is published for aviators, without contours, and with information as to camps, billets, &c., printed in red.

Of medium scales, there is a 1/60,000 reduction of the Belgian 1/40,000, and a direct reproduction of the French 1/80,000. Neither of these gives any information which is not on the originals, except that town and village populations are shown on the 1/80,000.

French army *plans directeurs* have been copied, and sometimes combined with enlargements from smaller scale maps.

On the Western Front the Germans use the 1/80,000 for general purposes, and the 1/25 000 as the normal trench map. Trench maps on scales of 1/10,000 and 1/5,000 are also issued.

Trench maps are squared with a kilometre grid, the squares being sometimes identified horizontally by letters and, vertically, by numbers, but more usually numbered on a system of geographical co-ordinates. The kilometre square is usually sub-divided into 25 secondary squares.

**7. Meteorological stations.**—There is a meteorological station (*Feldwetter-Station* or *Feldwetterwarte**) at the Headquarters of each Army in the field ; each of these has a number of forward stations (*Frontwetterwarten*) which send in observations for the daily weather forecasts. Weather reports are issued twice daily.

The meteorological stations work in conjunction with the divisional anti-gas officers, and with aircraft units.

The Army Meteorological Station is placed under the orders of the aviation commander at Army Headquarters.

Each Army Meteorological Station has also a number of wind observation posts (*Windwarten*), one of which is normally situated a mile or so behind the front in each Corps area, and is manned by two men.

In each divisional sector there is a collecting station for forward observations (*Gassammelstelle*) under the control of the divisional gas officer, which collects the weather reports sent in by the weather observation posts in the forward areas. There is normally one of these posts, consisting of three men in each regimental sector.

---

\* Abbreviated to *Fewewa.*

# German Railway Organization.

—

DIRECTOR OF RAILWAYS AT GENERAL HEADQUARTERS.

(*Feldeisenbahnchef.*)

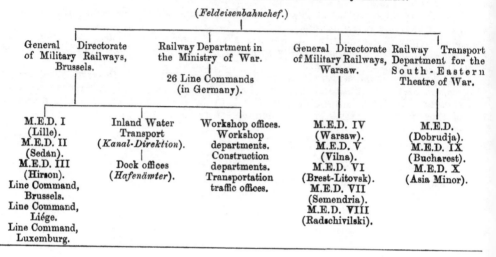

MILITARY RAILWAY DIRECTORATE
(*Militär-Eisenbahn-Direktion*)
or
LINE COMMAND
(*Linien-Kommandantur*).

Locomotive offices (*Maschinenämter*).  Operating traffic offices (*Betriebsämter*).  Transportation traffic offices (*Verkehrsämter*).  Independent Traffic and Constructional Units.

# CHAPTER XIII.

## TRANSPORTATION.

The Communication Troops (*Verkehrstruppen*) formerly comprised all the personnel dealing with communications, including air service, signals, railways and mechanical transport. During the war the Air Service and the Signal Service have been separated from the Communication Troops and organized as distinct corps.

All the railway and mechanical transport services are controlled by the General Inspectorate of Military Communications in Germany, and by the Quartermaster-General in the field. The transportation service in the field is divided into two branches:—

(*a.*) The Railway Service (*Feldeisenbahnwesen*).
(*b.*) The Mechanical Transport Service (*Feldkraftfahrwesen*).

### (A.) The Railway Service.

1. **Higher command and organization.**—The command of the entire railway service in Germany and in the field is centred in the Director of Railways (*Chef des Feldeisenbahnwesens* or *Feldeisenbahnchef*), whose central office is at General Headquarters. He holds the rank of a Corps commander. The diagram on the opposite page shows the general organization of the railway service in war. Traffic on the lines in Germany is maintained by the civil administration, working uuder 26 military control offices known as Line Commands (*Linien-Kommandanturen*).

2. **General directorate.**—As shown in the diagram, the executive control in each ot the two main theatres of war is exercised by a General Directorate (*Militär-General-Direktion* or *M.G.D.*).

The General Directorate at Brussels has supreme control of all railways in the occupied portions of France and Belgium. It has a large staff, divided into the following 8 branches:—

> Military,
> Interior economy,
> Finance,
> Construction,
> Transportation traffic,
> Locomotive,
> Operating traffic,
> Medical.

The General Directorate at Brussels administers the railway system through the medium of three "military railway directorates" at Lille, Sedan and Hirson, and three "line commands" at Brussels, Liége and Luxemburg. The administrative zones of each of these offices is shown by Plate 12.

Also under the direct control of the General Directorate at Brussels are the Director of Inland Water Transport (*Kanal-Direktion*), miscellaneous workshops and construction organizations, aud certain transportation traffic offices (*Verkehrsämter*).

3. **Railway representatives with armies.**—A railway representative (*Bahnbeauftragter* or *Bba*) is attached to the headquarters of each Army and Army L. of C. area on the Western Front. This officer is a representative of the General Directorate at Brussels, and is directly under the orders of that office, being independent of the military railway directorates. All requirements of the military authorities as regards troop movements, and transportation by rail or canal, are submitted to him for transmission to the railway and canal services. The railway representative also controls the constructional alterations to the railway and canal systems (including light railways and trench tramways) in the zone of the formation to which he is appointed.

4. **Military railway directorates and line commands.**—The military railway directorates (*Militär-Eisenbahn-Direktionen* or *M.E.D.*), of which there are three on the Western Front—at Lille, Sedan and Hirson—administer large zones, as shown by the map on Plate 12. Their staff, like that of the General Directorate, is divided into 8 branches, with somewhat similar functions.

As shown in the diagram, each military railway directorate administers a number of locomotive offices (*Maschinenämter*), operating traffic offices (*Betriebsämter*), and transportation traffic offices (*Verkehrsämter*). The directorates also control a number of independent construction and traffic units (*Bau-* and *Betriebs-Kompagnien*).

There are three line commands, at Brussels, Liége and Luxemburg, controlling the zones in Belgium and Luxemburg, adjacent to Germany (*see* Plate 12). The above remarks regarding the staff and the sub-offices and units controlled by the military railway directorates apply also to the line commands.

5. **Locomotive offices.**—Under the control of each military railway directorate and line command are two or more locomotive offices (*Maschinenämter*). Eighteen of these are known to exist on the Western Front, and seven on the Eastern Front.

Within their zones of control these offices are responsible for all mechanical questions, including the control of repair shops, the maintenance, disinfection and marking of rolling stock and the distribution of locomotives.

In the zone of each office and under its control there are three or four local repair shops, known as *Betriebswerkmeistereien*, situated at large stations, such as Meirelbeke, Bruges. Courtrai and Valenciennes.

The locomotive offices also control the mechanical personnel at all stations in their zone on technical matters.

6. **Operating traffic offices.**—Under the control of each military railway directorate and line command are a number (6 or 7) of operating traffic offices (*Betriebsämter*). About 40 of these are known to exist on the Western Front, about 20 have been identified on the Eastern Front.

Within their zones of control these offices are responsible for the running of time-tables, the signal arrangements, the speed and precedence of trains, and the use and disuse of stations.

These offices control the personnel of their branch at all stations in their zone.

7. **Transportation traffic offices.**—Under the administration of each military railway directorate and line command are two or three transportation traffic offices (*Verkehrsämter*). Fifteen of these have been identified on the Western Front. Certain of these offices are directly under the orders of the General Directorate, Brussels.

These offices differ from operating traffic offices in that they do not operate traffic, but deal with transportation in their areas, with the issue of tickets and passes, the control of traffic to other countries, the customs and freight regulations, the nomenclature of stations, and the distribution and use of rolling stock.

In departmental matters, these offices control the personnel of all stations in their zones.

8. **Railway personnel.**—The railway troops (*Eisenbahntruppen*) consisted in peace of :—

3 Prussian railway regiments, each of 8 companies.
1 Prussian railway battalion of 4 companies.
1 Bavarian railway battalion of 3 companies.
3 railway traffic companies, working the military railway from Berlin to Jüterbog.

The railway personnel is now organized in :—

(*a*.) Railway construction companies (*Eisenbahn-Bau-Kompagnien*). These include, at least, 80 Active, 60 Reserve, 6 Landwehr and 15 Fortress construction companies.

(*b*.) Railway traffic companies (*Eisenbahn-Betriebs-Kompagnien*). These include 100 Active and 7 Fortress traffic companies and, in addition, about 30 light railway traffic companies, numbered from 101 and 201 upwards.

There are also 5 railway workmen battalions, 9 supplementary battalions and 23 railway store companies.

At least 13 armoured trains (*Panzerzüge*) are known to exist.

Each railway construction and traffic company is affiliated to the depôt of the railway regiment from which it was formed, and wears the number of that regiment on the shoulder straps in Roman numerals under the " E," which distinguishes the railway troops.

Railway troops wear the Guard *Litzen* on collar and cuffs.

9. **System of traffic control.**—Early in the war, no railway time-tables existed in the occupied portions of France and Belgium. Trains started for a destination, getting through as best they could, passing from station to station as the line became clear.

In 1915, the " marche " system was introduced on the lines of the system in Germany, calculated for a mean speed of 30 km. per hour. This system has been in use ever since.

When the " marche " system was introduced, time-tables formulated from it came into operation. These schedules show the running of all regular express, passenger, leave, supply and goods trains. During troop movements, where such are protracted, the troop trains are interposed between trains on the existing time-tables, causing no change to the running of the regular trains beyond certain delays. During continuous and large troop movements, whole series of trains, especially of the less important natures, are cut out of the programme.

New time-tables for the Western Theatre of war appear to be issued frequently, necessitated possibly by the ever-changing restrictions to traffic of different varieties.

Normally, time-tables are punctually adhered to. A feature of certain time-tables is the fact that through " wagon-lit " accommodation was provided, at any rate up to November, 1917, between places such as—

Thielt and Cologne,
Douai and Strassburg,
Vouziers and Saarbrücken, &c.

The " block " system of signals appears to be universally employed. Pre-war sections have not been materially altered. A certain percentage of German appliances have been introduced.

**10. Speed and tonnage of trains.**—Captured time-tables show that 95 per cent. of goods trains keep to the basic speed of 30 km. per hour. In isolated instances they travel at 40 km. per hour ; on a few local lines 15 and 20 km. per hour are laid down.

As regards the faster passenger and leave traffic, in 1915 some of this ran at 80 km. per hour, which was soon afterwards reduced to 70. More recent information shows that fast trains do not now reach a speed greater than 50 to 60 km. per hour. In April, 1917, the maximum speed for Belgian engines was laid down as between 45 and 60 km. per hour.

The maximum tonnage carried on a truck lies between 12 and 15 tons. The tonnage carried on a goods train varies from 270 to 650 tons; in the majority of cases between 500 and 650 tons. For the purpose of engine haulage, tables have been drawn up which show the tonnage to be drawn on any particular stretch of line for every type of locomotive in use.

No train is allowed to exceed 110 axles in length.

**11. Control of troop movements.**—Orders for the movement of divisions are issued from the central railway office at German General Headquarters. The movement of smaller formations is arranged by the local railway authorities.

When a big troop movement is about to take place on the Western Front, the General Directorate at Brussels receives instructions from German General Headquarters as to the time of commencement and completion. Provided these instructions are complied with, the control of the movement within the zone of the Brussels authorities is entirely left to those authorities. The movement, including the entraining and detraining arrangements, is then regulated from Brussels. In the case of formations entraining on the Western Front, as soon as the order for the movement is received from German General Headquarters, instructions are issued by the Brussels authorities to the most favourably situated centres of rolling stock to make up a definite number of fixed pattern trains, to be sent to certain points by a certain time.

**12. Arrangements for troop movements.**—Experience has shown that the number of trains required to move a German division with its field artillery from one portion of a theatre to another portion of the same theatre is 40 to 45. The number required, however, to move a division from one theatre to a different theatre is very much larger, varying from 60 to 80. The extra trains in the latter case are accounted for partially by the fact that the longer journey necessitates the provision of more liberal accommodation for men and horses, and partially by the fact that heavy artillery also often accompanies formations in inter-theatre movements.

Experience also shows that the number of wagons on troop trains for constituted units lies between the limits of 40 and 60. There is, however, to a certain extent a standard in troop trains in that, for each type of unit, a train is made up of a fixed proportion of the different types of wagon. Such trains are kept made up ready at various forming-up stations.

The minimum interval allowed between trains on a clear line is 20 minutes. In practice trains are run at intervals varying from 20 to 40 minutes when necessary. The speed with which troop movements can be carried out, therefore, is usually dependent on the entraining and detraining arrangements. No fixed number of entraining and detraining points is laid down. Roughly, however, it takes the trains carrying a German division 4 days to pass a point when travelling between parts of any one theatre, and 6 to 8 days when travelling from one theatre to another. Entraining and detraining apparently requires to be spread over these periods in the case of a divisional movement. The average time taken to transport a single unit from the Western to the Eastern Theatre is 106 hours. From East to West the average time is 127 hours, the additional time being taken up by the disinfection of the troops on reaching the German frontier at special disinfecting stations (*Entläusungs-Anstalten*).

13. **Breakdown arrangements.**—Detailed arrangements exist for dealing with breakdowns. Breakdown trains are stationed at fixed intervals. Each carriage has allotted to it certain stretches of line, on which it will deal with all breakdowns. Breakdown trains only move when wired for, and are then given priority on all lines. The following list shows the position of the 19 carriages in the zone of the Military Railway Directorate at Lille (M.E.D.I.):—

Ghent (St. Pierre), Ostend, Orchies, Somain, Ledeberg, Courtrai, Ath, St. Ghislain, Meirelbeke (two), Lille (three), Tourcoing, Cambrai, Bruges, Tournai, Valenciennes (two).

14. **Light railway construction.**—Light railway (*Feldbahn*) construction has only been carried out in the zone of operations within 20 miles of the front.

Within this zone a complete network has been built up, based on the pre-war metre gauge system. On quiet fronts, the enemy has usually aimed at two lines of supply, either metre or normal gauge, per division in line. To these lines of supply have been added many transverse lines and branches to points of importance.

A feature of the light railway construction since midsummer, 1917, has been the tendency of the enemy to break bulk farther from the front. The transfer points of freight from normal to narrow gauge have been established at places averaging 16 miles from the front, as compared with a previous average of 5 to 6 miles.

It is of interest to note that the 60 cm. gauge system has not been adopted by the enemy to any extent, most of the light railway system being metre gauge. The 60 cm. gauge is only employed in the very forward areas, and usually in the form of trench tramways.

## B. The Mechanical Transport Service.

1. **General organization.**—In peace, the mechanical transport and the air service were jointly under the control of the Inspector of Military Aircraft and Mechanical Transport Services, but these services have been completely separated during the war, and the mechanical transport troops (*Krajtfahrtruppen*) were reorganized in December, 1916, and have now a separate inspectorate (*Inspektion des Kraftfahrwesens*), under the Inspector-General of Military Communications.

The command in the field is exercised by the Director of Mechanical Transport (*Chef des Feldkraftfahrwesens* or *Feldkraftfahrchef*), who holds the rank of a brigade commander, and is directly under the orders of the Quartermaster-General. The Director of Mechanical Transport controls all mechanical transport services in Germany, on the lines of communication and in the field. He also has the General Headquarters Mechanical Transport Park directly under his orders.

The uniform of the mechanical transport troops is similar to that of the railway troops, except that the letter " K " is worn on the shoulder straps instead of " E." Car drivers and motor cyclists wear a bronze collar-badge representing a car or motor cycle.

The shortage of rubber and petrol has considerably restricted the employment of mechanical transport by the Germans during the war. As a rule, it is employed only where the railway service is either insufficient or overstrained.

## 2. Organization in the field.—At the headquarters of each Army in the field there is a Commander of the Mechanical Transport Troops (*Kommandeur der Kraftfahrtruppen* or *K. d. K.*) holding the rank of an independent battalion commander, with a staff of 5 officers and 27 other ranks. Each Army has a mechanical transport park (*Armee-Kraftwagenpark*), a pool of cars and lorries (*Kraftwagen-Staffel*), a motor cyclist detachment (*Kraftradfahrer-Abteilung*), a postal lorry park (*Post-Kraftwagen-Park*), a motor ambulance convoy (*Sanitäts-Kraftwagenabteilung*), and an Army artillery tractor park (*Armee-Fussartillerie-Kraftzug-Park*).

## 3. Mechanical transport columns.—Attached to each Army is a varying number of lorry columns (*Armee-Kraftwagenkolonnen*, or *A.K.K.*). At the Lines of Communication Main Depôt of each Army in the field there is a mechanical transport park (*Etappen-Kraftwagenpark*), with a varying number of Lines of Communication mechanical transport columns (*Etappen-Kraftwagen-Kolonnen*).

Earlier in the war mechanical transport columns were allotted to Corps, but in 1916 these were split up and converted into divisional units. A Divisional Mechanical Transport Column (*Divisions-Kraftwagen-Kolonne*, or *D.K.K.*), consisting of from 6 to 12 lorries, is allotted permanently to each division. These units are numbered in regular series as follows :—

| | | |
|---|---|---|
| 500 and upwards | .. | with units in Palestine and Syria. |
| 530    ,, | .. | ,, Prussian, Saxon and Württemberg Active divisions. |
| 680    ,, | .. | ,, Bavarian Active divisions. |
| 700    ,, | .. | ,, Prussian, Saxon and Württemberg Reserve divisions. |
| 750    ,, | .. | ,, Bavarian Reserve divisions. |
| 760    ,, | .. | ,, Ersatz divisions. |
| 770    ,, | .. | ., Landwehr divisions. |

# DIAGRAM SHOWING THE LINES OF COMMUNICATION OF AN ARMY.

Supplementary Mag.ne
(Ersatz-Magazin)

Home base
(Etappen-Anfangs-Ort.)

Collecting Station
(Sammel Station)

Supplementary
Magazine.

Home base.

Military Railway
Directorate
(Mil.Eis.Dir.)

Frontier

Weigh-transshipping-station
or
Umschlage-stelle

Trains and Barges taking up
Supplies and Ammunition and
bringing back Sick & Wounded.

HOME TERRITORY
(Heimats-Gebiet)

Area under Government of a
Governor General.
(General Gouvernement.)

INVADED COUNTRY.

Broad Gauge Railway.
Light Railway (60-cm.)
Road.

L. of C. Main depot
(Etappen-Haupt-Ort)

L. of C. Main depot.
L. of C. Etappen.

Railhead.

Railhead
(Ausgabe-Stelle.)

Railhead.

Railhead.

Railhead.

| L. of C. MAIN DEPOT. |
|---|
| L.of C. Inspector. |
| " Commandant. |
| " Magazine. |
| " Am.n Depot. |
| " Hospital. |
| " Amb: Convoy. |
| " Medical Depot. |
| " M.T. Park. |

Area of Communications.
(Etappen-Gebiet.)

Area of Operations.
(Operations-Gebiet.)

Div.
Div.
Div.
Div.
Div.
Div.
Div.
Div.

HARRISON & SONS, LTH ST.MARTIN'S LANE, W.C.

# CHAPTER XIV.

## INTENDANCE AND SUPPLY.

1. **General organization.**—The supply of the German Armies in the field is carried out mainly through the agency of a semi-civilian branch known as the Intendance (*Intendantur*). The Intendance is controlled by the Army Administration Department of the War Ministry (*see* page 37), and the personnel is composed principally of military officials (*see* page 40).

The entire supply service of the German Army is under the Intendant-General (*General-Intendant des Feldheeres*), who is directly subordinate to the Quartermaster-General (*see* page 41.)

Each Army in the field has its own *Intendant*, and similarly there is a *Korps-Intendant* with each Corps Headquarters to control the supply arrangements. At each divisional headquarters there is a *Feldintendantur*, or administrative staff, which controls the divisional supply office (*Feld-Proviantamt*).

In Germany, the administrative work in each Army Corps District is carried out by a "deputy-intendant" (*stellvertretender Intendant*).

2. **Organization in the field.**—The Army Intendant has to ensure supplies reaching the troops and the resources of the country being utilized to the full ; he is responsible for money contributions and for magazines being established and filled. He is under the direct orders of the Chief of Staff of the Army, but under the Intendant-General for administration and accounts.

The Corps Intendant is responsible for the supply of his Corps, whether it is derived from local sources or from the Lines of Communication. He is responsible for the administration of all supply units in his Corps, such as supply columns and parks, field bakeries, &c. Under him are the field Intendance and field pay, supply and bakery offices.

At the headquarters of each infantry regiment there is a transport officer (*Bagage-Führer*), who is responsible for the regimental transport, and in each battalion there is a supply officer (*Verpflegungs-Offizier*) who is responsible for drawing and issuing rations. These officers carry out the arrangements made by the *Feldintendantur* as regards supply and transport.

Each infantry battalion has a paymaster (*Zahlmeister*), who is responsible to the *Feldintendantur* as regards the pay of the unit.

A Main Depôt (*Etappen-Haupt-Ort*) is established in the Lines of Communication area of each Army in the field, usually at a central railway junction, *e.g.*, Ghent, Ath, Maubeuge, Hirson.

Each Corps and divisional headquarters has a field supply office (*Feld-Proviant-Amt*), situated at the Corps or divisional railhead (*Ausgabestelle*), and draws its supplies and ammunition direct from the Lines of Communication Main Depôt of its Army.

3. **The Train.**—All the personnel of medical and supply units, except the trained medical, veterinary and mechanical transport personnel, is found by the Train. The Train corresponds to our Army Service Corps only in so far as it provides the personnel, horses and vehicles of transport and supply units.*

---

* The Train also provides personnel, horses and vehicles for regimental transport, bridging trains, &c.

Ammunition, supply, transport and bakery columns, as well as bridging trains, originally formed part of the divisional and Corps trains. These units were grouped in echelons (*Staffeln*), two to each division and one to each Corps. Each echelon had a permanent staff (*Staffelsbab*), which supervised the working of the columns. An echelon staff consisted of 5 officers and 15 other ranks.

Owing to the difficulty involved in moving so many administrative units when divisions and Corps were relieved, the supply service was completely reorganized at the beginning of 1916. The use of mechanical transport was largely extended, a number of Army M.T. columns being allotted to each Army, and one divisional M.T. column being allotted to each division. Army M.T. columns are allotted temporarily to Corps staffs as required. The divisional M.T. column is now the only transport unit which forms part of the divisional organization and moves with its division.

4. **Echelon staffs.**—All the horsed ammunition, transport and supply columns are now sector units, which are grouped under echelon staffs and allotted permanently to areas, at the rate of one echelon staff to each divisional sector and one to each Corps Headquarters. An echelon staff allotted to a divisional sector normally administers:—

> 2 light artillery ammunition columns (*l. Mun. Kol.*).
> 2 new pattern artillery ammunition columns (*Mun. Kol. n/A.*).
> 1 supply column (*Proviant-Kolonne*).
> 1 supply park (*Fuhrpark-Kolonne*).
> 1 field bakery column (*Feldbäckerei-Kolonne*).
> 1 divisional bridging train (*Div.-Brücken-Train*).

The echelon staffs attached to Corps Headquarters are similarly constituted, and each usually administers in addition a field hospital, a veterinary hospital and a field slaughtery.

The echelon staffs, and the train units which they administer, are now largely employed in exploiting the economic and agricultural resources of the occupied territories, and in administrating the civilian population in the forward zone. Each inhabited village forms an *Ortskommandantur*, administered by a town major (*Ortskommandant*), who is usually an officer temporarily appointed from one of the echelon staffs. Under the orders of the echelon staffs are placed the cart-horse columns (*Landespferdekolonnen*), economic companies (*Wirtschaftskompagnien*) and harvesting companies (*Erntekompagnien*) which may be allotted from time to time for agricultural purposes.

In addition to Corps and divisional train echelons, the Train forms a number of supply and transport units on the Lines of Communication, namely:—

> Depôt supply parks (*Magazin-Fuhrpark-Kolonnen*).
> Lines of Communication supply parks (*Etappen-Fuhrpark-Kolonnen*).
> Lines of Communication auxiliary bakeries (*Etappen-Hilfsbäckerei-Kolonnen*).
> Lines of Communication medical depôts (*Etappen-Sanitäts-Depots*).
> Lines of Communication remount depôts (*Etappen-Pferde-Depots*).

The *Feldintendanturen* of divisions and Corps draw their supplies direct from these Lines of Communication depôts during trench warfare.

5. **Depôt supply parks.**—The depôt supply parks (*Magazin-Fuhrpark-Kolonnen*) of the German Army constitute part of the Lines of Communication Train. They are under the orders of the *Kommandeur der Etappentrains*, who is himself directly under the orders of the Army *Etappen-Inspektion*.

*Magazin-Fuhrpark-Kolonnen* are auxiliary parks provided by the *Kriegs-Etappen-Ordnung* for special duties, such as the establishment of dumps intermediate between the Lines of Communication dumps and those of the front line, for the temporary reinforcement of the Lines of Communication supply parks and so forth.

Examination of prisoners has shown that the parks still perform these functions to some extent, but on the Eastern Front they also appear to be employed on the agricultural and forestry work in occupied territory.

In accordance with the establishment laid down by the *Kriegs-Etappen-Ordnung*, each park is allotted 60 lorries, and the personnel is provided by the *Feldtrain-Kompagnien*.

*Magazin-Fuhrpark-Kolonnen* constitute a single series, including Bavarian, Saxon and Württemberg parks. The series is numbered from 1 upwards, the highest number identified being 861. It is certain, however, that many gaps exist in the series, owing to the fact that a number of parks, for which the scheme in its entirety provided, were never formed, and also because many of those numbered from 1–100 have been renumbered in the series over 400.

It may be assumed that the minimum number of *Magazin-Fuhrpark-Kolonnen* in existence is about 200. Most of them are attached to the *Etappen-Inspektionen*, though a few have been attached, at least temporarily, to Corps or divisions.

6. **Rations.**—(*a.*) **Rations carried.**—The supplies carried with the troops consist of the field service ration (*Kriegsportion*) and the iron ration (*eiserner Bestand*). The numbers carried and their composition according to the peace establishment are shown in the following tables:—

| | On the man or horse. | In regimental supply wagons. | | In travelling kitchens. | In supply columns and parks. |
|---|---|---|---|---|---|
| | Iron ration. | Iron ration. | Field service ration. | Iron ration. | |
| **Cavalry—** | | | | | |
| Rations | 1 | 1 | 2* | .. | ⎫ |
| Forage | ½ | 3† | 1½‡ | .. | |
| **Infantry—** | | | | | |
| Rations | 2 | .. | 2* | 1 | |
| Forage | 1 | 3§ | 2 | .. | |
| **Horse Artillery—** | | | | | |
| Rations | .. | 3 | 2* | .. | Five days' rations and three days' forage for Corps and half cavalry division. |
| Forage | 1½ | 1½ | 3‖ | .. | |
| **Field Artillery—** | | | | | |
| Rations | .. | 3 | 2* | .. | |
| Forage | 2 | 2 | 3¶ | .. | |
| **Foot Artillery—** | | | | | |
| Rations | .. | 3 | 2* | .. | |
| Forage | 2 | 2 | .. | .. | |
| **Pioneers—** | | | | | |
| Rations | .. | 3 | .. | .. | |
| Forage | 1 | 3 | 2* | .. | ⎭ |

\* Cut down to one day's rations after the first day's march. Three days' extra groceries are also carried.
† For draught horses.
‡ Two days' for officers' horses only.
§ For riding horses on the horse and for draught horses in the wagon.
‖ For the wagon horses only.
¶ For the officers' horses only.

**(b.) Composition of rations prior to the war.**—At the beginning of the war the composition of the iron ration and field service ration was as follows :—

## Iron ration.—

| | | |
|---|---|---|
| 8·8 oz. biscuit | 250 | grammes. |
| 7·0 oz. preserved meat* | 200 | ,, |
| 5·3 oz. preserved vegetables | 150 | ,, |
| ·9 oz. coffee | 25 | ,, |
| ·9 oz. salt | 25 | ,, |
| 3·5 oz. packing | 100 | ,, |
| 26·4 | 750 | ,, |

## Iron forage ration.—

| | |
|---|---|
| Normal | 13¼ lbs. (6 kg.) oats. |
| Heavy draught horses | 26½ lbs. (19 kg.) oats. |

## Field service ration.—

| | | | |
|---|---|---|---|
| *Bread* | 26½ oz. bread *or* | 750 | grammes. |
| | 14 oz. egg biscuit *or* | 400 | ,, |
| | 17½ oz. field biscuit | 500 | ,, |
| *Meat* | 13 oz. fresh or frozen meat *or* | 375 | ,, |
| | 7 oz. preserved meat | 200 | ,, |
| *Vegetable* | 4½ to 9 oz. vegetables *or* | 125-250 | ,, |
| | 53 oz. potatoes *or* | 1,500 | ,, |
| | 2 oz. dried vegetables *or* | 60 | ,, |
| | a mixed ration of potatoes and dried vegetables | 600 | ,, |
| *Grocery* | 9/10 oz. coffee *or* | 25 | ,, |
| | 1/10 oz. tea | 3 | ,, |
| | 7/10 oz. sugar | 20 | ,, |
| | 9/10 oz. salt | 25 | ,, |

| Forage ration. | Hay. | Oats. | Straw. |
|---|---|---|---|
| Normal | 5½ lbs. (2·5 kg.) | 13¼ lbs. (6 kg.) | 3¼ lbs. (1·5 kg.) |
| Heavy draught horses | 16¼ lbs. (7·5 kg.) | 26¼ lbs. (12 kg.) | 6½ lbs. (3 kg.) |

**(c) Present composition of rations.**—*Meat ration.*—The daily fresh meat ration has undergone a considerable reduction, namely, from 350 g. (12¼ oz.) in December, 1915, to 288 g. (10¼ oz.) at the end of June, 1916. Further, one meatless day per week was introduced in June, 1916. According to a statement laid before the Reichstag in October, 1916, the fresh meat ration at that time had been still further reduced, viz., to 250 g. (8¾ oz.).

\* Or 6 oz. bacon.

The preserved meat ration was reduced during the same period from 200 g. (7 oz.) to 150 g. (5¼ oz.).

The above amounts are issued to the fighting troops, the fresh meat ration of staffs, columns and trains being only 200 g. (7 oz.) at the end of June, 1916.

*Bread ration.*—The normal daily ration for fighting and other troops is still 750 g. (1 lb. 10½ oz.), though this may be increased when the troops are undergoing unusual exertions. This is normal to peace conditions.

*Vegetable and grocery rations.*—In October, 1916, the daily vegetable ration consisted of 1,500 g. (3⅓ lb.) of potatoes or 250 g. (8¾ oz.) of beans, peas, &c.

Groceries at this date included—

| | |
|---|---|
| Coffee | 25 g. (·88 oz.) |
|   or | |
| Tea.. | 3 g. (·1 oz.) |
| Sugar | 17 g. (·6 oz.) |
| | (formerly 20 g.) |
| Butter | 65 g. (2·3 oz.) |

*Drink ration.*—The troops are provided with mineral water by the Intendance. Commanders may order a daily issue of—

·17 pint: brandy, rum or arrack,
·44 pint: wine,
·88 pint: beer,

when the medical officers consider such an issue desirable.

*Tobacco ration.*—The daily ration consists of—

Two cigars and two cigarettes, or
1 oz. of pipe tobacco, or
0·9 oz. of plug tobacco, or
0·2 oz. of snuff.

**7. Arrangements for feeding troops during a battle.**—Much stress is laid on the necessity for the troops taking several days' rations up with them into the line. The amounts considered necessary vary, but the general opinion is that 5 days' rations are the minimum; these need not necessarily be " iron rations."

In order to provide the troops with warm food, the Germans issued solidified alcohol with which food could be warmed up, or else took the food up in "food carriers"* and coffee cans. The latter method is, however, rarely applicable beyond the support trenches.

In addition to the rations carried by the troops, large ration depots, each containing several thousand rations, were formed close behind the positions; carrying parties brought these rations up into the trenches whenever pauses in the artillery fire permitted.

**8. Water supply.**—Generally speaking, most of the water in Northern France and Belgium is not fit for drinking purposes unless sterilized by boiling or other methods.

Soon after trench warfare became an established fact, the Germans organized local systems of water supply for the men in the trenches. As much use as possible was made

---

* Some of these "food carriers" are constructed on the principle of the "Thermos flask," and keep the food warm for several hours.

of existing systems, pipe lines being laid from existing waterworks, or branching off from existing mains. In other cases pipe lines were laid from wells, and pumps were installed; intermediate reservoirs were built, or the vats of breweries and sugar factories were employed as reservoirs. In some places new wells were sunk. The pipe lines were led into villages close behind the front or even into the support trenches.

These methods of supply sufficed until the battle of the Somme, when the pipe lines were soon cut by the heavy bombardment, and the water had to be carted or carried up to the trenches.

To meet these new conditions, the Germans established or took over existing mineral water factories behind the front, and stored large quantities of bottled mineral water in and close behind the line.

The men took two filled water-bottles with them into the trenches, or, in some cases, were issued with special large tin water-bottles.

# MEDICAL ARRANGEMENTS FOR THE "CAMBRAI" GROUP.

## EXPLANATION:

- ● Main Dressing Station.
- ⊞ Field Hospital (Casualty Clearing Station).
- ⊗ Sick and Wounded Collecting Post.
- 🚑 Motor Ambulance Convoy.
- ⊟·⊟ Bathing and delousing stations. Number dealt with daily shown in brackets.
- ⊳ Hospital field laundry.
- (⊞) Accommodation earmarked for field hospitals (casualty clearing stations) in the event of Cambrai being evacuated.
- ▣ Accommodation proposed for field hospitals of Divisions "P" and "Q" moving in.
- DA Skin disease stations.

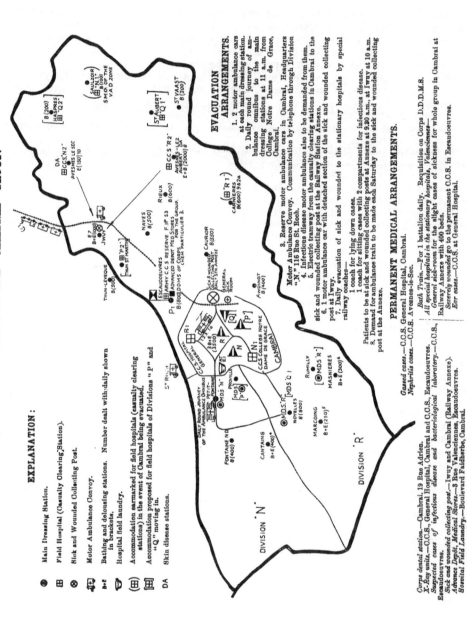

## EVACUATION ARRANGEMENTS.

1. 2 motor ambulance cars at each main dressing station.

2. Daily round journey of ambulance omnibus to the main dressing stations at 11 a.m. from College Notre Dame de Grace, Cambrai.

3. Reserve motor ambulance cars in Cambrai. Headquarters Motor Ambulance Convoy. Communication by telephone through Division "N." 116 Rue St. Roch.

4. Infectious disease motor ambulance also to be demanded from them.

5. Electric tramway from the casualty clearing stations in Cambrai to the sick and wounded collecting post at the Railway Station Annexe.

6. 1 motor ambulance car with detached section of the sick and wounded collecting post at Iwuy.

7. Daily evacuation of sick and wounded to the stationary hospitals by special railway coaches—
1 coach for lying down cases.
1 coach for sitting cases with 2 compartments for infectious disease.

Patients to be at sick and wounded collecting posts at Annexe at 9.30 a.m., at Iwuy at 10 a.m.

8. Demand for ambulance train to be made each Saturday to the sick and wounded collecting post at the Annexe.

## PERMANENT MEDICAL ARRANGEMENTS.

*Gassed cases.*—C.C.S. General Hospital, Cambrai.
*Nephritis cases.*—C.C.S. Avesnes-le-Sec.

*Bath Train.*—For 1 battalion daily. Requisition on Corps L.D.D.M.S.
*All special hospitals in the stationary hospitals, Valenciennes.*
*General sick-room for the slight cases of sickness for whole group in Cambrai at Railway Annexe with 400 beds.*
*Severely wounded* go to the permanent O.O.S. in Escaudoeuvres.
*Ear cases.*—C.C.S. at General Hospital.

*Corps dental station.*—Cambrai, 19 Rue Adrien.
*X-Ray units.*—C.C.S., General Hospital, Cambrai and C.C.S., Escaudoeuvres.
*Suspected cases of infectious disease and bacteriological laboratory.*—C.C.S., Escaudoeuvres.
*Sick and wounded collecting post.*—Iwuy and Cambrai (Railway Annexe).
*Advance Depôt, Medical Stores.*—3 Rue Valenciennes, Escaudoeuvres.
*Hospital Field Laundry.*—Boulevard Faidherbe, Cambrai.

*Consulting Surgeon.*—Stabsarzt. (Reserve) Prof, Dr, Raum, Escaudoeuvres. Telephone, Local Exchange.

# CHAPTER XV.

## MEDICAL AND VETERINARY SERVICES.

1. **General organization of the Medical Service.**—The Army Medical Service consists of the corps of medical officers (*Sanitäts-Offizier-Korps*); the medical rank and file consists of the *Sanitätsmannschaft*, forming the medical units in the field, and the *Militär-krankenwärter* or hospital orderlies. In addition to the above there is the regular establishment of regimental stretcher bearers (*Krankenträger*).

The medical service of the Field Army is under a Director-General (*Chef des Feld-sanitätswesens*). He is attached to General Headquarters and controls the medical service in the theatre of operations and on the Lines of Communication. With the Headquarters of each Army in the field there is a Director of Medical Services (*Armee-Arzt*) with the rank of *Obergeneralarzt*. Each Corps has a *Generalarzt* as Deputy Director of Medical Services (*Korpsarzt*). At the Headquarters of each Corps there is a consulting civil surgeon (*beratender Chirurg*). Each division has a *Divisionsarzt* as Assistant Director of Medical Services. For the grades of medical officers, *see* page 22.

2. **Medical organization in the field.**—The German medical organization for battle comprises the following échelons from the firing line to the back areas :—Regimental Medical Service; Bearer Companies (Field Ambulances); Field Hospitals; Motor Ambulance Convoy or Column; War Hospitals; Ambulance Trains and Temporary Ambulance Trains; Advanced Depôts of Medical Stores. (*See* diagram showing medical arrangements in force for the "Cambrai" Group during the fighting in September, 1917.)

3. **Regimental medical service.**—Normally there are with each battalion two medical officers, four medical non-commissioned officers (one with each company), and 16 stretcher bearers, with a senior medical officer for the regiment. At the end of May, 1916, a fifth medical non-commissioned officer was added to each battalion. The stretcher bearers are borne on the establishments as non-combatants and wear the Red Cross brassard.

In the trenches each company formed a medical dug-out or aid post just behind the fire trench, but owing to the large number of casualties amongst the medical officers, it was considered inadvisable to let the battalion medical officers go forward to the fire trench.

A large regimental aid post or dressing station (*Truppenverbandplatz*) is established further back, usually in or near the second support trench, and accommodated in well constructed dug-outs or in cellars. The dug-outs are constructed to hold 30 wounded. A telephone is provided, and supplies of lighting materials, extra rations, dressings and medical comforts to cover periods of five days or more are maintained in the aid post.

Similar aid posts are formed for groups of three or four batteries of artillery, if the latter are not too far apart.

The personnel on duty in a regimental aid post normally consists of three battalion medical officers, and a detachment of eight stretcher bearers with two stretchers from the bearer company. Wounded are brought to the regimental aid post by the battalion stretcher bearers, and are kept there as short a time as possible, being evacuated by the bearer company.

In back areas the regimental medical service opens a local medical inspection room and ward for detained cases (*Ortskrankenstube*), where patients may be kept up to five days.

4. **The bearer company** (*Sanitätskompagnie*) or field ambulance consists of elements equivalent to the bearer division and the tent division of our field ambulance. A bearer company is commanded by an *Oberstabsarzt*. There are 208 stretcher bearers in two sections, with non-commissioned officers and other ranks under officers who are not medical officers, and with a medical officer (*Stabsarzt*) in medical charge of the sections ; and there is also a main dressing station detachment of eight medical officers including the senior medical officer in command.

One of these companies forms part of each division. During the battle of the Somme this was not found sufficient, and there was a demand for two bearer companies for a division in the fighting line. The bearers of the one company became exhausted, and it was necessary to establish a relief company to cope with the work of collecting and bringing back wounded. An additional number of independent bearer companies was formed in 1917, in order to reinforce particular divisional sectors during a battle.

The posts established in action by the bearer company were :—

(*a*.) A wagon rendezvous ( *Wagenhalteplatz*).
(*b*.) A main dressing station (*Hauptverbandplatz*).
(*c*.) A collecting station for slightly wounded (*Leichtverwundeten-Sammelplatz*).

(*a*.) *The wagon rendezvous* is placed in advance of the main dressing station and about 4,000 yards behind the regimental aid post. Dug-outs are constructed at this post, and arrangements are made for giving hot food and drinks to wounded coming back. A dump for issue of medical and surgical material to the regimental medical service has also to be maintained by the bearer company at or near the wagon rendezvous. The post is provided with a telephone. The personnel consists of a small detachment of the stretcher bearers under a non-commissioned officer, and a medical officer is placed on duty there from time to time by order of the divisional Assistant Director of Medical Services. One or more of the ambulance wagons of the company are kept constantly at the wagon rendezvous, and go forward at night to meet the bearers bringing back wounded. The wagon rendezvous performs much the same function as our advanced dressing station.

(*b*.) *The main dressing station* is established in a shell-proof shelter in some village 6 or 7 miles from the front line. The personnel may be reinforced from the regimental medical services or from field hospitals ; but it is not to be used for reinforcing or replacing medical officers of either of these échelons. All wounded coming back from the regimental medical service must pass through this post. Two or more motor ambulance cars are allotted to it, and one motor omnibus.

The walking cases are sent back to the main dressing station, after being collected at the wagon rendezvous, in small groups and in march formation.

Every wounded man must have two diagnosis tallies (field medical cards) attached. These tallies have two red perforated margins. If a man is able to walk (*marschfähig*), both margins are torn off : if classed as fit for transport (*transportfähig*), one margin is torn off ; if unfit for transport (*nicht transportfähig*), the card is left intact. A man coming back to the main dressing station or wagon rendezvous without a field medical card, or without authority, is sent back to his unit, unless he is found to be suffering from sickness or wound, in which case the card is attached at the main dressing station and the unit informed. This procedure is adopted to prevent men straggling back from the front who have nothing the matter with them.

Amongst the special equipment attached to one of the main dressing stations in a Corps area is a water sterilizing wagon.

(*c.*) *The collecting station for slightly wounded* is established further back, at or near an entraining station. The walking cases are sent on from the main dressing station, either in march formation or in the motor omnibus or other vehicles.

**5. Field hospitals** (*Feldlazarette*), originally 12 per Corps, are now allotted on the scale of 2 per division and 2 per Corps staff. They are used, in the same way as we use casualty clearing stations, 'for the retention of cases unfit for transport and for special cases. The number of medical officers in each is six. Normally equipped for 200 beds, they are expected to expand to any extent. They are opened in various villages in the back area.

Field hospitals are organized during a battle to deal with special cases, advanced operating centres being arranged near the main dressing stations. There are also special field hospitals allotted for severely wounded, special surgical cases, Röntgen ray examination, dental cases, gassed cases and infectious cases. These field hospitals are army troops and remain semi-permanently in sectors.

**6. Motor ambulance convoys** (*Sanitäts-Kraftwagen-Kolonnen*).—The composition of these has not been definitely ascertained. There was no war establishment laid down for them before the war. They appear to be a collection of motor ambulance cars and omnibuses, parked under an officer at some village or locality in telephonic communication with medical units, and used for the conveyance of sick and wounded from the main dressing station to the entraining station or to field hospitals on demand.

One of these motor ambulance convoys is allotted to each Group (Corps).

**7. The ambulance convoy detachment** (*Sanitäts-Kraftragenabteilung*) is a definite unit, divisible into three sections and allotted in the proportion of one to each Army. Its personnel consists of seven medical officers with subordinate ranks, and its function is to open reception shelters, dressing stations and refreshment rooms at stations where sick and wounded entrain, and take care of them while awaiting evacuation by railway. It is also a distributing centre for classifying patients for evacuation to various field hospitals or war hospitals, opened for the reception of special cases in the villages in Army and advanced Lines of Communication areas. It makes arrangements for the comfort of sick and wounded during the journey back, and, with the special equipment held for the purpose in advanced depôts of medical stores, fits out empty returning trains as temporary ambulance trains.

**8. War hospitals** (*Kriegslazarette*) are used in much the same way as we use stationary hospitals in advanced areas. The number is not fixed and depends on localities available for opening them. Their equipment and personnel are obtained, as required, to a great extent from local resources or depôts of medical stores; but there is a nucleus of the personnel in the form of a definite unit called the War Hospital Detachment (*Kriegslazarettabteilung*), mobilized in the proportion of one for each Corps. Each detachment has 19 medical officers, a dentist, three pharmacists, and subordinate ranks. These units are now Lines of Communication troops. They are intended for the more or less continuous treatment of special classes of wounds and injuries, which are not sent back to Germany. Hospitals for infectious diseases (*Seuchen-Lazarette*) are also organized.

The unit is used for the same purpose as we use the evacuation section of our casualty clearing stations.

9. **Ambulance trains** (*Lazarettzüge*).—Ambulance trains normally run to within 10 or 15 miles of the front line. Both slightly and severely wounded are also sent back on narrow-gauge railways.

10. **Advanced depôts of medical stores** (*Gruppen-Sanitäts-Speicher*).—These are allotted to Corps sectors, and are usually situated near Corps Headquarters. The divisional bearer companies are responsible for bringing up stores to a dump for issue to regimental medical services. The advanced depôts refill from the Lines of Communication medical depôts (*Etappen-Sanitäts-Depots*).

11. **The Veterinary Service.**—The Army Veterinary Service consists of the corps of veterinary officers (*Veterinär-Offizier-Korps*) and sub-veterinary surgeons (*Unter-veterinäre*). Like medical officers, veterinary officers are assimilated in grade to combatant officers, but have no combatant rank. For the grades of veterinary officers, *see* page 22.

The Army Veterinary Service is under a Director-General (*Generalveterinär*). Under him are three principal veterinary officers (*Chefveterinäre*) in the Western, Eastern and South-Eastern Theatres.

The *Korpsveterinär* is the veterinary adviser of the Corps commander, and is responsible for all veterinary services throughout the Corps.

Each division has a veterinary hospital (*Pferde-Lazarett*) which is administered by the *Divisionsveterinär*, and corresponds to our mobile veterinary section.

With each cavalry or field artillery regiment there is a *Regimentsveterinär*, and the lower ranks of veterinary officers (*Oberveterinär* and *Veterinär*) are attached to cavalry squadrons and field artillery *Abteilungen*. According to the peace establishment, three veterinary officers are attached to each cavalry and field artillery regiment.

Besides the divisional veterinary hospitals there are also veterinary hospitals controlled by Corps and Armies, and the Lines of Communication remount depôts (*Etappen-Pferde-Depots*).

# CHAPTER XVI.

## LANDSTURM UNITS.

1. **General organization.**—All men between the ages of 17 and 45 who have not been found fit for war service, and who have not been specially exempted from military service, are incorporated in Landsturm units.

Landsturm units are sub-divided into—

(a.) Armed Landsturm (*mit Waffen*).
(b.) Unarmed Landsturm (*ohne Waffen*).

The Armed Landsturm consists of the men passed as " fit for garrison duty " (*Garnison-dienstfähige*); the Unarmed Landsturm consists of those passed as " fit for labour employment " (*Arbeitsverwendungsfähige*).

Every man in the Landsturm, Armed or Unarmed, is liable at any time to be re-examined ; if considered " fit for war service" (*Kriegsverwendungsfähig*), he is sent to the depôt of a field unit, and eventually takes his place in the ranks as a fighting man, though still retaining the designation *Landsturmmann*.

2. **Organization of the Armed Landsturm.**—The Armed Landsturm is organized in battalions, squadrons, batteries and pioneer companies.

The total number of Landsturm units identified up to the end of 1917 was as follows :—

| | |
|---|---:|
| Infantry battalions | 942 |
| Cavalry squadrons | 104 |
| Field artillery batteries | 35 |
| Foot artillery batteries | 75 |
| Pioneer companies (including pioneer park companies) | 136 |

Of the 942 Landsturm infantry battalions, about 120 have been grouped to form 40 Landsturm infantry regiments, which are mostly employed on the Russian Front.

The greater part of the Armed Landsturm is organized in independent battalions. These battalions are designated by a serial number in each Army Corps District ; thus, "Landsturm Infantry Battalion VIII/10" means the 10th Landsturm Infantry Battalion raised in the VIII Army Corps District. Landsturm battalions have also a subsidiary title dependent on their town of origin ; thus : " Landsturm Infantry Battalion VIII/10 " is also known as the " 2nd Landsturm lnfantry Battalion, Coblenz."

3. **Employment of the Armed Landsturm.**—A certain number of Landsturm battalions, principally those which have been incorporated in regiments, have been

employed in front line, but this procedure is still comparatively rare.   Landsturm units only appear in front line on the Eastern Front, or in quiet sectors of the Western Front such as Lorraine or the Vosges.   The employment of Landsturm units in front line will, however, probably increase.   There is a tendency to employ them in front line in quiet sectors, in order to liberate Active formations for employment elsewhere.

In general, the battalions of Armed Landsturm are employed as—

(*a.*) Garrisons of the coast defences.
(*b.*) Guards for neutral frontiers.
(*c.*) Garrisons of inland fortresses.
(*d.*) Guards for the Lines of Communication
(*e.*) Guards for prisoners of war.
(*f.*) Garrisons of the occupied territories.
(*g.*) Landsturm depôt and training battalions.

(*a.*) **Garrisons of the coast defences.**—The coast defences, which used to be almost entirely in the hands of the Admiralty, were in 1916 placed under an independent military commander.

In addition to naval units, the troops allotted to the coast defences consist of 50 battalions of Armed Landsturm belonging to the Army Corps Districts adjoining the coast (X., IX., II., XVII. and I.).   These battalions are distributed as follows :—

*North Sea* (20 battalions).

8 battalions (X.) defending the Frisian Islands, mainly at Borkum and Norderney.
4 battalions (IX.) defending the estuary of the Weser.
8 battalions (IX.) defending the west coast of Schleswig, mainly at Sylt.

*Baltic* (30 battalions).

12 battalions (IX.) defending the east coast of Schleswig, mainly at Alsen, Kiel and Lübeck.
10 battalions (II.) defending Stettin and the Island of Rügen.
 4 battalions (XVII.) at Danzig.
 4 battalions (I.) at Königsberg and Labiau.

(*b.*) **Guards for neutral frontiers.**—The troops allotted to guard the German land frontiers consist of about 40 Landsturm battalions.   The majority of these are concentrated on the Dutch and Swiss frontiers; only a few are on the Danish frontier.

(*c.*) **Garrisons of inland fortresses.**—The fortress garrisons consist of 20 garrison battalions drawn from the Armed Landsturm.

They exist at Posen, Breslau, Strassburg, Graudenz, Lötzen, Marienburg, Soldau, Ingolstadt and Regensburg.

(*d.*) **Guards for the Lines of Communication.**—About 12 Landsturm battalions are employed on the Lines of Communication Inspectorate (*Etappen-Inspektion*) allotted to each Army.

In all, about 200 Landsturm infantry battalions are employed in this way.

(*e.*) **Guards for prisoners of war.**—There are about 150 prisoners of war battalions (*Kriegsgefangenen-Arbeiter-Bataillone*). each consisting of about 2,000 prisoners of war guarded by 150 to 200 men of the Armed Landsturm.

(*f.*) **Garrisons of the occupied territories.**—The Military Governments (*General-Gouvernements*) in Poland, Belgium, Serbia and Roumania are safeguarded by permanent garrisons of Armed Landsturm battalions, as well as by the field units resting in the different areas.

In Belgium there are 90 Landsturm battalions forming the permanent garrison, and in Poland 40 battalions.

The Belgian garrison is distributed in groups of 5 to 12 battalions at the main railway junctions, such as Liége, Antwerp, Brussels, Namur and Ghent. The remaining battalions are distributed singly or in pairs along the main railway lines and along the Dutch frontier, which is also guarded by a number of Landsturm squadrons.

In addition to the ordinary Landsturm infantry battalions, there are a few permanent garrison battalions stationed at certain places such as Antwerp, Bruges, Brussels, Charleroi, Ghent, Hasselt, Liége, Luxemburg, Malines, Maubeuge, Namur, Soignies, St. Quentin and Tournai.

(*g.*) **Landsturm depôt and training battalions.**—Among the series of Landsturm infantry battalions formed in each Army Corps District are a certain number of *Landsturm Infanterie-Ersatz-Bataillone.* These units serve as depôt battalions: there is approximately one Landsturm depôt (*Ersatz*) battalion for every four Landsturm infantry battalions.

To these depôt battalions are sent all untrained Landsturm men and those rejected as unfit for service at the front, The men in these battalions are employed on light garrison duty in Germany, and are subjected to frequent medical examinations. Whenever they are considered fit for more active work, the men are drafted to Landsturm infantry battalions.

Of a similar nature are the training battalions (*Landsturm Infanterie-Ausbildungs-Bataillone*), of which there are one to three in each Army Corps District. These units, which assist in training men of the untrained Landsturm, are mainly composed of men of an inferior type to those incorporated in the depôt battalions.

4. **The Unarmed Landsturm.**—The Unarmed Landsturm is composed of the remaining men of the Landsturm category who are considered as "only fit for labour employment" (*Arbeitsverwendungsfähige*). This class is employed on various forms of labour, such as trench-construction, cultivation, road-making, forestry and harvesting.

The auxiliary units of this nature identified up to the end of 1917 were as follows:—

    220 Labour Battalions (*Armierungs-Bataillone*).
     60 Road Construction Companies (*Strassenbau-Kompagnien*).
     50 Lines of Communication Auxiliary Companies (*Etappen-Hilfs-Kompagnien*).
     30 Lines of Communication Collecting Companies (*Etappen-Sammel-Kompagnien*).
    150 Works Companies (*Wirtschafts-Kompagnien*).
     20 Harvesting Companies (*Ernte-Kompagnien*).

A certain number of skilled workers are incorporated in technical battalions (*Facharbeiter-Bataillone*).

# CHAPTER XVII.

## UNIFORM.

(*See* Plates 2 to 11, at end.)

1. **General.**—Before the war, the German Army possessed two different uniforms, one for parade and one for field service.

The field service uniform (*feldgraue Uniform*), which was introduced in 1910, is now the only pattern met with in the field, the old dark-blue uniform (*dunkelblaue Uniform*) being obsolete.

In 1915, a new field service uniform was introduced, comprising a tunic for wear in time of peace, and a jacket (*Bluse*) for wear on field service. A detailed description of the new field service uniform is given in Appendix A (page 156).

This new uniform had not been taken into general use at the beginning of 1918, although it had been issued to a certain number of units, principally artillery and engineer.

The colour of the field service uniform is "field-grey" (*feldgrau*) for all arms with the exception of the following units which wear a greener colour known as "grey-green" (*graugrün*) :—

(*a.*) All Prussian and Saxon *Jäger* battalions, but not Bavarian *Jäger* battalions.
(*b.*) The 108th *Schützen* Regiment and the Guard *Schützen* battalions.
(*c.*) *Jäger zu Pferde* regiments.
(*d.*) Machine gun units.
(*e.*) Staff orderlies.

2. **The field service tunic.**—All arms and units, except certain cavalry regiments, wear the single-breasted tunic (*Waffenrock*) with coloured facings, and eight dull metal buttons embossed with a crown (with a lion for Bavarian troops). The skirts at the back of the tunic are slashed and have six similar buttons. The tunic has side pockets closed by buttons.

The front of the tunic, as well as the skirt behind, is edged with scarlet piping (green for *Jäger* and *Schützen*).

The tunic has a stand and fall collar closed by a hook and eye. The collar is edged with coloured piping as follows :—

(*a.*) Scarlet for Infantry.
(*b.*) Green for *Jäger*.
(*c.*) Black for *Schützen*, Artillery, Pioneers, Air Service, Telegraph and Communication Troops.
(*d.*) Blue for Train.

The cuffs are either of the Brandenburg or Swedish pattern. The Brandenburg cuff has three buttons placed vertically; the Swedish cuff has two buttons placed horizontally The piping on the cuffs is of the same colour as that on the collar (*see* above).

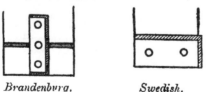

*Brandenburg.*          *Swedish.*

Guard and Grenadier units are distinguished by patches (*Litzen*) of white or yellow braid on collar and cuffs. The Brandenburg and Swedish cuffs have three and two *Litzen* respectively, one for each button.

The trousers (*Tuchhose*) worn by dismounted units are of the same colour as the field service tunic. *Jäger* units wear green piping down the seam, this piping being red in the case of all other units.

The pantaloons (*Reithose*) of mounted units are of field-grey cloth with red piping. *Jäger zu Pferde* regiments have green piping, and hussar regiments wear a braid stripe down the seam.

The wearing of puttees is sanctioned for aircraft units, assault battalions and mountain units.

The marching boot is a half-boot of the Wellington pattern.

3. **Shoulder straps of the field service tunic.**—The tunic is provided with field-grey (or grey-green) shoulder straps, which bear either the number or the monogram of the regiment worked in red (*see* Plate 2). Foot Guards and Horse Guards regiments have plain shoulder straps. Reserve, Landwehr and Ersatz regiments wear the same number on their shoulder straps as the corresponding Active regiment, but not the monogram.

The shoulder strap is fastened with a metal button which bears the number of the man's company, &c.

The shoulder strap is edged with piping,* the colour of which varies for different units as follows :—

*White piping.—*

1st, 3rd and 5th Foot Guards Regiments, and 1st and 5th Guard Grenadier Regiments.
Infantry regiments of the I., II., IX., X. and XII. Army Corps Districts and the 109th, 110th and 116th Infantry Regiments.
Field Artillery regiments of the I., II., IX., X. and XII. Army Corps Districts.
All Foot Artillery units (except Saxon).
All independent machine gun units.

*Scarlet piping—*

2nd Foot Guards Regiment and 2nd Guard Grenadier Regiment.
Infantry regiments of the III., IV., XIII., XV. and XIX. Army Corps Districts, and the 111th, 115th, 168th, 169th, 171st, 172nd Infantry Regiments and 2nd Bn. 89th Grenadier Regiment.
† 1st and 2nd Guard Field Artillery Regiments.
Field Artillery regiments of the III., IV., XI., XIII., XIV., XV. and XIX. Army Corps Districts and the 25th and 61st Field Artillery Regiments.
All Pioneer units.
Saxon Foot Artillery units.
All Bavarian units.

---

* In the field, shoulder straps without piping are frequently met with.
† The 1st Guard Field Artillery Regiment has also a narrow white piping inside the scarlet edging.

*Yellow piping—*

>3rd Guard Grenadier Regiment, Guard Fusilier Regiment.
>Infantry regiments of the V., VI., XVI. and XVII. Army Corps Districts, and the 112th, 118th and 142nd Infantry Regiments.
>3rd Guard Field Artillery Regiment.
>Field Artillery regiments of the V., VI., XVI. and XVII. Army Corps Districts.

*Blue piping—*

>4th Foot Guards Regiment and 4th Guard Grenadier Regiment.
>Infantry regiments of the VII., VIII., XVIII. and XX. Army Corps Districts, and the 40th, 113th, 145th and 170th Infantry Regiments.
>Field Artillery regiments of the VII., VIII., XVIII., and XX. Army Corps Districts.
>Train units.

*Green piping—*

>Infantry regiments of the XXI. Army Corps District, and the 114th Infantry Regiment.
>All *Jäger* battalions.
>Guard *Schützen* battalions.
>108th *Schützen* (Fusilier) Regiment.
>Field Artillery regiments of the XXI. Army Corps District

*Light grey piping—*

>Air Service, Telegraph and Communication Troops.

*　　*　　*　　*　　*

Prussian, Saxon and Württemberg field artillery units have a grenade, worked in red, above the number on the shoulder strap. In the case of field artillery units which wear a monogram instead of a number, the grenade is placed below the monogram.

Bavarian field artillery units do not wear a grenade on the shoulder strap.

*Minenwerfer* companies wear the letters "M.W." above the number of the company.

The following badges, worked in red above the shoulder strap number, are peculiar to Saxon units :—

| | |
|---|---|
| *Jäger* and *Schützen* | Hunting horn. |
| Foot Artillery | Grenade. |
| Pioneers | Crossed pick and shovel. |

The following special monograms or badges are worn on the shoulder strap by technical troops :—

Aeroplane units..

Airship and balloon units

| Railway troops | .. | .. | .. | .. | .. | .. | *E* |
| Telegraph and telephone units.. | | .. | .. | .. | .. | *T* |
| Mechanical transport troops | .. | .. | .. | .. | .. | *K* |

Experimental companies of pioneers and communication troops *V*

**4. Cavalry tunics.**—Cuirassier, Dragoon and *Jäger zu Pferde* regiments wear a tunic with a stand up collar (in place of the stand and fall collar worn by the infantry), Swedish pattern cuffs and coloured piping round the lower edge of the skirt. The colour of the piping on tunic and collar varies in different regiments. The collar and cuffs are also trimmed with braid (*Bortenbesatz*), the pattern of which varies for different regiments.

*Ulanen* and Bavarian *Chevaulegers* regiments wear a double-breasted lancer tunic (*Ulanka*), with two rows of seven buttons, a pointed cuff with one button, and a stand up collar. The seams of the back and sleeves are also edged with coloured piping (*see* Plate 3).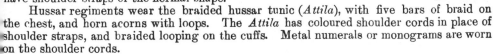

The shoulder straps of the *Ulanka* are rounded off at the corners, except in the case of the Saxon *Ulanen* regiments, 17, 18 and 21, which have shoulder straps of the normal shape.

Hussar regiments wear the braided hussar tunic (*Attila*), with five bars of braid on the chest, and horn acorns with loops. The *Attila* has coloured shoulder cords in place of shoulder straps, and braided looping on the cuffs. Metal numerals or monograms are worn on the shoulder cords.

**5. Head-dress.**—The black leather polished helmet, with metal spike, is worn by infantry, pioneers, train, and dragoon and *Chevaulegers* regiments. Artillery units wear a similar helmet with a ball instead of a spike, except in the case of Bavarian artillery units, which have a spiked helmet.

*Jäger* and *Schützen* battalions wear a black leather shako (*Tschako*).

*Ulanen* regiments wear a lance cap (*Tschapka*), and hussar regiments wear a busby (*Pelzmütze*).

Cuirassier regiments have a polished metal helmet with a spike (an eagle for Guard Cuirassiers), and *Jäger zu Pferde* wear a black polished metal helmet with spike.

In front of the head-dress is worn a metal plate which varies in design for the different States (*see* Plate 4).

In the field all the above forms of head-dress are provided with covers of field-grey cloth.

The number of the unit is sometimes stencilled in green on the helmet cover.

In addition to the various forms of head-dress described above, all arms wear a soft field service cap (*Feldmütze*), which usually replaces the helmet in the trenches. The cap is field-grey (grey-green) with coloured\* band and welt, the colours of which vary for the different arms as follows :—

| Arm of the service. | Cap band. | Welt. |
|---|---|---|
| Infantry .. .. .. .. .. .. .. .. | Scarlet | Scarlet. |
| *Jäger* .. .. .. .. .. .. .. .. | Green | Green. |
| *Schützen* .. .. .. .. .. .. .. .. | Black with green edging | Green. |
| Artillery, Engineers, Air Service and Communication Troops | Black with scarlet edging | Scarlet. |
| Train .. .. .. .. .. .. .. .. | Light blue | Light blue |
| Cavalry .. .. .. .. .. .. .. .. | Various | Various. |

In the field the coloured band is concealed by a strip of field-grey cloth.

The field service cap (*see* Plate 6) has two coloured metal cockades in front ; the upper one (*Deutsche Kokarde*) bears the German colours (black, white, red) in concentric rings ; the lower one (*Landeskokarde*) bears the colours of the State. The principal State colours are as follows :—

Prussia .. .. .. .. .. .. .. Black and white.
Bavaria .. .. .. .. .. .. .. Blue and white.
Saxony .. .. .. .. .. .. .. Green and white.
Württemberg .. .. .. .. .. .. Red and black.
Baden .. .. .. .. .. .. .. Red and yellow.

These cockades are also worn at the side of the helmet, forming the chin-strap attachment.

The *Dienstmütze*, or forage cap, provided with a black leather peak and chin-strap, is worn by all ranks in peace when off parade, but in the field it is usually worn only by officers and non-commissioned officers.

6. **Belt.**—All arms wear a leather belt (*Feldkoppel*). Mounted units wear a belt with a plain buckle in front ; the infantry belt has a buckle plate embossed with a crown and the national motto :—

Prussia and Baden .. .. .. .. .. "*Gott mit uns.*"
Bavaria .. .. .. .. .. .. .. "*In Treue fest.*"
Saxony .. .. .. .. .. .. .. "*Providentiae memor.*"
Württemberg .. .. .. .. .. .. "*Furchtlos und treu.*"

Attached to the belt is the bayonet frog or sword sling. The bayonet knot or sword knot varies in colour according to the company, &c.

7. **Badges of rank.**—Officers' uniform is of similar pattern to that of the other ranks, but is of finer material. All black facings are of velvet, and Guard patches, &c., are of silver or gold lace.

---

\* According to German Army Order No. 699 of the 20th July, 1917, a new universal pattern forage cap (*Einheits-Feldmütze*) is being introduced for all arms and ranks. This cap will have a grey band (grey-green for *Jäger* and *Schützen*) instead of the coloured bands formerly in use.

Field-grey cap-band covers will in future only be worn with forage caps of the old pattern ; no new ones will be issued.

There is no alteration in the pattern of the peaked cap (*Schirmmütze*).

Badges of rank are worn on the shoulder strap by officers and on the collar and cuffs by other ranks. Officers' shoulder straps bear the number of their regiment in metal numerals.

*Subaltern officers* (a) wear narrow flat shoulder straps of silver lace.

*Field officers* (b) wear slightly larger shoulder straps of twisted silver cord.

*General officers* (c) wear shoulder straps of twisted gold and silver cord mixed, and larger than those of field officers. The tunic worn by general officers has breast pockets, and scarlet collar patches with gold embroidery.

The badges of rank for officers are—

| | | | | | | |
|---|---|---|---|---|---|---|
| (a) | 2nd Lieutenant (*Leutnant*) | .. | .. | .. | .. | No star. |
| | Lieutenant (*Oberleutnant*) | .. | .. | .. | .. | One star. |
| | Captain (*Hauptmann* or *Rittmeister*) | | | .. | .. | Two stars. |
| (b) | Major (*Major*) .. | .. | .. | .. | .. | .. No star. |
| | Lieut.-Colonel (*Oberstleutnant*) | .. | .. | .. | .. | One star. |
| | Colonel (*Oberst*) .. | .. | .. | .. | .. | Two stars. |
| (c) | Major-General (*Generalmajor*) | .. | .. | .. | .. | No star. |
| | Lieut.-General (*Generalleutnant*) .. | | .. | .. | .. | One star. |
| | General (*General*) .. | .. | .. | .. | .. | Two stars. |
| | *General-Oberst* .. | .. | .. | .. | .. | Three stars. |
| | Field-Marshal (*General-Feldmarschall*) .. | | .. | .. | .. | Crossed bâtons. |

Non-commissioned officers wear the same uniform as the men, but are distinguished by the following badges of rank :—

| | | |
|---|---|---|
| *Gefreiter* | .. .. | A small button on each side of the collar. |
| *Unteroffizier* | .. .. | Braid round the base of the collar and one row of braid round the cuff. |
| *Fähnrich* | .. .. | Same as an *Unteroffizier*, but wears an officer's sword knot (*Portepee*). |
| *Sergeant* | .. .. | Same as an *Unteroffizier*, but has a large button on each side of the collar. |
| *Vizefeldwebel* | .. .. | Same as a *Sergeant*, but carries an officer's sword and sword knot (*Portepee*). |
| *Feldwebel* | .. .. | Same as a *Vizefeldwebel*, but has two rows of braid on the cuff and wears an officer's belt. |
| *Offizierstellvertreter* | .. | Same as a *Vizefeldwebel*, with braid round the shoulder strap and metal numerals. |
| *Feldwebel-Leutnant* | .. | Ranks as a commissioned officer ; wears officer's uniform, but has the braid and buttons of a *Feldwebel* on the collar. |

All *Portepee* ranks are entitled to wear silver cockades on the cap.

The *Portepee* is a double leather strap, about 15 inches long, hung from the sword hilt. The leather is interlaced with silver wire, and at the end is a knot of silver wire also. In war, it is carried on the side arm.

8. **Special badges and marks.**—*General Staff Officers* wear carmine collar patches and a treble carmine stripe on the pantaloons.

*Guard and Grenadier units* wear white or yellow patches (*Litzen*) on collar and cuffs.

*Musketry badges* are worn by individual marksmen, and consist of a plaited cord (*Schützenschnur*) from the right shoulder to the top button of the tunic.

*Machine gun marksman units* are distinguished by an oval badge, representing a machine gun, worn on the left sleeve (*see* Plate 7).

*Electrical detachments* (*Starkstromabteilungen*) are distinguished by a circular badge representing forked lightning on the left sleeve.

*Medical personnel and stretcher bearers* wear a lemon-yellow badge representing an Æsculapius' staff on the right sleeve and a Red Cross brassard on the left arm. Medical officers have dark blue collar patches edged with scarlet. Veterinary officers wear black collar patches with carmine edging.

Certain *Hanoverian, Brunswick and Nassau units,* which formed part of the King's German Legion, wear British battle honours; thus the 73rd Fusilier Regiment, the 79th Infantry Regiment and the 10th *Jäger* Battalion wear a light blue band on the right sleeve with the inscription " Gibraltar," and all the original Hanoverian regiments have "Waterloo" inscribed on the helmet plate. The 92nd Infantry Regiment and the 17th Hussar Regiment wear a metal Death's Head badge on the head-dress.

*Bandsmen and trumpeters* wear epaulettes (*Schwalbennester*), trimmed with stripes of white or yellow braid. These stripes are vertical for dismounted and oblique for mounted units.

*Pilots in the Air Service* wear a silver badge (*Abzeichen*) on the left breast.

*The Alpine Corps and the 200th Division* wear, above the upper cockade, a metal badge representing a stag's antlers with a sword and pine branches, with the motto " *Karpathen Korps* " on a scroll.

*Bavarian cyclists* wear green shoulder straps embroidered with the letter " *R* " in yellow.

## 9. Landwehr and Landsturm uniform.—*Landwehr* units wear the same uniform

as Active and Reserve units, and are only distinguished by having a white cross on the lower cockade of the cap and the letter " L " above the number on the helmet cover.

*Landsturm* units wear a field-grey uniform similar to the normal one, but the shoulder straps bear no numbers and are of different colours for the various arms as follows:—

| | | | | | |
|---|---|---|---|---|---|
| Infantry | .. | .. | .. | .. | Blue. |
| Pioneers | .. | .. | .. | .. | Black. |
| Field Artillery | .. | .. | .. | .. | Scarlet. |
| Foot Artillery | .. | .. | .. | .. | Yellow. |

Landsturm cavalry squadrons wear the uniform of their parent regiment, and are only distinguished by the Landwehr cross.

Landsturm units are distinguished by dull brass numerals worn on the collar. The Army Corps District is shown by a Roman numeral (" G " for Guard), and the number of the battalion, &c., by an Arabic one (*see* Plate 5).

*Feldwebelleutnants* of Landsturm units wear the numerical badges on the shoulder-straps.

Landsturm units in the field wear the helmet or shako ; the helmet cover bears the number of the battalion (but not of the Army Corps District), surmounted by the Landwehr cross. Units of the Unarmed Landsturm wear an oil-cloth cap with a brass Landwehr cross in front.

**10. Means of identification.**—German prisoners and dead may be identified by the following means:—

(*a.*) Distinguishing marks on uniform and equipment.
(*b.*) Identity disc.
(*c.*) Pay book.
(*d.*) Addressed correspondence and other documents.

(*a.*) **The distinguishing marks** denoting the various arms, grades and units have been described above. Besides these, regimental marks are frequently stencilled on the lining of the uniform, as well as the stamp of the Army Corps clothing depôt, *e.g.*, *B.A. IV.*, denoting the *Bekleidungs-Amt* of the IV. Army Corps District. Owing to the frequent transfers of men from one unit to another, and also to the fact that men on leaving hospital, or returning from furlough, may be issued with uniform from another clothing depôt, such means of identification are often deceptive.

The regimental markings on arms, accoutrements, gas masks, &c., are still less likely to afford true identifications.

(*b.*) **Identity disc.**—Every German officer and soldier carries a metal identity disc (*Erkennungsmarke*), which is intended to be worn round the neck. The identity disc is not an entirely reliable means of identification, as the transfer of a man from a depôt to a field unit or from one field unit to another is not always recorded.

Three patterns of identity discs are met with (*see* Plate 11). The old pattern (Fig. 1), which is oval in shape, and measures 2 inches by $1\frac{1}{2}$ inches, gives the man's regiment, company and individual number in the company. The lettering is apt to be confusing, the following abbreviations being used:—

| | |
|---|---|
| *I.* or *J.* | for Infantry. |
| *R.*.......... | for Regiment or Reserve. |
| *L.* or *Ldw.* | for Landwehr. |
| *E.* or *Ers.* | for Ersatz. |
| *C.* or *K.* | for Company. |
| *B.* or *Bay.* | for Bavarian. |

A second pattern of identity disc (Fig. 2) was introduced in September, 1915. The disc is of zinc, oval in shape, and measures $2\frac{3}{4}$ inches by 2 inches.

As soon as a man joins a depôt unit, the upper portion of his identity disc is stamped with the following particulars:—

(1.) Christian name and surname.
(2.) Last residence (in large towns, the street and number is added).
(3.) Date of birth.
(4.) Depôt unit.
(5.) Company, squadron or battery (at the depôt).
(6.) Regimental number (at the depôt).

When the man is drafted to a unit in the field, the following information is added on the lower portion of the identity disc:—

(1.) Unit.
(2.) Company, squadron or battery.
(3.) Regimental number (in his company, &c.).

The markings of the depôt unit are not struck out.

When a man is transferred from one unit in the field to another unit, the markings of the old unit are struck out and the new markings inserted below.

In November, 1916, a third pattern of identity disc was introduced. This pattern (Fig. 3) is similar in shape to the second pattern, but the disc is divided into two halves, upper and lower, by a perforated line. Each half bears identical markings; the name, address and depôt unit are marked on the front, and the field unit on the back. When a man is killed, the lower half of his identity disc is broken off and forwarded to Germany, the upper half being buried with the body.

(*c.*) **The pay book** (*Soldbuch*) forms the best means of identifying a prisoner or dead German.

The pay book is a small book 5½″ by 3½″, with a brown paper cover, marked :—

> " *Soldbuch für den*...............................................................
> *Nr. der Stammrolle.*".....................

on which is written the man's name and regimental number.

The book contains the following particulars :—

(1.) Name in full ...............................................................................
Date of birth.......................................................................
Place of birth  ...................................................................
District ..............................................................................
Province (Prussia, Bavaria, Saxony, &c.).....................................

(2.) Parents'
(*a*) Profession  ...........................................................
(*b*) & (*c*) Names in full................................................
(*d*) Residence  .........................................................
(*e*) District  ..............................................................

(3.) Religion.....................................................................

(4.) Profession or trade  .....................................................

(5.) Married to....................................................................
Wife's residence  ...........................................................
District ........................................................................
Number of children............................................................

(6.) Date of first joining the Standing Army  .................................
Unit  .............................................................................
Date of being called up·for active service...............................
Unit  ............................................................................

(7.) Medals and decorations .................................................

(8.) Description  ...............................................................
Measurements of foot.........................................................

This page is usually stamped with the regimental stamp.

Then follows a statement of the daily rate of pay to which the man is entitled, and a record of the payments which have been made to him.

The book also records the number of times the man has been inoculated.

The private soldier in the German Army is known generally as *Gemeiner* and officially as *Soldat* or *Infanterist*. Technically, however, the private is designated in his pay book according to the arm or unit to which he belongs as follows:—

| | | |
|---|---|---|
| *Schütze* .. | .. | = Private in a *Schützen* regiment or battalion, or any machine gun unit. |
| *Jäger* .. | .. | = Private in a *Jäger* battalion. |
| *Gardist* .. | .. = | ,, ,, Foot Guards regiment. |
| *Grenadier*.. | .. = | ,, ,, Grenadier regiment or battalion or assault battalion. |
| *Füsilier* .. | .. = | ., ,, Fusilier regiment or battalion. |
| *Musketier*.. | .. = | ,, ,, Line infantry regiment. |
| *Pionier* .. | .. | = Sapper. |
| *Kanonier*.. | .. | = Gunner. |
| *Fahrer* .. | .. | = Driver. |

Cavalry soldiers are designated *Kürassier, Dragoner, Husar, Ulan*, &c., according to their regiment.

The above terms only apply to "Active" soldiers. The other categories are officially designated as "*Reservist*," "*Ersatz-Reservist*," "*Wehrmann*," "*Landsturmmann*," &c.

156

# APPENDIX A.

# THE NEW GERMAN FIELD SERVICE UNIFORM.

## I.—SUMMARY OF CHANGES.

Certain changes affecting the uniforms of the German Army in peace and war have recently been published, and may be briefly summarized as follows:—

(a.) The abolition of the old "dark blue" peace uniform (except in the case of the full dress of the Gardes du Corps, Guard Cuirassiers and certain Hussar regiments) and the substitution of a new field-grey (grey-green) uniform for all arms, for wear in time of peace.

(b.) The introduction of a new universal pattern field service jacket (*Bluse*) of field-grey (grey-green) cloth for all arms and ranks, for wear on field service.

(c.) The introduction of a field-grey greatcoat of universal pattern for all arms and ranks.

(d.) The introduction of a field-grey peaked cap of universal pattern for all arms.

(e.) The abolition of the special grey-green field service uniform for machine-gun batteries; all machine-gun units will wear the uniform of the unit to which they are allotted.

The regulations referred to deal only with Prussian troops, and no information is yet available concerning the changes in the uniforms of Bavarian, Saxon and Württemberg troops, though these will doubtless conform in the main to the Prussian pattern.

## II.—DESCRIPTION OF NEW FIELD SERVICE UNIFORM.

(a.) **Jacket** (*see* Plate 3).—The field service jacket (*Bluse*) of universal pattern for all arms and ranks is shown in the Plate, and consists of a loose-fitting jacket of field-grey (grey-green) cloth, fastened down the front by hooks; turned-back cuffs of the same material as the jacket; stand and fall collar of special field-grey (grey-green) cloth used for badges (*Abzeichentuch*); shoulder straps of various materials and colours (*see* below), fastened by dull metal buttons bearing a crown; side pockets closed by similar buttons. The collar patches worn by certain regiments (Guards, Grenadiers, Fusiliers, and certain units of the Communication Troops) are shown in paragraphs II.d and III.A.

(b.) **Shoulder straps.\***—There are considerable alterations to the shoulder straps of the jacket and greatcoat of the field service uniform; the particulars of the colourings of shoulder straps are summarized in the following table. It will be observed that each arm or branch of the service can at once be distinguished by the colour of the cloth of which the strap is made, except in the case of *Ulanen* and Horse and Field Artillery, for both of which it is scarlet.

---

\* An Army Order, dated April, 1917, lays down that:—

(a.) Men belonging to light and divisional ammunition columns will in future wear scarlet shoulder straps with a grenade above the number.

(b.) The personnel of divisional and Corps bridging trains will wear black shoulder straps with red edging, and the number of the pioneer depôt from which the unit was formed.

THE NEW FIELD SERVICE JACKET.

A man of the Guard Field Artillery wearing the new field service jacket, helmet with cover but without ball, and chin strap instead of chin chain.

| Arm, &c. | Shoulder straps. | | |
|---|---|---|---|
| | Cloth. | Edging. | Badge. |
| Infantry .. .. .. .. | Field-grey.. .. | White (1) .. .. | Red. |
| *Jäger and Schützen* .. .. | Grey-green .. | Light green (2) .. | Red. |
| Cavalry— | | | |
|   Cuirassiers .. .. .. | White .. .. | As at present* .. | Golden yellow (3). |
|   Dragoons .. .. .. | Cornflower-blue .. | As at present* (4) .. | Red (5). |
|   Hussars .. .. .. | Cords of the same | colours as at present.* | Golden yellow (6) or white cloth. |
|   Lancers (7) .. .. .. | Scarlet .. .. | As at present* (8) .. | Lemon-yellow. |
|   *Jäger zu Pferde* .. .. | Light green .. | As at present* (9) .. | Red (10). |
| Artillery— | | | |
|   Horse and field .. .. | Scarlet .. .. | Nil (11) .. .. | Lemon-yellow. |
|   Foot .. .. .. .. | Golden yellow .. | Nil .. .. .. | Red. |
| Pioneers .. .. .. .. | Black .. .. | Scarlet .. .. | Red. |
| Communication Troops.. .. | Light grey .. | Nil .. .. .. | Red. |
| Train— | | | |
|   Train detachments .. .. | Cyanine-blue .. | Nil .. .. .. | Red. |
|   Stretcher bearers .. .. | Crimson .. .. | Nil .. .. .. | Yellow. |
|   Sick attendants, &c. .. .. | Dark blue.. .. | Cornflower-blue .. | Yellow. |

(1.) Except 2nd Foot Guards, 2nd Grenadier Guards and 8th Grenadiers, which are scarlet; 3rd Foot Guards, 3rd Grenadier Guards, Guard Fusiliers, and 7th and 11th Grenadiers, which are lemon-yellow; 4th Foot Guards, 4th Grenadier Guards, and 145th Infantry Regiment, which are light blue ; and the 141st Infantry Regiment, which is light green.

(2.) Except Guard *Schützen* Battalion, which is black.

(3.) Crimson for 2nd Cuirassiers.

(4.) Except for 22nd Dragoons, which is now black only.

(5.) Except for 3rd Horse Grenadiers, 7th and 15th Dragoons, which are pink, and 11th and 12th Dragoons, which are crimson.

(6.) White for 4th, 6th, 7th, 9th, 10th and 17th Hussars ; remainder golden yellow. The 1st Body Hussars now wear the Imperial Monogram.

(7.) *Ulanen* now wear angular shoulder straps instead of the former special oval shape.

(8.) Except that the scarlet edgings of the 2nd Guard *Ulanen* and 2nd and 6th *Ulanen* are abolished and the edging of the 13th *Ulanen* is now light blue.

(9.) Those of the more recently formed 9th, 10th, 11th, 12th and 13th Regiments are identical with those of the 2nd, 3rd, 4th, 5th and 6th Regiments respectively, while that of the 7th Regiment is pink.

(10.) Except for 1st Regiment, which is lemon-yellow, and 7th, which is pink.

(11.) Except for 1st Guard Field Artillery Regiment, which is white, 3rd Guard Field Artillery Regiment, lemon-yellow, and 4th Guard Field Artillery Regiment, light blue.

(c.) **Shoulder cords (officers').**—"Field shoulder cords" will be worn by officers on the jacket (*Bluse*) and greatcoat; for officers below the rank of General they have a uniform width of $1\frac{3}{4}$ inches without any stiffening; they consist of a cloth strap of various colours, corresponding to those of the

* The colours vary and are too numerous to quote here.

shoulder straps of the rank and file (in the Infantry and *Jäger* the colours correspond to those of the *edging* of the shoulder straps of the rank and file). This strap forms a foundation for the cords and badges, which are "dull" and of a size corresponding to the present size for captains.

The only exceptions to the above are as follows:—

| | |
|---|---|
| 1st Foot Guards .. .. .. .. .. | the cloth strap is edged with silver lace. |
| 109th Body Grenadiers .. .. .. .. | ,, ,, ,, ,, ,, ,, ,, ,, |
| Gardes du Corps .. .. .. .. .. | ,, ,, ,, ,, ,, ,, ,, ,, |
| 19th Dragoons . .. .. .. .. | ,, ,, ,, ,, ,, ,, ,, ,, |
| 1st Flying Battalion .. .. .. .. | ,, ,, ,, ,, ,, ,, white. |
| 2nd ,, ,, .. .. .. .. | ,, ,, ,, ,, ,, ,, scarlet. |
| 3rd ,, ,, .. .. .. .. | ,, ,, ,, ,, ,, ,, lemon-yellow. |
| 4th ,, ,, .. .. .. .. | ,, ,, ,, ,, ,, ,, light blue. |

**(d.) Collar patches of all arms except Infantry.**—The details of the collar patches of Infantry regiments and *Jäger* battalions have been shown for convenience in the table on pages 159 and 160; the remainder are shown in the following table:—

| Unit, &c. | Collar patches: grey. | | |
|---|---|---|---|
| | Shape. | Centre. | Upper and lower stripes. |
| *Cavalry*— | | | |
| Gardes du Corps .. .. .. .. | Double .. | Scarlet .. .. | White. |
| Guard Cuirassiers .. .. .. | ,, .. | Cornflower-blue .. | ,, |
| 1st Guard Dragoons .. .. .. .. | ,, .. | Scarlet .. .. | Yellow. |
| 2nd ,, ,, .. .. .. .. | ,, .. | ,, .. .. | White. |
| Body Guard Hussars .. .. .. | ,, .. | ,, .. .. | Yellow. |
| 1st Guard *Ulanen* .. .. .. | ,, .. | ,, .. .. | White. |
| 2nd ,, ,, .. .. .. .. | ,, .. | ,, .. .. | Yellow. |
| 3rd ,, ,, .. .. .. .. | ,, .. | Golden yellow .. | White. |
| *Artillery*— | | | |
| 1st—4th Guard Field Artillery Regiments | ,, .. | Black .. .. | Yellow. |
| Guard Foot Artillery Regiment .. .. | ,, .. | ,, .. .. | ,, |
| *Pioneers*—. | | | |
| Guard Pioneers.. .. .. .. | ,, .. | ,, .. .. | White. |
| *Communication Troops* — | | | |
| All except Telegraph Battalions 2—6, Airship Battalions 3—5, and Flying Battalions 1—4 .. .. .. .. | ,, .. | ,, .. .. | ,, |
| Flying Battalions 1—4 .. .. .. | Single .. | Nil .. .. | ,, |
| *Train*— | | | |
| 1st and 2nd Guard Train Detachments .. | Double .. | Cyanine-blue .. | ,, |
| Guard Stretcher Bearers .. .. .. | ,, .. | Crimson .. .. | ,, |

**(e.) Trousers and pantaloons.**—No alterations to these have been published, except that officers' pantaloons must correspond in width and cut to those of the rank and file.

**(f.) Helmets, etc.**—Helmets and lance caps will be fitted with removable spikes or balls or upper portion, which will not be taken into the field. Chin straps will replace chin chains for wear with helmets, shakos, busbies and lance caps (*see* Plate facing page 156).

**(g.) Field service cap.**—A new field service cap has been introduced for officers (details have not yet been published) and the field service cap for the rank and file will, in future, be a peaked cap of field-grey (grey-green) cloth. There are no alterations to the colours of the cap bands (*see* page 150), but a field-grey (grey-green) band is worn in the field to cover the coloured cap band.

**(h.) Greatcoat.**—A universal pattern greatcoat of field-grey cloth is being introduced for mounted and dismounted branches of all arms. The polished buttons are being replaced by dull metal buttons. The shoulder straps for Infantry and *Jäger* will be made of the same cloth as the greatcoat and will have the same edgings as the shoulder straps of the jacket (*Bluse*); for all other arms the shoulder straps are identical with those on the jacket (*Bluse*).

**(i.) Leather Equipment.**—The following changes have been introduced :—

(*a*) A field service belt (*Feldkoppel*) of dark brown grained leather for officers instead of the old officer's waist belt (*Feldbinde*). Sashes will no longer be worn in the field by adjutants, who will then, like all other officers, wear the field service belt (*Feldkoppel*).

(*b*) Black laced boots and gaiters for officers.

(*c*) A universal pattern of cavalry boot.

(*d*) Leather equipment, boots, and cases for field glasses, pistols and maps must be blacked. (There is no change in the colour of saddlery and harness.)

## III.—DETAILS OF DISTINGUISHING MARKS.

### A.—Infantry.

1. INFANTRY OF THE GUARD AND OF THE LINE.

#### Jacket (*Bluse*).

*Cloth*—Field-grey.  *Collar*—Stand and fall.
*Shoulder straps*—Field-grey, edging as shown below.
*Badge on shoulder strap*—Red.
*Buttons on shoulder straps and pockets*—Dull with crown, material as shown below.

| Unit. | Shoulder straps: field-grey. | Collar patches: Grey. | | | Buttons. |
|---|---|---|---|---|---|
| | Edging. | Shape. | Centre. | Upper and lower stripes. | |
| 1st Foot Guards .. .. .. | White .. .. | Double .. | Scarlet .. | White .. | Nickel. |
| 2nd „ „ .. .. .. | Scarlet .. .. | „ .. | „ .. | „ .. | Tombak.* |
| 3rd „ „ .. .. .. | Lemon-yellow .. | „ .. | „ .. | „ .. | „ |
| 4th „ „ .. .. .. | Light blue .. | „ .. | „ .. | „ .. | „ |
| 5th „ „ .. .. .. | White .. .. | Old Prussian .. | .. | „ .. | Nickel. |
| 1st Guard Grenadiers .. .. | „ .. .. | Double .. | Scarlet .. | „ .. | Tombak. |
| 2nd „ „ .. .. | Scarlet .. .. | „ .. | „ .. | „ .. | „ |
| 3rd „ „ .. .. | Lemon-yellow .. | „ .. | „ .. | „ .. | „ |
| 4th „ „ .. .. | Light blue .. | „ .. | „ .. | „ .. | „ |
| 5th „ „ .. .. | White .. .. | Old Prussian .. | .. | Yellow .. | „ |
| Guard Fusiliers .. .. .. | Lemon-yellow .. | Double .. | Scarlet .. | White .. | Nickel. |
| Grenadier Regiments, Nos. 1 to 6.. | White .. .. | Single .. .. | .. | „ .. | Tombak. |
| 7th Grenadiers .. .. .. | Lemon-yellow .. | „ .. | .. | Yellow .. | „ |
| 8th „ .. .. .. | Scarlet .. | „ .. | .. | White .. | „ |
| 11th „ .. .. .. | Lemon-yellow .. | „ .. | .. | „ .. | „ |
| 80th Fusiliers .. .. .. | White .. .. | Old Prussian . | .. | .. | „ |
| 109th Body Grenadiers .. .. | „ .. .. | Double .. | Scarlet .. | White .. | Nickel. |
| 114th Infantry Regiment .. .. | Light green .. | .. | .. | .. | Tombak. |
| 145th „ „ .. . | Light blue .. | .. | .. | .. | „ |
| All other Prussian Line Infantry Regiments. | White .. .. | .. | .. | .. | „ |

\* Tombak is an alloy of zinc and copper ; its colour is that of reddish brass.

## 2. Jäger and Schützen.
### Jacket (*Bluse*).

*Cloth*—Grey-green.
*Collar*—Stand and fall.
*Shoulder straps*—Grey-green, edging as shown.
*Badge on shoulder strap*—Red.
*Buttons on shoulder straps and pockets*—Dull with crown, tombak.

| Unit. | Shoulder straps: Grey-green. | Collar patches: Grey. | | | Buttons. |
|---|---|---|---|---|---|
| | Edging. | Shape. | Centre. | Upper and lower stripes. | |
| Guard *Jäger* Battalion .. .. | Light green .. | Double .. | Light green. | Yellow .. | Tombak. |
| Guard *Schützen* Battalion .. .. | Black .. .. | ,, .. | Black .. | ,, | ,, |
| All other Prussian *Jäger* Battalions | Light green .. | .. | .. | .. | ,, |

## B.—Cavalry.

**Jacket.**—All the special pattern tunics (*Attila, Ulanka,* &c.) of the cavalry have been abolished for field service, and cavalry will wear the universal pattern jacket (*Bluse*) of field-grey (grey-green) for *Jäger zu Pferde*) cloth, with stand and fall collar, as described in paragraph II.a (*see* Plate 3).

**Shoulder Straps.**—These are no longer of field-grey (grey-green) cloth, but each branch of the cavalry has its own distinctive colour for the cloth of the shoulder strap, as shown in the table in paragraph II.b.

It should be noted that the shoulder straps of *Ulanen* Regiments are now angular instead of the former special oval shape.

**Collar Patches.**—*See* table in paragraph II.d.

## C.—Artillery.

**Jacket.**—Universal pattern jacket (*Bluse*) of field-grey cloth, with stand and fall collar, as described in paragraph II.a.

**Shoulder Straps.**—These are no longer of field-grey cloth, but are of scarlet cloth for horse and field, and golden-yellow cloth for Foot Artillery, as described in the table in paragraph II.b.

The badges for Foot Artillery units are altered by the addition of two crossed grenades, with the numeral of the present pattern shoulder strap beneath them.

**Collar Patches.**—*See* table in paragraph II.d.

## D.—Pioneers, Communication Troops and Train.

**Jacket.**—Universal pattern jacket (*Bluse*) of field-grey cloth, with stand and fall collar, as described in paragraph II.a.

**Shoulder Straps.** – *See* table in paragraph II.b.
**Collar Patches.**—*See* table in paragraph II.d.

## E.—Medical and Veterinary Officers.

The changes in officers' uniforms apply also to medical and veterinary officers, whose shoulder straps, however, remain unchanged.

## F.—Landsturm Formations.

The regulations lay down that the existing distinguishing badges, &c., for Landsturm formations will remain in force during the war.

These distinctions consist of shoulder straps on the tunic, jacket (*Bluse*), or *Litewka* and greatcoat, and numerals on the collar of these articles of uniform.

**Shoulder Straps.**—These are of different colours to distinguish the arms of the service, and bear no numeral. The colours are :—

| | | | | | | | |
|---|---|---|---|---|---|---|---|
| Infantry | .. | .. | .. | .. | .. | .. | Blue. |
| Pioneers | .. | .. | .. | .. | .. | .. | Black. |
| Field Artillery.. | .. | .. | .. | .. | .. | .. | Scarlet. |
| Foot Artillery .. | .. | .. | .. | .. | .. | .. | Yellow. |

**Numerals on Collar.**—These are worn by men of the arms mentioned above on both sides of the collar of the tunic, jacket (*Bluse*), or *Litewka* and greatcoat. They are made of dull brass, and consist of the Army Corps number in Roman figures (G for Guard Corps) with the number of the battalion, &c., below in Arabic figures, the latter running consecutively from 1 upwards in each Army Corps, and including *Landsturm Ersatz* formations.

# APPENDIX B.

## Conventional Signs used to represent Artillery Units, &c.

| Conventional sign. | German abbreviation. | English equivalent. |
|---|---|---|
| F | *Mast-Fernrohr* | Giant periscope. |
| | *Flieg. Abt.* | Reconnaissance flight. |
| | *Ballonzug* | Balloon section. |
| | *Kraftwagen-Kol.* | M.T. column. |
| | *Fahrb. Brieftauben-St.* | Mobile pigeon loft. |
| | *Feldsignal-Trupp* | Signal section. |
| | *Scheinwerfer-Zug* | Searchlight section. |
| | *M.G.* | Machine gun. |
| | *3·7 cm. Rev. K.* | 3·7 cm. revolver gun. |
| | *5 cm. K.* | 5 cm. gun. |
| | *Belg. 5·7 cm. K.* | 5·7 cm. Belgian gun. |
| | *F.K. 96 n/A.* | 7·7 cm. field gun. |
| | *K. i. H.* | 1916 pattern field gun. |
| | *l. F.H.* | 10·5 cm. light field howitzer. |
| | *9 cm. K. 73/88.* | 9 cm. field gun (1873/1888 pattern). |
| | *Franz. 90 mm. K.* | 90 mm. French gun. |
| | *Flak.* | Anti-aircraft gun. |
| | *10 cm. K.* | 10 cm. gun (old pattern). |
| | *10 cm. K. 04* | 10 cm. gun, 1904. |
| | *10 cm. K. 14* | 10 cm. gun (1914 pattern). |
| | *s. 12 cm. K.* | 12 cm. heavy gun. |
| | *frz. kz. 120 mm. K.* | 120 mm. French short gun. |
| B | *Belg. s. 12 cm. K.* | 12 cm. Belgian heavy gun. |
| | *13 cm. K.* | 13 cm. gun. |
| | *15 cm. R.K.* | 15 cm. gun with chase rings. |

## Conventional Signs used to represent Artillery Units, &c.—*continued.*

| Conventional sign. | German abbreviation. | English equivalent. |
|---|---|---|
| | *lg. 15 cm. R.K.* | 15 cm. long gun with chase rings. |
| | *lg. 15 cm. K.* | 15 cm. long gun. |
| | *15 cm. K. i.S.L.* | 15 cm. gun with overhead shield. |
| | *Russ. l. 15 cm. K.* | 15 cm. Russian light gun. |
| | *s. F.H.* | 15 cm. heavy field howitzer. |
| | *s. F.H. 02* | Ditto (1902 pattern). |
| | *s. F.H. 13* | Ditto (1913 pattern). |
| | *21 cm. Mrs.* | 21 cm. mortar (old pattern). |
| | *Mrs.* | Ditto (new pattern). |
| | *lg. Mrs.* | Long 21-cm. mortar. |
| | *Russ. 20·3 cm. H. 77* | 20·3 cm. Russian howitzer '77. |
| | *Schw. Küstenmörser B. 96, Mrs.* | 30·5 cm. mortar. |
| | *Kz. Mar. Kan. 14* | 42 cm. short naval gun on wheeled carriage. |
| | *42 cm. Mrs.* | 42-cm. mortar on platform bed. |
| | *l. M.W.* | Light *Minenwerfer.* |
| | *s. M.W.* | Heavy *Minenwerfer.* |
| | *l. M.K.* | Light ammunition column. |
| | *24 cm. K.* | 24 cm. gun. |

*Note.*—For further information, *see* S.S. 618 and S.S. 618A, "German Conventional Signs," which contain full details of the authorized conventional signs of various types, and is more up-to-date than the above.

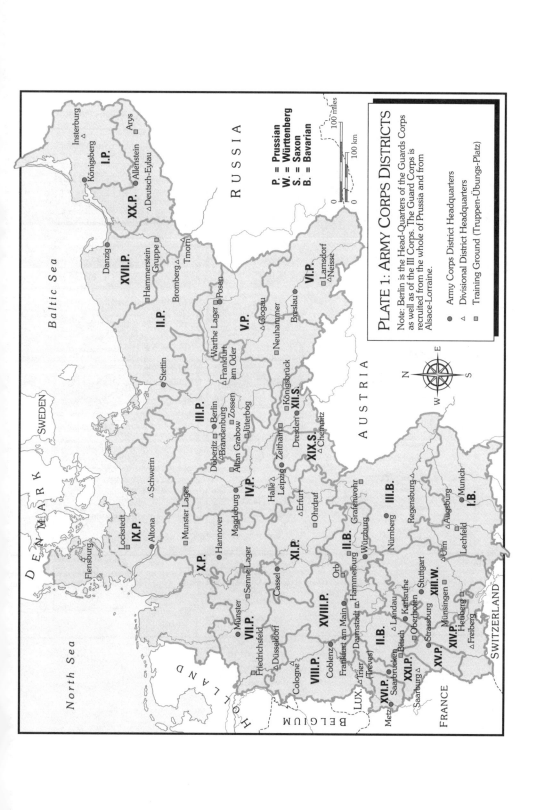

# PLATE 1: ARMY CORPS DISTRICTS

Note: Berlin is the Head-Quarters of the Guards Corps as well as of the III Corps. The Guard Corps is recruited from the whole of Prussia and from Alsace-Lorraine.

P. = Prussian
W. = Württemberg
S. = Saxon
B. = Bavarian

● Army Corps District Headquarters
△ Divisional District Headquarters
▢ Training Ground (Truppen-Übungs-Platz)

Plate 2.

Titular Monograms on the Shoulder Straps of certain German Infantry Regiments.

GUARD GRENADIER REGIMENTS.

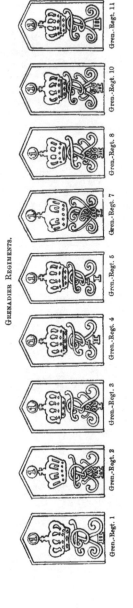

1., Garde-Gren.-    2. Garde-Gren.-    3. Garde-Gren.-    4. Garde-Gren.-

GRENADIER REGIMENTS.

Gren.-Regt. 1    Gren.-Regt. 2    Gren.-Regt. 3    Gren.-Regt. 4    Gren.-Regt. 5    Gren.-Regt. 7    Gren.-Regt. 8    Gren.-Regt. 10    Gren.-Regt. 11

BAVARIAN INFANTRY REGIMENTS.

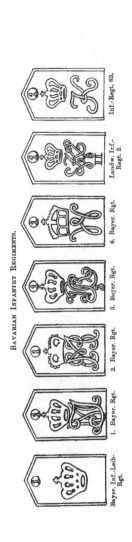

Bayer. Inf.-Leib-Rgt.    1. Bayer. Rgt.    2. Bayer. Rgt.    3. Bayer. Rgt.    6. Bayer. Rgt.    Landw. Inf.-Regt. 2.    Inf.-Regt. 63.

165

INFANTRY REGIMENTS.

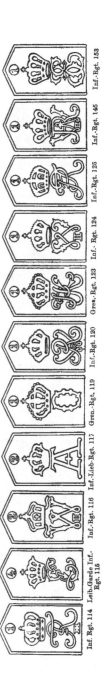

PLATE 3.

# Jacket (*Bluse*) for all Arms.

Front View.

Back View.

## Field Service Tunics, &c.

Front View.
(4th Gd. *Reiter* Rgt.)
Tunic with turned down collar.

Back View.
(Inf. Regt.)

Tunic with stand-up collar
(8th Cuir. Regt.)

Front View.
(2nd Gd. *Ulanen* Rgt.)

Back View.
(15th *Ulanen* Rgt.)

(12th Hus. Rgt.)

PLATE 4.                    166

# Helmet and Shako Ornaments.

Troops of the Guard.    G. du Corps and    Body Gd.    G. Jäger, Train    Gren. R. 2, 7, 8.    Old Prussian
            G. Cuirassiers.    Hussars.    and Schützen.    Drag. No. I.    Eagle.
                                               Horse Gren. R. No. 3.
                                                 (Silver.)

Eagle worn by    N.C.O.'s Schools.    Drag. Regts.    Hus. Regts. 1    Hus. Regt. 7.    Hus. Regt. 17.    Bavaria.
Line Regts.                                      and 2.

Saxony.    Württemberg.    Baden No. 109    Baden.    Hesse.    Meckl.-Schwerin.
                        Gren. R.

Meckl.-Strelitz.    Oldenburg.    Saxe Weimar.    Brunswick.    Brunswick.    Anhalt.
                                              Inf. Reg. 92, III Battn.

Saxon Duchies.    Schwarzburg.    Reuss.

### Infantry Private in Marching Order.

The man belongs to the 239th Res. Infantry Regt., as shown by the number on helmet cover and shoulder strap. The shoulder strap has a coloured strip as a further distinguishing mark; this is peculiar to some divisions and is not regulation.

The cuff is of the new turned back pattern instead of the older Brandenburg type.

The photograph shows the normal way of carrying the pack, greatcoat, ammunition pouches and entrenching tool, but the man is not carrying the tent-square which is normally strapped above the greatcoat.

### Landsturm Infantry Private in Marching Order.

The man belongs to Landsturm Infantry Battalion XI/22, as shown by the copper numerals on his collar. The helmet cover also bears the number 22, and the Landsturm cross. The rifle and bayonet are of an old pattern, but otherwise the equipment is the same as that of infantry of the line.

PLATE 6. 168

### Infantry Uniform.

private of the 28th Inf. Regt. or 28th Res. Inf. Regt., as
rn by the number on the shoulder strap. The tunic
ons are embossed with the Prussian crown; the shoulder
button, which bears the number 1, shows that the
er belongs to the 1st company of his regiment.
he red band of the forage cap is concealed by a strip of
cloth. The upper cockade is the imperial one, black,
e and red; the lower cockade is black and white, the
sian colours.

### Infantry Uniform.

A *Vizefeldwebel* belonging to the grenadier battalion of the
109th Res. Inf. Regt. On the collar he wears grenadier braid
patches (*Litzen*), as well as the lace and button which are
the rank badges of a *Feldwebel* or *Vizefeldwebel*.

The forage cap is of the peaked type hitherto worn only by
officers and non-commissioned officers. The red band is
covered by a grey strip. The upper cockade on the cap is the
imperial one, black, white and red. The lower cockade is red
and yellow, the Baden colours.

The non-commissioned officer is wearing the ribbon of the
Iron Cross, 2nd Class.

## Machine Gun Unit.

A gun crew belonging to a machine gun marksman company (*M.G. Scharf-schützen-Kompagnie*). All the men wear the machine gun marksman's badge on the left sleeve.

The gun commander, on the right, is an *Unteroffizier*, as he has lace on his collar and wears a peaked cap. The second man from the right is a lance-corporal (*Gefreiter*), and wears a button on each side of the collar.

The State (lower) cockade on the forage-cap is hidden in each case by the grey cap band cover.

The man on the left is wearing turn over cuffs of the new pattern.

The machine gun is of the ordinary '08 pattern with telescopic sight.

The cross-belts, which are peculiar to machine gunners, are worn in action by the detachments; they serve to carry the equipment.

PLATE 8.                    170

### Field Artillery.

The man on the right is a gunner, and the man on the left is a driver of the field artillery. The helmet has a ball instead of a spike. The gunner is armed with a rifle* and bayonet, and wears the infantry belt.

The driver is armed with sword and revolver and wears a belt of the cavalry pattern.

---

\* Gunners are normally armed with the carbine.

## Cavalry.

Two corporals (*Unteroffiziere*) of the 20th *Ulanen* Regiment, as seen by the regimental monogram on the shoulder strap; they wear the double-breasted lancer tunic with pointed cuffs.

The rank is denoted by the lace on collar and cuffs.

The lower cockade of the forage cap bears the Württemberg colours, red and black.

## Pioneer in Marching Order.

The man belongs to a field company of the 14th Pioneer Battalion, as shown by the number on helmet cover and shoulder strap.

The cuff is of the Swedish pattern instead of the Brandenburg cuff worn by the infantry.

The pouches differ from those of the infantry, and the bayonet has a saw-back.

A long-handled spade is carried in place of the short infantry entrenching tool.

The tent-square can be seen strapped above the greatcoat and pack.

PLATE 10.                    172

### Pioneers.

A group of pioneers belonging to a field company of the 8th Pioneer Battalion, as shown by the black cap band and number on the shoulder strap.

The man on the extreme left is a lance-corporal (*Gefreiter*) as shown by the button on his collar.

The left-hand man in each row is wearing the new field service jacket (*Bluse*) with turn-over cuffs, black shoulder straps, and fastened with hooks and eyes instead of buttons. There is a black piping down the seam of the trousers.

The men are seated in one of the steel half-pontoons which form part of the equipment of a Divisional bridging train.

## Identity Discs.

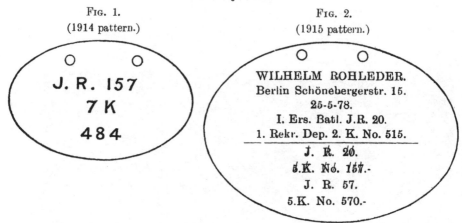

FIG. 1.
(1914 pattern.)

J. R. 157
7 K
484

FIG. 2.
(1915 pattern.)

WILHELM ROHLEDER.
Berlin Schönebergerstr. 15.
25-5-78.
I. Ers. Batl. J.R. 20.
1. Rekr. Dep. 2. K. No. 515.
J. R. 20.
5.K. No. 157.-
J. R. 57.
5.K. No. 570.-

FIG. 3.
(1916 pattern.)

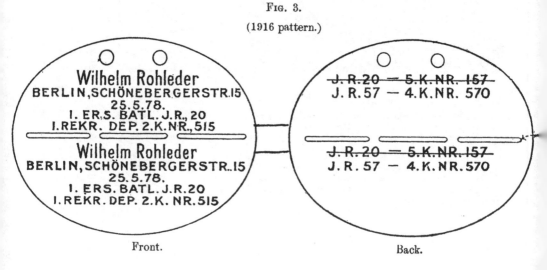

Wilhelm Rohleder
BERLIN, SCHÖNEBERGERSTR.15
25.5.78.
I. ERS. BATL. J.R., 20
I. REKR. DEP. 2.K.NR., 515

Wilhelm Rohleder
BERLIN, SCHÖNEBERGERSTR..15
25.5.78.
I. ERS. BATL. J.R.20
I. REKR. DEP. 2.K. NR.515

J.R.20 — 5.K.NR. 157
J.R.57 — 4.K.NR. 570

J.R.20 — 5.K.NR.157
J.R.57 — 4.K.NR.570

Front.            Back.

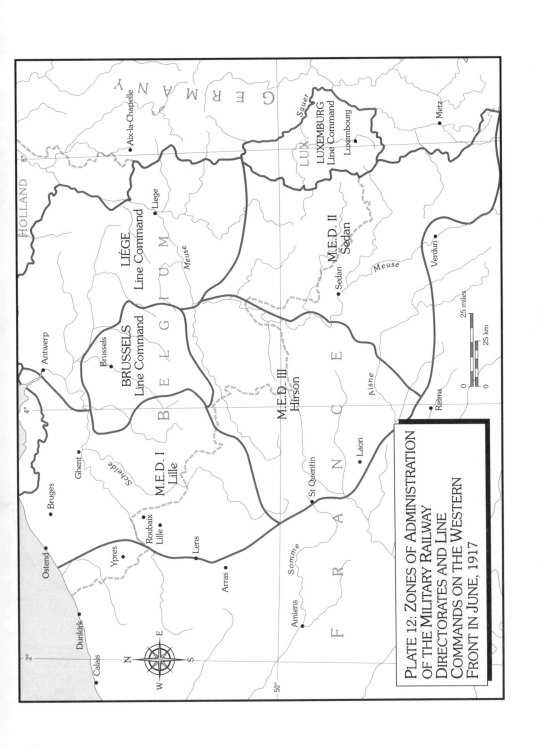

HOLLAND

GERMANY

Aix-la-Chapelle

LUX.

Sauer

LUXEMBURG
Line Command

Luxembourg

Metz

6°

Liège

LIÉGE
Line Command

B E L G I U M

Meuse

M.E.D. II
Sedan

Sedan

Meuse

Verdun

Antwerp

Brussels

BRUSSELS
Line Command

M.E.D. III
Hirson

Aisne

Rèims

4°

Ghent

Scheldt

M.E.D. I
Lille

Laon

0     25 miles

Bruges

Roubaix
Lille

Lens

St. Quentin

0     25 km

F R A N C E

Ostend

Ypres

Somme

50°

Arras

Amiens

Dunkirk

N
E
W
S

2°

Calais

PLATE 12: ZONES OF ADMINISTRATION
OF THE MILITARY RAILWAY
DIRECTORATES AND LINE
COMMANDS ON THE WESTERN
FRONT IN JUNE, 1917

Plate 13.

1916 Pattern Field Gun ("**F.K. 16**").

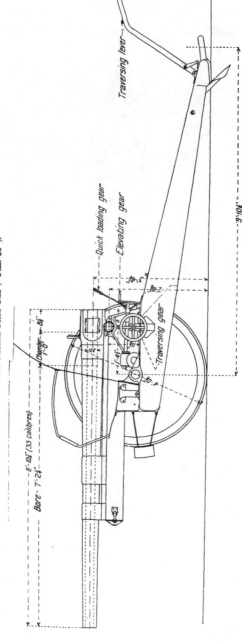

PLATE 14.

15-cm. Long Heavy Field Howitzer '13.   lg. s.F.H. 13.

PLATE 15.

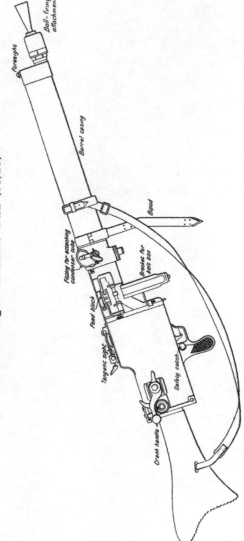

German Light Machine Gun (08/15).

Foresights

Ball-firing attachment

Barrel casing

Fixing for attaching condenser tube

Bipod

Feed block

Bracket for ammn box

Tangent sight

Safety catch

Crank handle

PLATE 16.

The 21-cm. Mortar (Mörser or Mrs.).

PLATE 17          180

7.6cm. Light Minenwerfer (new pattern)

# INDEX.

## A.

## S.

Saddlery, cavalry, 64, 65.
Schools—
    Cadet, 23.
    For non-commissioned officers, 25, 26.
Searchlight sections, 102.
Service, liability to, 9.
Service, men unfit for, 9.
Signal service—
    Carrier pigeons, 121.
    Commands, 117,
    Director of, 117.
    Earth current telegraphy, 119.
    Lamp signalling, 120.
    Listening sets, 119.
    Message-carrying projectiles, 121.
    Messenger dogs, 121.
    Peace organization, 117.
    Regimental signalling detachments, 45, 117, 118.
    Telegraph troops, 117, 118.
    Telephone detachments, 118.
    Wireless stations, 119, 120.
Ski battalions, 46, 47.
Sound ranging, 123.
Staff, administrative, 39.
  ,, college, 38, 39.
Supply parks, 134, 135.
  ,, officers, 44, 133.
Survey units, 122–124.
Sword, 64.

## T.

Telegraph troops, 117–119.
Telephones—
    Artillery, 76.
    Cavalry, 65.
    Detachments with higher formations, 118, 119.
    Infantry, 52.
Tools, infantry, 53.

Train, 133, 134.
Training centres, 18, 19, 69, 107, 108, 113.
Transport—
    Field artillery, 69.
    Infantry, 44, 45.
Transport officer, 133.
Transportation (*see* under mechanical transport and railway troops).
Trench guns, 91, 103–105.
  ,, mortars, 103–105.
Tunnelling companies, 99, 100.

## U.

Uniform (*see* also under various arms)—
    Field service, 146–155.
    New field service, 156–161.

## V.

Veterinary officers, 20, 22, 139, 142.
  ,, service, 41, 142.
Volunteers, 11, 24.

## W.

War Bureau, 37, 38.
War Ministry, Prussian—
    Army Administration Department, 37.
    Central Department, 36.
    General War Department, 36, 37.
    Medical Department, 37.
    Pensions and Justice Department, 37.
    Quartering Department, 37.
    Remount Inspection, 37.
Water supply, 137, 138.
Wireless station, 121.